Akram Midani
New York 1960

D1246798

PITTSBURGH FILMMAKERS
477 MELWOOD AVENUE
PITTSBURGH, PA 15213

MY FATHER,
Charlie Chaplin

RANDOM HOUSE

New York

PITTSBURGH FILMMAKERS
477 MELWOOD AVENUE
PITTSBURGH, PA 15213

MY FATHER,
Charlie Chaplin

by CHARLES CHAPLIN, Jr.
with N. and M. RAU

FIRST PRINTING

© Copyright, 1960, by Charles Chaplin, Jr., and N. and M. Rau
All rights reserved under International and Pan-American Copyright
Conventions. Published in New York by Random House, Inc., and
simultaneously in Toronto, Canada, by Random House of Canada,
Limited.
Library of Congress Catalog Card Number: 60-5537
Manufactured in the United States of America
by Haddon Craftsmen

DESIGN: Patricia de Groot

To my daughter,
Susan

Memo to my father:

In your account of your trip around the world in 1931, when you recalled meeting Lord Birkenhead, son of the famous British jurist and statesman, the Earl of Birkenhead, and hearing that Lord Birkenhead was writing a life of his father, you wrote: "This was quite a task, I thought, and wondered if a son, in doing such a biography, could sufficiently detach himself from the subject so as to see the deep shadows as well as the highlights which are necessary to a true portrait of a great man."

Since this book will come as a surprise to you, I hope I have achieved that detachment you questioned of Lord Birkenhead. As for your being a great man, I have found that even your rankest enemies concede that in your realm of talent you have no peer.

Respectfully,
Your son, Charles

I remember, I remember
The fir-trees dark and high;
I used to think their slender tops
Were close against the sky:
It was a childish ignorance,
But now 'tis little joy
To know I'm farther off from heav'n
Than when I was a boy.

—THOMAS HOOD

MY FATHER,
Charlie Chaplin

I

There was always the scream I heard, the scream that seemed to be coming from someone else, the scream at something whose face I could never see but whose malignant presence I could feel—scream after scream in the dark, the utter loneliness. And then suddenly there was the light. There were people caressing me, putting cold compresses on my head, for I was almost rigid in my terror.

"There, there now, Charlie," I heard their comforting voices. "It's all right. Wake up! Wake up!"

They were the voices of people, real people. I was not alone any longer. I would open my eyes and smile, because they were all there around me—my grandmother, my great-grandmother, my mother and sometimes even my great-grandfather. Sydney, my younger brother, would be sitting upright in his bed, blinking at me in astonishment.

How different Sydney and I always were. He seemed better equipped to fight the loneliness. He was more independent. When he was two years old he got tired of home one day and just wandered off. They found him around the block still going. I would never have done that.

We had one thing in common, though. We were both stubborn. Syd's was the rambunctious kind of stubbornness, mine was more quiet. Mother didn't really know how to cope with either of us. She was so glamorous and young, more like a big sister to us. And shortly after I was three she went back East to appear as a singer in night clubs and then we saw her only at intervals.

For the longest time Syd and I didn't see our father at all. We were too young to be impressed by the fact that he was the great Charlie Chaplin. And certainly we didn't remember the bitterness of his brief marriage to our mother that ended in separation and divorce. It was a story I was to hear in later years under unhappy circumstances.

My mother, Lillita McMurray, or Lita Grey, the name she chose for the stage, is half Scottish, half Spanish-English. My maternal grandmother, Mrs. Lillian Grey, whom Syd and I still call Nana, is descended on her mother's side from an old California family of Spanish ancestry. Louisa Carrillo was the maiden name of my great-grandmother, who was Grandma to us. She died in 1950 at the age of eighty-three. The screen star Leo Carrillo is supposed to be our distant relative. My great-grandfather, Nana's father, William Edward Curry, was an Englishman. My grandfather, Robert Earl McMurray, my mother's father, is Scottish. He and Nana were separated when my mother was very small.

Mother was just six when she and my father first met in a small neighborhood restaurant which he sometimes visited. He was so attracted by her little-girl charm that he took time to talk to her and entertain her with a few simple match tricks. After that chance meeting they did not see each other again for six years. The next meeting, too, had an element of chance about it. Chuck Riesner, who was Dad's associate director at the time, lived in the same block as Mother and Nana, and Mother used to play with his little boy, Dinky. Mr. Riesner noticed her and mentioned her to my father, suggesting that he take a look at her. Dad came by one day and saw Mother, who was out on her front lawn. He was so impressed with her appearance that he signed her to a year's contract and immediately put her in *The Kid*, which was then being filmed with Jackie Coogan.

Recently I asked Jackie what it was like working under my father's direction. Jackie shook his head.

"I don't remember much about your father," he said, "except that whenever he wanted me to cry for the camera he would tell me sad stories until the tears started rolling down my cheeks. I was so small—only four."

Then his face brightened.

"I do remember your mother, though. We used to play together on the set. She was always so gay."

After *The Kid*, Mother and Nana did bit parts in Dad's two-reeler, *The Idle Class*. Then Mother's contract expired and she disappeared out of my father's life for several years. She probably would never have seen him again if one afternoon after school she hadn't dropped by his studio with a girl friend, Merna Kennedy, to prove her boast that she actually did know the famous Charlie Chaplin. At the time my father was casting about for an unknown to play opposite him in *The Gold Rush*.

When he saw Mother he was captivated all over again, but in a different way. At sixteen, Mother was no longer a gay little girl but had blossomed into a beautiful young lady, a brown-eyed, vivacious brunette. My father asked her to test for his picture. Mother did so and Dad was pleased with what he saw and signed her for the part. So fate or chance or

5

whatever you want to call it took a hand again and threw my mother and father together more closely than ever before. It all ended with my parents' surprise marriage in November of 1924, in the little village of Empalme, Mexico, where they had fled to escape the reporters with their constant barrage of questions.

After the elopement my father took his bride, my mother, to his big new house on Summit Drive in Beverly Hills. My mother gave up her part in *The Gold Rush* to Georgia Hale and became a housewife. At Dad's request Nana came to stay with Mother, and I was born the following year. June 28, 1925, my birth certificate reads. I was born at home, as my mother had been. My birthplace was the east bedroom, the room that became Syd's and mine when in later years we came to live at our father's house.

My father was very apprehensive before my arrival. He had been married once before—to another young girl, named Mildred Harris—and their child had died within a few days of its birth. My father had grieved for months over the child's death, grieved so bitterly that Miss Harris later maintained it was the chief reason for the breakup of their marriage.

When I was born there was fresh cause for anxiety. The umbilical cord was wrapped so tightly around my neck that I was almost strangled. The doctor had to put gauze over my mouth and blow into it. I was spanked vigorously as well. At last I started crying and everyone relaxed.

Before my birth my father had often expressed a preference for girls, but since I was his first-born and healthy as well, he welcomed my arrival with satisfaction. I was named Charles Spencer, after him, though there was a family quarrel over it. My father objected strongly, saying that bearing his name would mean having to live up to his reputation, which might prove a strong handicap to me in later life, especially if I chose his profession. My mother, knowing my father's tremendous ego, could not help feeling that his real objection was to having two Charlie Chaplins in the family, and con-

6

tinued to press her point until she won. During my grandfather's lifetime my father had been known as Charlie, Jr. Now I was to fall heir to this title.

I must have been the first baby my father had ever been in close contact with. I was more than a baby to him. I was a symbol of home and home life, of all the things he had missed as a child—just about everything, really. You have to understand that to understand my father.

My father was born April 16, 1889, at 3 Parnell Terrace, Kennington Road, London. The three-story brick building (which was bombed out during the Second World War) was built in the nineteenth century and had a drab, depressing appearance. Both my father's parents were British subjects. My grandfather was a mixture of French and Irish—the Chaplin name is of French origin. My grandmother had Gypsy blood —French or Spanish—inherited from her mother. My father has always been inordinately proud of that wild Romany blood.

Both my grandparents were rather well known in the London music halls of the day. My grandfather was a ballad singer with a baritone voice that was pleasing enough to win him bookings in New York. My father's mother, Hannah Chaplin, who went on the stage at an early age under the name of Lily Harley, sang and played the piano, was for a while a member of a Gilbert and Sullivan troupe that toured England, and acted out parts in the little skits which were so popular on the music-hall programs.

My father had two half brothers. One was the late Wheeler Dryden, the son of Leo Dryden, the actor. Uncle Wheeler was, I believe, brought up by his own father, so that in those early days my father was far closer to Uncle Sydney, his other half brother. Uncle Sydney was four years older than my father. After Grandmother Chaplin divorced Uncle Sydney's father and married my grandfather, Uncle Sydney took the name of Chaplin. Because of a chance resemblance to his stepfather—some people said he looked more like Grandfather in many ways than my father—he was often taken for a full-blooded Chaplin.

The children of theatrical people usually lead a life subject to constant change. My father's was made even more insecure by Grandfather Chaplin's addiction to alcohol, which kept him from providing adequately for his family. He died in his thirties of an illness which had been brought on by his drinking.

Almost from the first my father had a bleak childhood. He was often cold and hungry. When he was five he went through an experience so bitter that he was to remember it with horror all his life. He and Uncle Sydney were placed in an orphanage by their mother because it was impossible to provide for them at home any longer. He had been failed by his father and now his mother was failing him too, or so it must have seemed to a small boy of five.

There was never enough to eat at the orphanage, never enough to wear. The children were always cold and hungry. They were treated like criminals for the offense of being poor. The discipline was harsh. It was on the military order, and one can easily imagine what this meant at the turn of the century, when the disciplining of children in general was far more severe than it is today. There were floggings, deprivations and solitary confinements for the smallest infractions. There seemed to be a concerted effort on the part of the orphanage personnel to break the will and the spirit of the children in their charge.

To add to his loneliness, Dad's mother seldom visited him during those two years of his stay in the orphanage. But when he was seven she came to take him home again. The release entry reads, "Sydney Chaplin handed back to mother, March 10, 1896. Charles, ditto." He came out a quiet, well-mannered boy—or at least that is how Cyril Holden describes him to

8

me. Mr. Holden, who is the son of Fred Holden, former manager of the Canterbury Theatre, and who is exactly my father's age, used to see my father often when they were eight, because Grandfather Chaplin was at that time playing the theater. My father had learned well the manners that poverty teaches. It was only when Mr. Holden looked into his ice-blue eyes that he could see something there that was unbroken, something single-minded, intense, much bigger than his small, wiry body. Call it my father's colossal ego if you wish. It kept him going when there was nothing else.

"You have to believe in yourself, that's the secret," he told me once. "Even when I was in the orphanage, when I was roaming the streets trying to find enough to eat to keep alive, even then I thought of myself as the greatest actor in the world. I had to feel that exuberance that comes from utter confidence in yourself. Without it you go down to defeat."

My father needed that dream. The Chaplins' period of prosperity was only temporary, and it wasn't long before he was again cold and hungry and neglected. But he didn't go back to the orphanage. He became scarcely more than a London street waif, begging for a living, sleeping heaven knows where, and just barely keeping body and soul together. His naturally wiry body became so wizened that his great handsome head, with its black curls, looked grotesque perched on top of his thin shoulders. There in the tough and ribald slums, where incongruities are often considered fit objects for ridicule, his appearance evoked ribald jokes and jeers. He was still knocked about, too, but at least he had his freedom. And occasionally he was fortunate enough to get a chance job which made life more secure—lather boy in a barber shop, janitor in a music hall, or, following early in his parents' footsteps, small comic and dancing parts in vaudeville skits.

There was one long period when, as a member of the Eight Lancashire Lads troupe, Dad knew relative security so far as physical needs were concerned. But he suffered in other

9

ways from that experience. The troupe made a long tour through the mining towns of the North of England. They were dismal towns over which cold, damp, smoky air always hovered. Drunken brawls were a frequent occurrence, and the sight of them acted on my father's spirit like a physical pain. He shrank, too, from the long, lonely nights which he spent with his young fellow troupers all crowded together in one small cold room, homesick and motherless. Motherless and fatherless—perhaps those words sum up the greatest lack my father felt in his childhood.

"Only mother love lasts," he was once quoted as saying. But I don't think he was ever convinced he had truly possessed that love. He frequently told the outside world that it was poverty that had caused all his childhood unhappiness, but to my maternal grandmother he admitted an even deeper source of hurt, a feeling that his mother had failed him when he had needed her most.

To add to the tragedy of my father's boyhood, his mother began to develop symptoms of mental illness that were never to leave her but were to become more pronounced with the passing years. Her ailment was not characterized by violence but was, instead, a kind of withdrawal from the world of reality. There were times when she became unable to recognize her own sons and had to be hospitalized.

My grandmother's illness must have preyed greatly on my father's mind, for he spoke of it often to Syd and me in later years. His light treatment of it did not deceive us.

"Thank God you're born with two hands and two feet and two legs and one head," he would say. "That you're normal, because sometimes you know . . . And of course you could have been this other way. There's something in the family, something . . . Oh, you had me definitely worried." He spoke jokingly, but he would then knock on wood as though the very mention of that family specter had brought it nearer than was comfortable to him.

Specters—the tragic figures of my grandmother and grandfather, the gray streets of Kennington, this was the background against which my father stood looking down at me that night with more than the usual anxiety of a man for his first-born son. I was healthy and normal in every way, the doctor assured him, laughing.

2

Before my birth things had not been well between my parents, but for a little while afterwards there was a spirit of reconciliation between them. They were united through a child. They were a family. Nana tells me that during those pleasant weeks my father seemed to change in nature, to become less taciturn, more gentle; but so far as I personally was concerned, I don't believe I ever, as a baby, got beyond the stage of being a symbol to him. He must have been in complete awe of me, for he never picked me up.

He was busy, too, with his work on *The Gold Rush* at the studio. We never saw much of him. But every morning before he went to work he would come into the room where I slept with Nana, who had the constant care of me, to greet me and see how I was. When he came home at night he would drop in again to look at me in the same way.

Though my father didn't know quite what to do with me, still, he was proud that he had a son. Many times the ways in which he showed off his pride were as quixotic as he is by nature. One morning on his way to work he stopped by the crib where I was lying, completely naked, and bent over me. He was wearing a white suit which I, with all the abandon of a small child, proceeded to soil with a gargantuan stream of water. My father didn't trouble to change the suit. He went to the studio wearing that obvious yellow stain like a medal of honor, and when he was asked what had happened he threw back his chest as though he had just been decorated.

"My son did this," he said proudly. "Isn't that something?"

On March 30, 1926, my brother Sydney was born in the middle bedroom of the Chaplin house on the hill. My father's desire for a girl had by this time become so overpowering that he was almost furious with disappointment when Sydney arrived. But my brother was soon forgiven his error.

Sydney was named Sydney Earl Chaplin, after Uncle Sydney, though my mother wanted to call him Thomas Edward. My father won this battle.

There were no complications to Sydney's birth. He was a lusty boy from the start. A nurse was brought in to care for him and he shared the middle bedroom with Mother. My father's itinerary now included two stops on his way to work. He would go in first to look at Syd and then he would come to look at me. From there down the stairs he would go, out the front door and on to the studio. It was the same routine when he returned from work.

It was shortly after Syd was born that I made my first acquaintance with the Little Tramp who was to play so great a part in my life in coming years. It was late in the day. Sydney lay in bed with Mother. I was sitting on Nana's lap when suddenly the door opened and in walked Dad. Too tired to take off his costume at the studio, he appeared before me

13

wearing the baggy pants and the silly little mustache that had become a beloved symbol to the whole world. I stared at him with eyes growing wider and rounder. Who was he? Out of what strange world had he come to penetrate our family circle? They tell me I was never an obstreperous child. I began to cry silently.

"Why are you crying?" the strange little man said. "It's only Daddy. It's Daddy."

But even the sound of that familiar voice could not stop my tears. Then the Little Fellow reached up and pulled off one corner of his mustache and said, "See? It's Daddy."

I went on crying, so he pulled loose the next section of his mustache.

"It's Daddy," he repeated again.

Caught between astonishment and tears, I stared at this weird apparition that was half my father, half a very peculiar-looking stranger. Then he pulled loose the last section of his mustache, saying once again as he did so, "See, it's Daddy."

But I had already broken into a wide, pleased smile. The Little Tramp who had made millions laugh had frightened his own small son to tears—frightened him with the thought that the father whom he saw so seldom but still loved, had loved from the very start of his life, had been metamorphosed into something alien. For how completely that familiar face had changed before my very eyes, like quicksilver—a personality I couldn't grasp, a nature to which I couldn't cling . . . something unreliable that was there and gone again.

I suppose a lot of people thought Syd and I were very fortunate boys. Our mother was young and beautiful. Our father was famous around the world. We had, besides, two grandmothers and two great-grandparents to make over us.

Sometimes Great-grandfather and Great-grandmother Curry came to the hill to visit and to admire their grandsons. Great-grandmother Curry was always very fond of Dad. Great-grandfather Curry and my father got along well together too, then, though there had been some differences between them before my father and mother were married. Both being English, the two men had similar ways and customs. They had an equal amount of stubbornness and pride and they shared the same outlook on life, especially where children were concerned. They both approved of them, but in their place.

But my great-grandfather felt Dad went much too far when he maintained that children should be taken away from their parents when they were young and brought up by the state. This wasn't the "communist" propaganda it appeared to be, because the idea of being subservient to a state is repellent to my father, who is such an individualist himself. Nor was it, as Great-grandfather and Nana supposed, because my father felt children brought up by the state would not be spoiled but would be trained properly. It was really just because my father had suffered so deeply as a child that he wanted to spare all other children the same fate. He saw the state as an all-wise, wealthy and humanitarian being that would never let a child down. It was just one of his many impractical and completely idealistic theories to bring about a Utopia—a Utopia in which no one would suffer.

Every week we would have a visit with Grandmother Chaplin too. My father would send his chauffeur to bring her to the house, or we would all go out to her little place on Lankershim Boulevard, in the San Fernando Valley near Hollywood. My father had brought Grandmother Chaplin to this country about four years before he and Mother were married. He had always been devoted to his mother. When through Uncle Sydney's connections he joined the Fred Karno theatrical company and began to earn a steady salary of some thirty dollars a week, he put her in a private nursing home in England. After his phenomenal rise to success in Hollywood he began working to bring her over here so that he could more easily look after her. It hadn't been easy to do. Her mental condition made Grandmother Chaplin ineligible for citizenship, and as an alien she was considered undesirable, because there was always the possibility that she might one day become a ward of the state. It took my father several years to get through all the legal difficulties which stood in his way. But at last, after agreeing to post an annual bond as guarantee of her care, he was given special permission to bring her to this country.

For most of the seven years which remained to her, Grandmother Chaplin lived in the little rented house on Lankershim Boulevard. My father hired the couple from whom he rented the house to care for her, and provided her with all the medical and nursing attention she needed. When he discovered that she delighted in sightseeing, he put his car and chauffeur at her disposal. He did everything in his power to make her comfortable and happy—everything but visit her. I don't know whether he was perturbed because of her unfortunate mental condition or whether it was because she brought back so vividly all his unhappy boyhood, but he could never see her without feeling a depression that was sometimes as acute to him as physical pain, that would last for days afterwards, preventing all concentration on his work.

It was my mother, used to the gregarious spirit in her own closely knit family, who persuaded my father to see Grandmother Chaplin more often. And so evolved that weekly visit with her.

When people saw my father and grandmother together they realized at once how much they resembled each other. Though my father has a large head—seven and three-quarter inches in circumference—which he inherited from his father, his small size comes from his mother. He has her beautiful glass-blue eyes, her full lips and roguish smile, and her delicate, expressive hands.

Both Mother and Nana found Grandmother Chaplin a very charming woman, as did all those who knew her. It was only after you talked to her for a while that you realized she lived in a different world from yours—a world of fantasy.

Sometimes Grandmother Chaplin would gravely discuss the air raids which the big German Zeppelin had made over London in the war just past and which had so terrified her. At other times she would prattle on about Grandfather Chaplin, whom she remembered with affection. Sometimes she would content herself with expressing her pride and love of Dad in one glowing exclamation which she would reiterate over and over again, "My son! My son!"

She never talked about the early days, the days of her youth, the days of my father's boyhood, the unhappy days of want and privation. Perhaps she had forgotten them. Yet there were those who saw her on numerous occasions who found her much quieter, more subdued and thoughtful when she was with my father.

Sometimes, though, Grandmother Chaplin would be in a gayer mood. She still remembered the stage routines of her youth and she would play the piano and sing for us. Presently she would jump up from the piano seat and start to do the numbers with which she had once pleased audiences in the London music halls. Twirling round and round and lifting her skirts as she did so, she would perform a merry dance just out of reach of my hands stretched out to her.

Then Grandmother Chaplin would suddenly stop before me and laughingly bend over to pick me up. This always alarmed my father. He would shake his head at Nana and Mother, afraid that Grandmother Chaplin would be careless with me.

"Watch her! Oh, do watch her," he would whisper warningly. "Don't let her pick him up. Please! She might drop him out the window by mistake."

It was useless for Mother and Nana to assure him there was really nothing to fear, that in essential ways Grandmother Chaplin was quite dependable. Dad has a runaway imagination that pictures things in hyperbole and often envisions the direst consequences from the most commonplace incidents.

17

3

To understand the position of our family in Hollywood during those days you have to know something of the history that catapulted my father from the obscurity of the Kennington slums to his place in the movies as King of Comedy. In this town his overnight success has always been considered one of our brightest phenomena. But you might say the miracle began with his mere survival from his rugged childhood experiences. Yet beyond that something else was preserved, perhaps even intensified by everything he suffered— something bright and effervescent, the spirit of fun that couldn't be killed, though it had to filter through tragedy to break the surface.

My father first drew attention to himself when as a child

of eight he appeared at the Hippodrome in London with the Eight Lancashire Lads. Dressed as a dog, he brought down the house with impromptu realistic business, first with a prop tree and then by sniffing among the other little dogs. The management, frantic with fear the police would close the theater, got him off stage as quickly as possible.

In his teens he toured the North Country again, this time with the Sherlock Holmes Company as Billy the Shoeshine Boy. Whenever in later years I talked about my stage work, my father would say, "Oh, you know your father is a stage actor, too. He's had a little stage experience." At first I expected him to follow up this remark by saying he had played Hamlet or Cyrano. Instead he would boast, "Yes, when I was fourteen I did Billy the Shoeshine Boy in 'Sherlock Holmes.' " Hearing my father talk so often in such a nostalgic vein about this part, I couldn't help feeling that secretly he might have preferred the stage to pantomime and the movies.

My father was about seventeen when he joined Uncle Sydney with the Fred Karno troupe. He was never a star in England, but always played the supporting roles. When the Karno Company toured the Continent, my father brought down the house at the Folies-Bergère in Paris with the dog act which had aroused such enthusiasm in London audiences when he innovated it at the age of eight. One night he was invited to join Claude Debussy, who was in the audience, and received the composer's enthusiastic congratulations. My father has always considered those moments with Debussy one of the highlights of his career. He spoke of it often to me when I was a boy.

It was my father's unique work even in bit parts that led to his being invited to join the second Karno troupe, which was touring America. The credit for bringing him to this country goes to Amy Reeves, wife of the late Alfred Reeves. At the time Alf was in charge of booking for the second troupe.

Amy first became aware of Dad's talents in 1909. Then

unmarried, she was a dancer with the Karno Company in London and she and Dad had small parts in one of the sketches. Uncle Sydney was the star of the show. A year later, after Amy had married Alf and was touring America with him and the second Karno Company, she remembered my father. At the time Mr. Reeves had just been struck by a familiar malady. His leading comedian had left him for greener pastures. He returned to London and, at Amy's suggestion, looked in on my father's acting, signed him at once and took him back with them as the star of the show. This was in 1910.

My father toured the United States for three years with the company. In 1912 he received an offer from another outstanding comedian, Ed Wynn, who was to become his close friend in later years. Wynn, who had his own troupe at the time, saw Dad's act and so admired it that he offered my father sixty-five dollars a week to join his troupe. Dad held out for seventy-five dollars, but Wynn shook his head.

"Oh, you'll never earn that much in this country," he remonstrated.

In 1913 Dad signed his first motion-picture contract. He was in Philadelphia when he received the telegram from Adam Kessel asking him to get in touch with the New York office of Kessel and Bauman, the owners of Keystone Films. The telegram was addressed to Mr. Charles Chapman.

Actually it was Mack Sennett who instigated the sending of that telegram. He discovered my father on a chance visit to the American Music Hall, where Dad was playing the role of the drunk in *A Night in an English Music Hall.* "Though he was great, I think if he had not been seen by me that day in the theater in New York he would probably have gone back to England," Mr. Sennett says. "He would have been a great music-hall actor; but I don't think he would ever have been in movies, because they weren't making comic movies in England in those days. Hollywood was the only place for that."

My father's opinion of what he would have been except for Mr. Sennett's chance intervention differs greatly. Dad says that at the time he and a fellow vaudevillian had been saving their money to buy an Arkansas farm and raise hogs.

My father hesitated a long while before going to Hollywood. He had a secure place with the Fred Karno Company, and as the star of the show he had a comfortable salary of fifty dollars a week. Even after he had managed to talk Keystone Films into paying him the astronomical weekly sum of a hundred and fifty dollars, he still wasn't convinced he was making the right move. He doubted whether the new medium would last and whether he could fit himself into it. Mack Sennett must have shared his views when he saw my father for the first time without makeup. Amy Reeves says his extreme youth always astonished everyone, because in makeup he looked like a forty-five-year-old man.

"Are you really the drunk?" Mr. Sennett asked with a sinking heart.

In reply my father did a little comedy routine and bowed. It was just a cover up for his lack of confidence. In later years he himself was to admit that once he was in Hollywood, his nervousness kept him from appearing at the studio for three days, and only a phone call from Mr. Sennett to his modest hotel on Bunker Hill brought him out of hiding at last.

My father's appearance at the studio caused some startled glances. Ford Sterling, whose place he was filling, gave him a quick once-over and roared with laughter.

"You've been taken, Mack," he told Mr. Sennett. "You've been taken by a little greenhorn who just doesn't have what it takes for the movies."

Most of the people on the lot were inclined to agree with Sterling. My father was so British in speech and action—he even called motion pictures "flickahs"—that no one could see how he could go over in America. He was a shy, unobtrusive young man who lived a frugal life and kept quite a bit to himself in his cheap hotel. He had a very Cockney outlook, with a Cockney's close eye for thrift. He told Mr. Sennett one day that after he had made his first hundred thousand dollars he was going to retire. I suppose he meant it then—as much as he has meant it ever since. That talk of retiring has been periodic with my father ever since those Keystone days. I can't recall his finishing a single big picture without telling me it was his last, that he was through for good.

My father's subtle sense of humor seemed particularly out of place at Keystone, where cast and crew were like one big boisterous family, always clowning among themselves and pulling practical jokes. One morning they couldn't resist trying a prank on my father, because he seemed such a shy little odd-ball. The joke had been originally planned only for Jess Dandy, the oversized comic, who spent a lot of time in the washroom reading the morning paper. They wired the toilet seat and when Dandy went in they turned on the juice. In an instant out charged the comic, yowling that he'd been killed. When a little later, oblivious to what had gone on, Dad walked in and headed for the washroom, the pranksters turned on the juice again.

But this time no one came flying out the door. Instead there was a loud thump and then a silence which grew and grew. Everyone got uneasy. Then someone muttered that the electric charge might have been too much. At last they all went quietly to the washroom and pushed open the door, fearing the worst. There lay my father sprawled out, face down, motionless. But while they stood there staring in horror he suddenly lifted his head, revealing the impish smirk that has since bedeviled so many millions from the screen. Insolently he lay there thumbing his nose at them.

I guess my father was considered insolent in other ways as well, or at least noncooperative. Though he was polite and quiet, he was also stubborn and argumentative with the director about how he should play his parts. In those days comedy was fast-paced and depended on plenty of action, just so it was rough and tough. My father's pantomime routines relied on delicacy, a graceful, almost ballet tempo of movement. When he tried to bring them to the screen, the director balked. He said they were too slow and wasted too much footage and wouldn't hold the interest of the audience. It looked as though the director was right when my father's first picture came out. It was a flop. Everyone was convinced that the "obscure little Englishman" Mr. Sennett had picked up was a real dud.

The story goes that at this time the whole cast of the studio got together to dream up a more photogenic costume than the British frock coat and top hat Dad had worn for his first picture. And so out of odds and ends the Little Tramp costume came into being. But my father told me once that the costume had really originated years before. One night while he was janitoring in a London music hall the frantic manager came to him with the dismal news that the star comedian was sick and he needed a fill-in. Would Dad help out? The comedian was a big man, and his clothes were oversize for Dad—the pants baggy, the shoes too large. But the derby was too small, because Dad's head was larger than the comedian's.

"I just put them on and there was my tramp outfit," my father told me. "I went out and everyone laughed to see the little guy in the big guy's pants. I evolved a nightly routine which ended with my falling into a tub of water on stage. The pants would blow up and I'd float around with air in them."

With the tramp outfit came the tramp personality. It wasn't a studied character. It was just released whole from somewhere deep within my father. It was really my father's alter ego, the little boy who never grew up: ragged, cold, hungry, but still thumbing his nose at the world.

Now that Dad was firmly established at Keystone he was able to reciprocate Uncle Sydney's good turn of getting him into the Karno troupe by sending for him to join the Keystone cast.

"Sydney was all right," Mr. Sennett recalls, "though he wasn't as good an actor as your father by a long shot. But he had the business brains of the family. He took over the management of your father's affairs."

As time went by and my father's popularity soared, his self-confidence grew. He began to assert himself more and more about how scenes should be played. He wasn't arguing just to be different. He simply wasn't the kind of man who could be content to be the personality and let someone else plan the framework in which he should be exhibited. From the moment he walked into those studio gates he began to study motion-picture techniques with all the intensity he puts into everything, whether it's work or play.

"Night after night he was the last performer to leave the studio," Mr. Sennett recalls. "He stayed to watch the other companies in action. He took in everything—everything. He was a terrific student."

By the end of the year my father was doing his own writing and directing. He made thirty-five films for Keystone in 1914, and in 1915 went over to Essanay at ten times his weekly salary with Keystone. He did fourteen films for Essanay, and then in 1916 signed with the Mutual Company for ten thousand dollars a week, with a bonus of a hundred and fifty thousand dollars. This totaled six hundred and seventy thousand dollars a year, a figure that made headlines around the world and set the precedent for the fabulous salaries other film personalities were to demand and receive. My father was twenty-six years old at the time. Two years before he had been only a music-hall pantomimist.

"How the hell could he make ten thousand dollars a week after just two years in this country?" says Mr. Sennett. "Because he was a genius, that's how. That little English boy was a pretty bright boy."

My father had no idea of the extent of his popularity until he made his famous trip to New York, where Uncle Sydney had preceded him, to close the Mutual contract. He was shaving in the men's lavatory when the train stopped at Albuquerque, New Mexico. He looked idly out the window and saw a crowd of some two thousand people gathered in front of the train. Thinking they were there to greet some dignitary aboard, Dad went out to see who it was, his face half lathered. To his amazement, someone in the crowd suddenly shouted, "There he is! There he is! There's Charlie Chaplin!"

Dad found this same tumultuous welcome awaiting him all across the country. Even the dignified *New York Times* banner-lined his arrival in New York with the exclamation, "He Is Here!" The dream of the little boy of the Kennington slums had been fulfilled—and in short order. He had become the greatest, the best-known, the best-loved comedian in the world. But there must have been a peculiar flatness about that moment of glory.

"I was a celebrity that everyone knew," Dad was to tell me in later years. "But I didn't know anyone in the whole city of New York except your Uncle Sydney. I was loved by crowds, but I didn't have a single close friend I could talk to. I felt like the loneliest man alive."

However, despite his loneliness, Dad put his amazing popularity to good use. He tripled his salary demand on Mutual and got it. I can imagine how much the company regretted not having signed him quietly in Hollywood.

4

My father made twelve comedies for Mutual and then went
over to First National Exhibitors' Circuit, a newly formed releasing company, where he could be his own producer. His
astronomical salary continued. He was to receive a million
dollars, with a fifteen-thousand-dollar bonus for signing and
an equal share of profits above costs. In return he was to make
eight pictures in the following eighteen months.

Now that he was to be a producer with perfect freedom in
the making of his films, my father began to build his own
studio on the corner of La Brea Avenue and Sunset Boulevard
in Hollywood. The cornerstone of the building bears the imprint of his tramp feet and the date, 1918, the year the studio
was completed.

As soon as Dad had signed the contract with First National he sent a cablegram to Alfred Reeves, the former booking agent of the Karno Company, asking him to come to Hollywood. "When I make my way in pictures I'm going to have Alf for my manager," Dad had told Amy Reeves three years before.

The First World War was in progress when Alf Reeves came over, and he found the United States seething with martial spirit. In the spring of 1918, Dad did his part by joining Douglas Fairbanks and Mary Pickford on a two-month tour to sell bonds for the Third Liberty Loan. The close friendship that developed between the three was to result in 1919 in the forming of the famous United Artists Releasing Corporation, which from 1923 on was to distribute all my father's pictures.

When Amy Reeves joined her husband in Hollywood, after the signing of the Armistice, she found that Dad, who was then twenty-nine, had just married Mildred Harris, a sixteen-year-old film personality. In later years Miss Harris was to write a series of poignant newspaper articles about that unhappy marriage. She told of my father's moodiness, his periods of abstracted silence, his intense need to be alone, his long, lonely walks at night, the weird, sad music he used to improvise by the hour. She soon discovered that where his work was concerned—and when he is making a picture that work continues day and night—she was nonexistent. The inevitable separation took place after the birth and death, a few days later, of their baby in the summer of 1919.

The separation, with its concomitant charges and countercharges, broke in the papers with lurid headlines. They were the first of a series of flaming front-page stories that throughout the years have punctuated my father's career. It is a paradox that Dad, who craves privacy more than any other man I know, should have had the exquisite torture of seeing so many of his intimate troubles detailed in print by the newspapers.

It was, of course, natural that they should carry the amusing account of a fist fight between him and the late Louis B. Mayer, at that time Mildred Harris' production manager, which took place while the divorce was pending. The story goes that Dad heard Mayer had been influencing Miss Harris not to accept the twenty-five-thousand-dollar settlement he had offered. As usual, my father lost his head and solemnly vowed to knock Mayer down the next time they met.

It didn't take Dad long to regret that idle threat. In those days Hollywood was a much more closely knit and dramatic town than it is today, and Dad's wild statement was taken at its face value. The word went around that he was out for Mayer. From then on my father felt like the hero of some Western melodrama stalking the town with his hand at his holster. Only he was a very reluctant hero, for above all things he didn't want to attract further unfavorable publicity to himself. Instead of hunting down his enemy he was doing his best to avoid him. Unfortunately, he wasn't successful, and one night he and Mr. Mayer found themselves together in the dining room of the Alexandria Hotel in downtown Los Angeles.

Dad knew his big moment had come. All the other guests were staring at him in hushed expectancy. He waited for Mr. Mayer in the corridor of the hotel.

"Take off your glasses, Mayer," my father said, and then made a desultory swing at him and missed. After which Mayer struck Dad, and the two men clinched. It was in this position that Dad slipped and went down, striking his head on a scaffolding placed there to make some repairs. The house detective rushed forward to stop the fight, and several guests helped Dad up. Both he and Mr. Mayer quietly disappeared.

My father could never remember that incident without a certain amount of embarrassment. "I trapped myself into something by talking too much," he told me.

During the upheaval over Mildred Harris my father feared for his picture, *The Kid*, for his reputation in general and his career in particular. But in November of 1920 he made a settlement to his estranged wife of a hundred thousand dollars together with some community property, and the divorce went through quietly. Publicity died out and my father was left to finish his picture in peace. I think it is interesting to note that the pretty dark-haired girl of twelve who appeared as the flirting angel in the dream sequence of *The Kid* was to be my father's next wife and my mother.

In 1921, when *The Kid* was completed, my father took his first trip abroad after his rise in Hollywood. His position in life had changed greatly from the days he had been just another music-hall performer. Now he was returning to England as an idol, and he found himself treated as an equal by such celebrities as George Bernard Shaw, James M. Barrie, Thomas Burke and H. G. Wells.

In later years my father was to explain that his chief purpose in going to England had been to look up a boyhood sweetheart, a girl by the name of Hetty Kelly. But upon his arrival he discovered that Hetty, a vivacious brunette just a little older than he, had recently died. My father's idyllic dream of Hetty continued to haunt him through the years— perhaps it was partly because she became inaccessible to him that his feeling of tenderness for her lasted so long.

In October of 1921, Dad returned to Hollywood and buried himself in work again. At the same time he found the leisure to entangle himself romantically with a succession of beautiful women—Pola Negri . . . Claire Windsor . . . Clare Sheridan. It was a condition which was to run true in all the periods of his life when he was unattached.

But my father was no hedonist. Though he had become one of the richest men in Hollywood he was, up until this time, still living in modest, nondescript apartments and rented houses. Even his dressing room at the studio was so small and dingy that it brought protests from his friends, especially Douglas Fairbanks and Mary Pickford, who had been married in 1920.

"You should have a room worthy of your position," Doug would lecture him. "One like mine."

My father would look at Fairbanks' elegant dressing room and shake his head.

"If I had a room like that," he would say, "I couldn't possibly portray the Little Tramp. I need a place that looks like him."

Doug Fairbanks and Mary Pickford weren't able to persuade my father to modernize his dressing room, but finally they needled him into buying six acres of the barren slopes below Pickfair, which they had recently built. I think it was Mary who was really responsible, for my father is more susceptible to the pleas of women and he had a great admiration for her.

When he bought the land on Summit Drive it was only a wild waste, the home of rabbits and coyotes. He began work on it at once, hiring Mexican gardeners to cover the barren slopes with trees because he loves the loneliness of woods, hiring contractors to crown the top of the hill with the house that he himself had designed. I can only imagine the emotions that stirred him as he watched that stout yellow fortress, a combination of Basque and modern Spanish architecture, rising on its hill. It was the first real home he had ever known. It seemed impregnable, solid as the old hill itself, looking down on the small town of Beverly Hills that lay scattered out below it.

At the time my father built his house, a decade after he had been signed by Keystone, the more subtle humor-pathos comedy which he had inaugurated had won out over the old slam-bang style of the Keystone comedies. Comedians were adopting the techniques he had innovated. Producers and directors were studying his methods of film making. He had become not only wealthy and famous but influential as well.

There were those who had known him in the old days who maintained my father had been changed by his success, that he was no longer the shy, unobtrusive Englishman who had left the Karno troupe for an uncertain career in Hollywood. They said he had become an egocentric of the greatest magnitude, who couldn't bear to be crossed in anything. There were others, though, who said he had remained surprisingly unchanged, that what looked like tyranny was only the wholehearted concern of the artist for perfection. But all were agreed that he was a genius and that his position in Hollywood was as secure as the house he had built on the hill. That was how things stood when he brought my mother to his home as his bride. That was how things were when Syd and I were babies.

5

My mother and father's marriage wasn't right from the very start, and nothing could have been done to make it so. If you had looked all over the world you couldn't have found two more divergent personalities. Today Mother looks philosophically at that strange marriage of opposites.

"You learn a sense of humor with the years," she says. "I can see now that the whole thing was ridiculous from the start, the hilarious story of two people who were definitely mismatched in age and everything else."

But it wasn't humorous then. Except for that brief period which followed my birth, it was the torture of complete incompatibility for two years. My father had a feeling of having been harnessed to a domesticity which he did not in the least understand, not its obligations or the essential give and take of its nature. It had been the same when he married Mildred Harris. He was the first to recognize his deficiency in this field.

"I am not so sure I should ever marry," he said once. "I like to be free to travel; free to eat at any time and free to do as I please. When I work I am oblivious to the world and it's difficult to ask any woman to be happy when at times I forget her very existence."

Mother was certainly not the person to be happy under such conditions. She was only sixteen when she married my father, a lively young girl who should have still been in high school, enjoying parties and dates and all the things that go with teenage living.

From the first she was in awe of my father, who, at thirty-five, was more than twice her age. Though he was her husband by law, in fact he was a great figure, the great Charlie Chaplin, wearing, or so it seemed to her, an aura of mystery and power. She couldn't understand his complex nature with its strange blend of introverted darkness and extroverted gaiety, or his almost fanatic devotion to work. She, too, began to have a feeling that she had exchanged her freedom for a prison in which she found nothing that resembled her romantic teenage dreams of love and marriage.

What went on over Syd's and my heads in those melancholy years! There were bitter recriminations from my father, hysterical tears from my mother.

"I'm not coming home to you, Lita," Dad would exclaim in the heat of his anger. "I don't intend to be a husband to you."

And then he would stay away night after night. Night after night my mother would listen in vain for his return. The Christmas Day that followed their marriage she and Nana heard him in the early morning hours. His weaving footsteps coming up the stairs and groping uncertainly down the hall told them he was drunk. My father drunk! That tells me more

33

than anything else the extent of his anguish and despair, because it is the only time I have ever heard of his drinking too much. He has always had an aversion to liquor.

As the atmosphere around the house became more unbearable, Mother and Nana began to take Syd and me away on short trips to relieve the tension. On one of these vacations at the seaside town of Coronado I learned to walk. I was a year old then. When I came back I amused my father with my talents. But I still remained a symbol to him, I'm sure. Had Syd and I both become symbols of something that now looked to him like a gigantic trap? He lived within himself and his own misery those days.

That summer of '26 my father, who had released *The Gold Rush* in August of the previous year, was well into his picture *The Circus* and growing more and more tense, as he always does during his periods of creation. Finally he complained to Mother and Nana that he couldn't concentrate with so many people in the house. He suggested that they take me on a trip to Honolulu. He would keep Syd behind with his nurse because, as he explained, you couldn't get the proper milk for a baby aboard ship.

Mother and Nana accepted the offer gladly. It was only after they had boarded the ship that they began to wonder why he had kept Syd. Had he really meant it about the milk, or did he plan to kidnap my younger brother? When they got back would Syd be gone, perhaps sent to England out of their reach? All sorts of suspicions run rife in the kind of atmosphere that then prevailed in our home.

After three weeks of worry about Syd, Mother and Nana came back home with me, ignoring Dad's pleas for us to stay away longer.

No one could expect a marriage like this to last. It came to an end on the first of December, 1926, when Syd was eight months old and I was a year and a half.

I guess there always has to be one final incident, one last

dramatic exclamation point about which people can say, "That was when . . ." In this instance it was a dinner party which my mother and Nana gave at the Biltmore for some friends who were visiting in town. At eleven thirty that night they brought their guests up to see the house on the hill. They didn't expect my father to be there—he had taken to staying away from home until much later. But suddenly in the midst of the gay chatter and the playing of the phonograph he appeared at the head of the stairs and peremptorily ordered the visitors from the house. Everyone was shocked. The guests left, subdued, and my mother was mortified beyond all hope of forgiveness.

The next day, while our father was at the studio, she left the house with Syd—I had spent the night with our great-grandparents. Nana stayed behind to tell my father, then she too left.

If my mother and father had been just an ordinary couple breaking up, their separation and subsequent divorce would have been got through with the usual amount of unpreventable bitterness followed by the inevitable adjustment. But there would have been no complications from outside sources to add to their misfortune. Unhappily Dad's name made him front-page copy again. The headlines were much more lurid than they had been at the time of his divorce from Mildred Harris. First Mother's separation from him hit the front pages of the newspapers. Then excerpts from her bitter forty-two-page divorce complaint were aired. Dad responded by saying that it was a plot to blast his reputation.

From then on Dad and Mother's private affairs became a three-ring circus for the public to enjoy. Everyone got into the act. Attorneys for both sides were busy making their own statements. Mother and we boys were pictured as starving, Dad as a monster who was refusing to pay any support money. Clubwomen made a flamboyant gesture of taking up a collection for us. Intellectuals in France signed a petition saying that the lives of artists should be their own affair.

A judge ordered Dad to pay Mother four thousand dollars a month alimony pending the divorce settlement, and denied him visitation rights to his children. Attorneys for Mother threatened to have Dad jailed if in sixty days he had failed to comply with the injunction. And anonymous letter writers threatened the judge for fixing such a high alimony.

A temporary casualty was *The Circus*, upon which Dad, who had gone to New York on business, no longer had the heart to work. There was speculation that he might never finish the picture. He himself spoke of deserting Hollywood and the stout yellow house on the hill which he had intended for his permanent home. He talked only of getting away from the scene of his disaster, of going to England for good.

Then the government slapped more than a million dollars' worth of liens on his properties for back income taxes. It came as an added shock to my father, who has always employed others to compute his taxes for him. He was now in real difficulties and his contemplated avenue of escape was sealed to him.

"Uncle Sam holds the only winning hand in this three-sided game," a newspaper promptly reported.

And still that divorce scandal kept ballooning up out of all proportion to its importance. Irrational statements made in the heat of anger, and supposedly in confidence, were blazoned across the papers for everyone to see. It is not surprising that the bitterness on both sides increased until it looked as though it could never be bridged.

My father even accused Nana of breaking up his home. "My wife's mother is responsible for my misfortune. She caused the separation and now she wants me to give her daughter nearly everything I possess," he was quoted as saying. "She will stop at nothing to attain her purpose."

But Nana would not believe that Dad meant what he was saying. She had always been on the closest of terms with him. A short while before the separation, Dad had come into her bedroom one morning while she was still in bed. He walked over and sat down on the edge of it.

"I want you to have something very beautiful," he said to her. "You've been so wonderful. You've never never interfered in our lives."

Then he opened the little box he was holding, took out a magnificent diamond pin from Cartier's and handed it to her. Nana was so touched she could scarcely thank him, and he bent over and kissed her on the cheek, as he usually did, and went away.

"So much of it was the newspapers' fault," Nana says now, looking back. "They had to have copy, so the reporters would go to your father and say, 'Lita said so and so.' Then they would come to your mother and say, 'Mr. Chaplin said so and so.' And so it was built up and built up. It was awful."

Five months after Mother filed her complaint, Dad's answer and cross-complaint made headlines along with Lindbergh's historic hop to Paris. There were ninety-one pages to his document, excerpts of which were duly quoted along with Dad's request for custody of Syd and me. It looked as though a bitter, sensational court fight was in the making; but it was a fight that failed to materialize.

The divorce, which was granted on August 22, 1927, was headlined in the papers of the twenty-third, along with the fact that Sacco and Vanzetti had been executed. Both of Mother's pleas, for the divorce and for custody of Syd and me, were uncontested by my father, who did not even appear in court. To the disappointment of a crowd of spectators, Los Angeles Superior Court Judge Walter Guerin ruled that all sensational matters be deleted from the suit. My father, whose earning powers had been at zero since the separation, agreed to a property settlement for Mother of six hundred and fifty thousand dollars, and he agreed as well to establish a two-hundred-thousand-dollar trust fund for Syd and me. He also had to pay the costs of the trial, which some enterprising reporter estimated at nine hundred and fifty thousand dollars, not inclusive of his own attorney's fees. The whole procedure took far less than an hour, and with the final settlement the Chaplin divorce case disappeared from the newspapers for good.

But the scars that Dad and Mother suffered from their unhappy marriage and divorce went far deeper than the public's interest in their affairs. During the height of the worst publicity my father suffered a nervous breakdown in New York and had to spend almost two weeks in bed under a doctor's care. Unable to retain any solid food, he was put on a liquid diet and his weight dropped from a hundred and thirty-five pounds to a hundred and eighteen. Reporters commented on his haggard appearance and subdued manner.

Mother suffered two serious breakdowns in later years, and during the first all the bitterness of the marriage relived itself in terrifying fantasy. For a long time she could not bear classical music in general and would flee the room in anguish when she heard Wagner. Classical music reminded Mother too strongly of the nights she had spent with Dad at the Hollywood Bowl concerts, and of my father himself, with his strange and somber depths which so frightened her because she could not understand them. As for Wagner, he has always been my father's favorite composer. My mother heard his music so much during her unhappy marriage that she came to associate those rich, somber, often sensual strains with the melancholy futility of the years she had spent as Dad's wife. To this day she prefers light modern music to the classics.

But at the time of the divorce everything seemed equably settled and properly adjusted. Our father's reputation had been only dented, after all, and he went back to work on *The Circus* with renewed energy. The bitter tensions of the divorce behind her, our mother, with Nana's help, started drawing up plans for a beautiful home in Beverly Hills. Syd and I were amply provided for with our individual hundred-thousand-dollar trust funds, and would never have to worry about food or shelter or the necessities of life as our father had in his childhood.

We were now living as quietly at our great-grandmother's home in Beverly Hills as before we had lived in our father's house. On January 24, 1928, five months after the divorce, Mother, who had been baptized a Catholic herself, had both Syd and me christened at the Church of the Good Shepherd in Beverly Hills. Father hadn't wanted this while we lived with him. He believed that children should be free to pick their own religion when they were old enough. But now all that life was gone, and we were starting from the beginning again. Everything was as if the life on the hill had never been.

Syd and I had lavish attention because we were living in the very home of our doting great-grandmother. Actually, only one face among those we had learned to love and trust was missing. But surely we were too young to notice. Yet somehow something without a name came into my life at this time, making it impossible for me to start everything afresh even though I was so young. An apprehension had worked itself into my unconscious mind and lifted its head occasionally in dreams. It was then I began to wake up at night screaming. At the same time, my family discovered that when I went in the ocean I would break out in giant hives.

6

The days, the weeks, the months went by without our father's making a move to see us, though that move would have entailed only a telephone call. Our father is a very stubborn man—perhaps that's where Syd and I get our stubbornness. He was bitter as well—so bitter that he had apparently lost all interest in us. Our mother's family had been hurt just as deeply and they were equally bitter. They didn't care whether we ever saw our father again—except for Grandma Curry. She just couldn't help feeling that whatever had happened between the grown folks, we shouldn't be deprived of our father. She kept hoping he would phone to claim the visitation rights the court had granted him.

Whether Dad gave any thought to us in those days I don't know. He was engrossed in completing *The Circus*, so long delayed by his private troubles, and I doubt if he had much thought for anything else. Work on *The Circus* came to an end by the close of the year, and the picture opened in January of 1928. It proved to be a great success at the box office and won Dad a special Academy award for 1927-28. The citation reads, "For his versatility and genius in writing, acting, directing and producing *The Circus.*

When Syd and I were older, Dad used to tell us about winning that Oscar. He said he hadn't even gone to the banquet, the first of its kind, which was held on May 16, 1929, at the Hollywood Roosevelt Hotel, so they had had to send his Oscar over to him. Dad said it was his opinion the whole institution of Academy awards was foolish.

"I don't think it's much of an honor when a small group of people decides I have the best picture," he would say. "I want my acclaim from the public. If they like my work that's reward enough for me."

He told us that in the beginning he had valued his Oscar so little that he used it for a doorstop. But ever since I can remember he has kept it on a high shelf with a bust of himself and his treasured Dresden and Staffordshire figurines. Even in Vevey, Switzerland, where he now lives, I saw it still occupying this place of honor. So perhaps his opinion of the Academy awards has improved with the years.

A very short while after my father finished *The Circus* he plunged into preparing his script for *City Lights.* But on the eve of production a major crisis hit the motion-picture industry. Nineteen twenty-eight was a historic year for Hollywood. Talkies had passed through the experimental stage and were now emerging as a commercial reality. Producers had to install new equipment, discard old techniques, put dialogue as well as plot and scenery in their stories, and find actors with good speaking voices to play in these pictures. This was a period of eclipse for many stars high in public favor, while unknowns with good speaking voices quickly rose to prominence.

Dad had a good voice, had used it on stage for both singing and acting parts. But he was uncertain about how it would go over on the screen. And he wasn't convinced of the artistic quality of the new medium, feeling that it brought too much realism into a make-believe world. He closed down production to mull over his problem. Only other producers of the time could know what anxiety he experienced in those days of indecision. He was chiefly concerned that the Little Tramp, through whom he had been able to express so many of his inner feelings and whose chief appeal rested on pantomime, might be destroyed by talkies. It was as though throughout that long spring and summer he were contemplating the death of a very dear though imaginary relative—his alter ego.

There were two real deaths in our family that year. Great-grandfather Curry died April 2, 1928, and Grandmother Chaplin died August 28, with my father at her bedside. Friends say that Grandmother Chaplin's death threw Dad into a melancholy state of mind for weeks.

By this time he had decided that *City Lights* should be a silent picture. I know he explained to some people that his decision was influenced by purely commercial reasons. The Little Tramp, with his universal language of pantomime, had become popular the world over; to limit him to the English tongue would reduce his market by millions of potential customers. But knowing my father, I'm sure there was a deeper reason than this for his decision. He simply could not make the move that might destroy the Little Tramp. *City Lights* was my father's signed reprieve.

What that decision cost him in emotional turmoil I can only guess. He drove his crews day and night, shooting thousands of feet of film—most of it to be discarded. He drove himself along with the crew, thinking no more of his own health than that of others. He was so run-down that in the early spring of 1929 a severe attack of ptomaine poisoning went into intestinal flu and ended in a close brush with pneumonia. He had to stop production and close down the studio for a week or so until he recuperated.

It was sometime that spring, after Dad had recovered from his illness and was back at work again, that Great-grandmother Curry decided to take matters into her own hands. Nana had left on a trip with Mother, and now that Great-grandfather Curry had passed away Grandma had no one to interfere with her. One day, almost two years after the divorce, she picked up the phone and asked Dad if he didn't want us to visit him.

Our father didn't hesitate. He told Grandma to bring us up at once. He was amazed to see us. We were no longer the babies who had been such an enigma to him. We were three- and four-year-old boys who walked and talked freely, not only in English but in Spanish, for Grandma Curry, who wanted us to know her native tongue, had hired a full-time Spanish maid to take care of us. Dad, who could speak only a few phrases of Spanish himself, was highly amused to hear us prattling away so fluently in a foreign tongue.

That first visit of ours broke the ice. After that Dad phoned Grandma often to tell her he would like to pick us up and take us to the studio with him. He delighted in showing us off to everyone. He was very proud of us.

I'm sure it was more than pride with Dad, that Syd and I helped to fill some emptiness in his life. My father is so re-served that often it's difficult to know what he's thinking or feeling. But sometimes he gives himself away in his sentimental gestures, such as his keeping the large picture of Syd and me in a place of honor on the piano in his living room. When Syd and I grew older we would have preferred to have our father exchange that picture for a more up-to-date portrait, because everyone said we looked like little girls, but Dad stubbornly clung to it.

When Nana and Mother returned from their trip, the relationship between Dad and us had been firmly established. Nana now took over the chore of driving us to Dad's place or getting us ready for him to pick up whenever he pleased. Nana never went in to see our father when she brought us to him. There was still the wall of separation between them and it was even mixed with some fear on Nana's part. In the past, in his bitter anger, my father had at times made vague but ominous threats—or at least it had seemed so to Nana, who is a rather timid person. She would leave us at the front gate with the servants and either wait for us or come back later. But one day shortly after Nana had turned us over to the servants we came running out again, hair flying, breathless with excitement.

"Nana, Nana," we called, "Daddy wants to see you. He said to come in."

Slowly Nana got out of the car, and with us tugging at her hands went up to the front door. It had been a long while since she had last gone inside the big house. Our father was waiting for her in the vestibule, somewhat aloof but friendly. He put out his hand. Nana took it.

"I wanted to tell you what wonderful boys they are," he exclaimed. "You've brought them up with such good manners I'm proud of them." It was his way of making the first overtures.

After that Nana went in with us every time we visited Dad. While she hovered in the background Syd and I would run up and kiss him on the cheek. Dad was shy about our kisses, about admitting how much he liked them, but we could see that he was truly pleased. Dad loves affection, even though he's so reserved about giving it. Syd and I have always been more outgoing. Even now that we're grown men we still kiss our father whenever we visit him. And he still reacts in the same embarrassed but pleased way. Shyly he'll kiss us back, or pat us on the shoulder. It wasn't long before he and Nana were kissing each other on the cheek too, just as they had when he and Mother were still married.

Syd and I soon discovered our father was completely different from all the other fathers we had ever seen. No one had such a funny father as ours. All the time we were with him he kept us laughing. We learned later that it didn't matter to him whether he had a big audience or just two small boys. If he felt like entertaining and the audience was friendly, there was no limit to what he would do for a laugh.

He used to go through the Little Tramp routines for us—a pathetic shuffle of the feet, a quick kick and a prat fall. He always executed those usually clumsy movements with such grace that there was an air of ballet about them.

"Have you seen the way a chicken walks?" he would say every now and then out of the blue, and he would strut around, flapping his wings and cackling. It was the bit he did in full chicken regalia—head, feathers, talons—for a sequence in *The Gold Rush*. But he really didn't need that costume. His performance was realistic without it.

At our father's studio Syd and I found a land of real make-believe. In his dressing room we watched him turning into the Little Tramp before our eyes. First he would get out the big sheet of black crepe hair which provided him with innumerable little mustaches. He'd cut one out, glue it on carefully and trim it down to size. Then he'd turn around and give Syd and me a cocky smirk.

"Well, what do you think of your father now?" he'd ask.

And he would start screwing his face into all sorts of grimaces. Next he would climb into the baggy pants, and after that on would go the oversize shoes. He would take a few turns around the room, shuffling about on those ridiculous shoes. We didn't realize at the time that he was working himself into character. We just sat fascinated while he kept up a continual line of patter.

"Of course," he'd run on, "you know why the Little Fellow has to walk with his feet out. Because the shoes are too long and he couldn't walk lifting his knees up all the time. He'd bump into himself. So, boys, that's the way we have to walk."

While Dad was keeping up this chatter he was shrugging into his tight-fitting coat, clapping the too-small derby on his head, twirling the cane. Syd and I couldn't help laughing. At every peal of merriment the Little Tramp would get a jauntier

45

set to his shoulders. And there he was at last completely in character. He seemed altogether different in his Little Tramp outfit, less reserved, more assured, more a child like ourselves.

Our father was just as fascinating to us out on the set. While the camera ground with its whirring rhythm and the hot lights beat down, he would perform against a background of other people. You always noticed him most. He was funny. People around the set laughed. Syd and I always laughed. When people laughed he seemed to get an even cockier tilt to his head. His eyes sparkled. He was obviously having fun.

And this was our father's work. It seemed more like play to Syd and me. People said that it was acting and that our father was an actor. Since we weren't at an age to see movies, it never occurred to us that what our father did all day ever got beyond the sets in his studio. Yet we knew he was important in some way. We were made aware of that whenever we went out in public with him.

One of our father's simpler pastimes was to stroll down Hollywood Boulevard, and sometimes he would take us with him. We would all just walk along, relaxing, window shopping, face shopping. Our father always liked to look at faces and study mannerisms on our strolls. Sometimes he tried to hide his identity behind dark glasses. But even then it wasn't long before he was recognized.

"Charlie Chaplin!" someone would exclaim. "Charlie Chaplin and his sons!" And a crowd would quickly gather, thrusting their autograph books at Dad. Dad would start obligingly signing them, but after a while he would wave the rest away.

"I'm tired now and I want to go home," he would say. "Please send them to the studio."

Then, taking our hands, Dad would hurry us along very fast to where the car was waiting to whisk us back up to the hill.

"As you can see, boys, I'm quite some fellow," he would say, half laughing, pleased with the afternoon. "Oh, very important indeed!"

46

He was important and he was an actor, whatever that was, and we loved him, Syd and I. We loved this pixie father who had such a jaunty way about him. We wanted to be with him. But there were long periods when he didn't call up, when he didn't come around for us.

We used to look at the picture we kept of him in our bedroom and wonder when he'd send for us again. We couldn't just go to him when we pleased because the world belonged to grownups and you had to do as they wished. I became resigned to that early. I found it was easier that way. Syd was different. He was always ready to tackle them, even though he knew each time that he would go down in defeat.

"I'm going to be an actor when I grow up," Syd said.

I understood what he meant. He was going to take that whole fairy world for himself one day, so he wouldn't have to wait to be invited into it. I thought over the idea a minute. It looked good.

"Me too," I agreed.

7

In February, 1931, after the New York premiere of *City Lights*, Dad left for an extended trip around the world. But he wasn't to be the only traveler in the Chaplin family. It had been decided that Syd and I, who were five and six at the time, should make a long trip ourselves. Mother, who had been sightseeing in Europe the year before, thought it would be nice for us to spend some time in France and learn another language while we were small. Nana was to take us.

By this time Syd and I had discovered that our father had a sure formula for getting attention. We had only to imitate him as the Little Tramp to be greeted everywhere with applause and laughter. But we weren't yet aware of his true stature in the outside world. That was brought home to us the day we boarded the *Ile de France* in New York Harbor. Just before sailing time a swarm of newspapermen scrambled aboard to talk to us. There must have been about twenty photographers with shutters clicking and flash bulbs popping, recording the momentous fact that the Chaplin boys were going to Europe.

When we landed in France we received the same jubilant reception. Perhaps it was even more enthusiastic, because our father, known to Frenchmen as Charlot, has always been extremely popular there.

"So you're the Chaplin boys," people would say to us in awed tones. "Do you know what a famous actor your father is? You should be proud to be the sons of the great Charlot."

Everyone seemed to know him. Everyone idolized him. Everyone lavished attention on us because we were his sons. Before it was all over we even appeared on a radio program. We sang songs in both French and English and answered questions about our father like authorities. Dad had always been just a very funny man to us. But now, limned in this constant spotlight, he seemed to swell into an almost legendary figure before our eyes.

We spent most of our year abroad at Nice, where Nana's boy friend was also staying. He was a millionaire by the name of Victor Bresler and he was in love with Nana and wanted to marry her, but Nana turned him down to devote herself to us. I have always been grateful to her for her sacrifice. How could Syd and I ever have gotten along without her!

France to me was like a great fairyland. I remember it as a montage of colorful scenes—the wonderful sights which Mr. Bresler showed us, the lovely parks where we rolled hoops and gleefully dodged the photographers who seemed to be always after us, the gay Gallic children who were our companions. At first we were at a loss, for we couldn't speak their language; but presently we were forgetting the Spanish we knew and jabbering away in colloquial French.

Somewhere there in sunny France the nocturnal terror disappeared and I no longer woke up screaming at night. Nana said I had outgrown it.

Meanwhile our father, on his trip around the world, was proving his popularity all over again. He was greeted by enormous crowds in England, Germany, Italy, France and later Japan. He met such political figures as Ramsay MacDonald and Lloyd George. He renewed acquaintance with Winston Churchill and Albert Einstein and, in the literary field, with George Bernard Shaw, H. G. Wells, Frank Harris and Emil Ludwig. He met kings, princes, dukes and Mahatma Gandhi. He learned to ski with Douglas Fairbanks at St. Moritz and sailed with Uncle Sydney to the Orient, visiting Ceylon, Singapore and Bali and ending up in Japan, where he was received like royalty.

In Japan he experienced some real adventure. Members of the Black Dragon Society, an old-fashioned clique which wanted to keep Japan in her medieval state, assassinated the Prime Minister, Tsuyoshi Inukai, while my father was there. My father told me in later years that the clique hated him, too, because they thought his popularity with the Japanese people was bringing about a more sympathetic attitude to the West. His life had actually been in danger. Police were ordered to keep guard over him, and he had to change hotels once to throw his would-be assassins off the track. Shortly after his departure from the first hotel two members of the society were caught there—looking for him and bent on violence.

Finally, after an absence of fifteen months, our father returned to America. Almost every incident that had befallen him during his long tour had been reported in the papers, and since we were his sons what little that happened to us had also made news. But it was always just a reflection of his glory. Now, a year after we had come to France, something suddenly occurred that made us feel we were soon to be celebrities in our own right. It was in the form of a cablegram to Nana from Mother.

David Butler, the director, was interested in doing a picture with us and we were to come home at once. We packed excitedly, and I recall how, on the boat back, Syd and I enthusiastically discussed our coming careers. When we reached New York there was a still greater hullabaloo. We were interviewed by reporters and they weren't asking about our father. They wanted to know all about us.

"I am going to be a great actor," I told them solemnly.

I was bragging, perhaps. But it wasn't just bragging. I was thinking about a man who was the greatest comedian in the world. I was his son with his name. So I had to be good. More than anything else in the world I wanted him to be proud of me.

Mother accompanied us back from New York to Hollywood, and one night shortly afterwards Mr. Butler came over to the house for dinner and the contract was signed. Meanwhile Nana phoned Dad, who had just returned himself, and asked him if he wanted to see us. Of course he did, he told her, so Nana took us to him at once.

We were back in the big house on the hill with our father, whom we hadn't seen for almost a year and a half. Diffidently we went up and kissed him. Then he smiled and put his arms around us. He seldom made the first affectionate move, and if he did it was usually a formal gesture—as though he were afraid of giving too much of himself and being rebuffed.

"Can you speak French, boys?" he asked almost at once.

He was always so interested in the things that Syd and I learned, so proud of us when we mastered anything in the educational field. We talked in French for him and he laughed as though it were something special. To Syd and me it was nothing. Millions of other children spoke French daily. But we were about to do truly big things.

"We're going to be great actors like you," we bragged.

We expected him to be pleased. Instead he looked strangely

grave and didn't even comment on our acting plans. Unknown to us, our father had already voiced his disapproval of our going into pictures. But Mother didn't think he would actually interfere. After all, he came from a family of actors and had appeared on the stages of music halls at an early age himself. It was natural for his children to follow in his footsteps. It was in the blood.

Perhaps it was just because our father had been a child actor and remembered too painfully the warping of his own childhood under the demands of a difficult profession that he was dead serious about keeping Syd and me out of pictures. When he learned that the deal was set and the contract signed he asked his lawyers to take the case to court. It proved to be another legal battle between him and Mother, or rather between their attorneys. The newspapers got hold of the story and blew it up. Everyone who could read knew about the fight—everyone except Syd and me.

Our father's argument against our being in pictures was an impressive one to the court. He was, he said through his lawyers, interested only in our happiness and well-being. He wanted us to have a normal childhood. He was afraid that entering show business so early would interfere with our education. The judge was in agreement and decided in our father's favor. The contract was nullified.

When Syd and I were told we weren't to make a picture after all, the disappointment was so great that we broke into tears. Later, up on the hill, Dad tried to explain his reason for breaking the contract.

"If you're really in earnest about wanting to act, going into it now would be the worst thing in the world for you, boys," he said. "You'd be typed as child actors. When you reached the gawky stage they'd drop you. Then you would have to make a complete comeback and you'd have a hard time of it, because everyone would remember you as those cute little juveniles. But if after you're grown up you still want to act, then I won't interfere."

Today, when I see the tough time former child stars like Jackie Coogan have had in making a comeback, I realize my father's wisdom. But then his explanations didn't make much sense to Syd or me. What did he mean when he told us we should wait until we were grown up? Shirley Temple, whom we were soon to number among our playmates, was even younger than we—only three years old and yet she was starting on her career. We could have been, too, if our father hadn't stopped it all, we told each other resentfully.

8

But life doesn't move always on the downbeat. We had lost our careers before they had even started, but at the same time a compensation came into our lives that was pleasurably to affect all our boyhood.

Paulette Goddard! She was number five or so in the list of leading ladies my father's wizardry had raised to prominence throughout the years. Edna Purviance, Georgia Hale, Merna Kennedy, Virginia Cherrill, they had all glowed for a spell under his tutelage. Paulette was the only one of them who remained as well known after she left my father.

Dad first met her when they were both guests on a yachting party given by Joseph M. Schenck, the producer. She was then a chorus girl under contract to Hal Roach, where she was doing quickie comedies to get experience before the camera.

My father, on the other hand, was one of the most prominent and popular figures in Hollywood. At the time he met Paulette there was gossip that he had more than a passing interest in Marion Davies. He was a frequent guest at her beach home. Her wit amused him and he admired her courage and her spirit of independence and her generosity. But though Miss Davies had so many qualities that appealed to my father, she lacked the most important one in his eyes. She didn't need him. She was at the time already a success in pictures.

Paulette, on the other hand, was still an unknown. From the very beginning her life had been hard. Her father and mother separated when she was very small and her mother had to go to work to support them both. At the age of fourteen Paulette became a Ziegfeld Follies girl and from then on she was the breadwinner of the family. At sixteen she married Edgar James, from whom she was divorced in Reno in 1931. Dad told me later that she was only twenty-one when he met her the following year. He found her a delightful person who seemed to be always laughing.

My father has an intuitive feeling toward people. He recognizes the intrinsic qualities that lie at the core of their personalities. In Paulette he didn't see just another run-of-the-mill chorine. He saw a girl with a great spirit of independence and courage, a girl who dared show an impudent pluck in the face of adversity.

She had all the qualities he needed for the gamin-like character who was to be the heroine in his next picture, *Modern Times*, the script of which he was then preparing. The story was to be a satire on the machine age, and he had been led to do it by the depression, which had shocked him deeply when he returned from his trip abroad to find millions idle in a land overflowing with plenty. He had already traced his heroine in vague outline, but before she could take concrete form he had to find the right person to play the part. Much of my father's success in being able to get good performances out of the girls he chose was due to his writing the parts with them in mind.

Almost immediately after my father's meeting with Paulette the girl in *Modern Times* began to emerge with her flesh-and-blood lineaments. At the same time he bought up her contract from Hal Roach and took her completely under his wing. He became her mentor. Dad is a born teacher at heart—teaching others is one more way of satisfying his ego.

He found Paulette an apt pupil. She read the books he suggested and many others besides, because she was as avid for education as he. She was the first of his wives who, despite her youth, was mature intellectually. She was able to talk with him on his level. It made for a closer companionship between them.

Paulette studied hard under the singing and dancing instructors my father provided for her, and sopped up all his dramatic coaching. She even followed his advice in the selection of her clothes. But most important of all to her, inasmuch as she was an unknown, my father began to take her everywhere with him, dating her almost exclusively.

Newspapers around the world had a field day over that. From the first they began predicting an early marriage for Paulette and my father. When he kissed her at the airport as she set off for a trip to New York in the fall of '32 it was grounds for open speculation. The speculation increased by the spring of 1933. That summer, a French newspaper came out with a "scoop" that Dad and Paulette had been married at sea.

When Dad bought his yacht, the *Panacea*, and started having it remodeled, newspaper accounts referred to it as the "honeymoon" yacht. In April of '34 the steady flow of rumors solidified into another "definite" story that my father and Paulette had been married aboard the *Panacea* by Captain Dave Anderson, the skipper, who had subsequently been paid by Dad—for reasons known only to him and Paulette—to tear the telltale page out of his log book. This fantastic story was repeated with variations all through the summer. In the fall of '34, when Paulette, to tease the newspapermen, began to wear a wedding band set with diamonds, a new twist was added to the old story. My father, so the story went now, had obtained the marriage license in London under the name of Spencer for himself and Mrs. Edgar James for Paulette. In February of '35, reporters bared the gossip that my father himself, at a recent party, had admitted a secret marriage to Paulette more than a year before. And in November of '36 no less a person than Randolph Churchill said solemnly, "I am not at liberty to quote Mr. Chaplin directly but I can definitely say that they are married. They have been married for more than a year."

To all these rumors both my father and Paulette replied with a discreet silence that only ballooned the subject up out of all proportion to its importance. I think my father, with his quixotic sense of humor, got a lot of amusement out of the flurry he and Paulette were causing. Perhaps he'd come to the conclusion that since he was to live in a fish bowl anyway he might as well have some fun at it. As for Paulette, she's always been a pixie—but a pixie with a purpose, too.

"If you don't admit or deny a story it keeps going and going," she told me once. "The minute you affirm or deny it—then it's dead, and I'm not so stupid as to do that."

Paulette was the unknown and my father was the known. As long as her name could be kept linked to his in a frantic guessing game she could count on appearing frequently in the papers. It was valuable publicity for her.

I remember the day Syd and I first met Paulette. It is as plain to me as though it had happened only yesterday, instead of more than a quarter-century ago. Our father brought her to the house where we were living with Nana and Grandma to introduce her to us and pick us up for an afternoon with him. He jumped out of the car, came around, opened the door and helped out a beautiful platinum blonde. Syd and I, who were waiting side by side on the porch, were so thunderstruck we could only stare. Her pale, shining hair framed a piquant heart-shaped face alive with sparkling blue-green eyes. As she came up to Syd and me, our father introduced us.

"These are my sons, Charles, Jr., and Sydney," he said gravely. And then, turning to us, he added, "This is Paulette Goddard, boys. Now what do you say to the nice lady?"

Syd and I lifted our heads and looked into that friendly face with its mischievous conspiratorial smile, and we lost our hearts at once, never to regain them through all the golden years of our childhood. Have you ever realized, Paulette, how much you meant to us? You were like a mother, a sister, a friend all in one. You lightened our father's spells of somber moodiness and you turned the big house on the hill into a real home. We thought you were the loveliest creature in the whole world. And somehow I feel, looking back today, that we meant as much to you, that we satisfied some need in your life, too.

9

The year 1933 marked the third and last of the legal battles between our parents, and it was over money. Syd's and my trust funds were handled by the Citizens National Bank, which invested them in stock. Our mother, who was our legal guardian, had full control of the monthly revenues, but she was expected to send our father an itemized monthly report of all expenses. I can well imagine what anguish keeping those accounts must have been to my mother, who, like me, isn't good at figures.

After the tangle she had with Dad over the movie contract, it suddenly occurred to her that he might one day call her to account for her expenditures on us. It was then that she hired a bonded CPA, Mrs. Julia Bergh, to take care of our business affairs. I remember Mrs. Bergh in her makeshift office on an upper landing in our home on Rossmore Avenue. There she would be behind her desk, her fingers flying over the typewriter keys as at the end of the month she knocked out page after page of items. The lists included even the most insignificant expenditures, from a haircut for Syd at $2.50 to the removal of a wart from one of my fingers at $5.00.

Month after month our father, carefully going over all these lists, began to feel a growing alarm at the amount of money being spent on us. His concern was based on a belief that money is about the most important security in the life of any individual, and he thought that as much of ours as possible should be laid away for our future.

My mother says today that she wishes Dad had come to her privately with his proposal to put a quarter of each of our monthly incomes in an irrevocable savings account, to be made available to us on our twenty-first birthdays. She would have seen the wisdom in it and agreed with him, and all the subsequent court hassle could have been avoided.

But my father, who had made up with Nana and was seeing us regularly, must have still felt some sense of estrangement toward my mother, because apparently it never entered his head to speak to her directly. Instead he called in his attorneys and put the matter in their hands. And there it was all over again—the public wrangling for the newspapers to pick up.

My father didn't go to court throughout the whole hearing. My mother made an appearance to testify and became hysterical. There on the witness stand she expressed the feeling of being relentlessly pursued, persecuted and hounded by my father. I suppose even then tensions were building dangerously in the hidden places of her psyche. For her conviction that my father had sinister motives toward her was to become magnified a thousandfold when she suffered her nervous breakdown a few years later.

The court battle died out quietly when the judge decided in favor of my father's proposal, and at the same time gave

Mother a moral victory by releasing her from those onerous monthly reports which had been such a burden to her. When our twenty-first birthdays came around, Sydney and I were both grateful to our father's wisdom, for we realized seventeen thousand dollars apiece from the savings accounts. But I cannot say we did not suffer at the time from the emotional tension of our contending parents.

An even more disturbing influence in our lives at that time was the aftermath of a tragedy which affected not only us but the children of prominent people everywhere. The day after the newspapers carried the story of the kidnaping of the Lindbergh baby, workmen came to equip all the windows of our house on Rossmore Avenue with burglar alarms. But our family didn't think the alarms were enough for our bedroom. We also had to sleep with the windows closed all night long. On hot evenings when we tossed and turned with our covers thrown back, our bodies flushed and sweaty with heat, we wondered what it was all about. It didn't make sense.

Then one night the screen of one of the windows was cut and the burglar alarm went off. In seconds the house was in a turmoil. All the lights flashed on and the police were called. Syd and I ran through the rooms, staring at the cut screen and the big uniformed policemen. From all the speculation that was going on we learned that whoever it was had been after us and that it was a real cops-and-robbers game. We were excited and childishly proud to be the center of so much excitement.

It was only later, after the bustle had died down and the officers in their dark uniforms had gone away, that we saw the gravity on the faces of the grownups and began to feel a vague fear for the first time. After that, as long as we stayed in that house on Rossmore, the fear was always with us.

For the first weeks after the scare we weren't allowed outside. Finally this ban was lifted, but we were no longer permitted even to step out the front door without an adult. And of course the homes of our friends were now off limits to us. If they wanted to see us they had to come to our house. Nana took us to our private day school and brought us home again. She escorted us to parties, even if they were in the neighborhood. We knew just one other person who was supervised as closely as we—Shirley Temple, who always invited us to her parties. By this time she was an established film celebrity, having left us far behind.

But Shirley was a girl, while Syd and I were seven- and eight-year-old boys—too old, we felt, to be supervised like kindergarteners. It was with a feeling of relief that we learned in the fall that we were to go away to boarding school the next January.

Boarding school was our father's idea. He felt we were surrounded by too many women. Counting Mrs. Bergh and our governess, there were five of them in all—an overwhelming number to my father, whose experiences with the opposite sex so far had made him somewhat wary of it in general. He sent Mother a list of schools of which he approved and asked her to pick one for us. Mother and Nana decided on Black-Foxe Military Institute. It was in Hollywood, so that it would be easy for us to come home on week ends. A number of children of prominent movie people went there, and, though Nana wasn't so sure about it, Mother felt the military training would be good for us. She notified our father of her choice and he expressed his satisfaction with it. I don't suppose he ever thought—either then or later—of how inconsistent it was for him, who had always voiced such a strong objection to war, to be sending his sons to a military academy.

It was a crisp January morning when we set out for our new school, jubilant over the prospects before us. But the minute I walked inside the gates with Syd and Nana, who had driven us over, I felt something was wrong. The sinking feeling increased with every step forward. It reached its climax when I said good-by to Nana, and found myself separated even from Syd. All our lives we had shared a room, and now for the first time we were not to be together. I had quarters, instead, with two young strangers. Our room was small and unpretentious, the beds narrow but comfortable. We shared a bathroom with the boys in the bedroom on the other side. Everything seemed somehow empty and bare.

I burst into tears. The school nurse, who had accompanied me to my room, must have been used to such exhibitions. She tried to comfort me.

"Everything will be all right. You'll get used to it and then you'll like it," she said.

It took me three weeks to "get used to it." I cried on and off, quietly, where no one could see or hear me. Once I walked in my sleep, and so did Syd. The nurse told Nana that was natural to newcomers.

The worst thing about the school in my eyes was the strict regimentation. From sunup to sundown everything seemed as carefully ordered as if you were a pawn on a chessboard.

There were penalties if you broke the rules. Whispering in class might result in a painful feruling on the palm of your hand. Talking in line could earn a visit to the physical instructor's office, and a paddling. I'd been paddled at home by Nana with a slipper, but that was different. When Nana spanked me I felt hurt mostly because I loved her and didn't want her disappointed in me. But a spanking at school was such an impersonal thing I felt both resentful and humiliated —humiliated because I was so much smaller I never had a chance to fight back or even to talk back. A really serious offense might bring you to the office of the headmaster, where something worse than a feruling or a paddling awaited you. Then you ran the danger of having a letter sent home to your father.

In those early days at school, life seemed something like running the gantlet, with a bunch of grownup ogres ready to pounce on you for the least offense. It was a far cry from the feminine love and justice we had known at home. Though I

63

didn't share a room with Syd, I saw him often and learned from him that he hated everything as much as I.

It's easy to imagine how Friday affected not only Syd and me but the whole school. It was a red-letter day. On Friday we paraded in front of an audience made up of relatives and friends, and showed off what we had learned during our week's drill.

Nana came every Friday to watch the parade. Mother came occasionally, and Dad only a few times. He was always reserved, as he is with strangers. He didn't make a point of visiting the teachers as the other parents did, or mixing with the parents themselves—not even Nana. Was it because the sight of that well-ordered school with its attractive buildings and spacious grounds brought vividly to mind the dingy orphanage where he had spent two years of his life? And did the memory tie his tongue again with the restrictive politeness drilled into the children of the poor?

One day, though, my father made his way through the spectators to Nana's side.

"You know, as we grow older we mellow," he said suddenly, out of the fullness of an emotion Nana could never comprehend. "Time takes care of a lot of things. I'm sure everything's going to be all right between us from now on."

And it was. Those words were the seal to the last bitterness between my father and mother. There were no more court battles and no pulling at cross-purposes over our welfare.

I remember our father those few times he came. I can see him plainly yet, standing with his hands behind his back, his blue eyes bright with amusement, and a pleased, almost gloating expression about his lips. Perhaps he was feeling a kind of amazement and pride that he was able to provide his sons with such a well-ordered, sheltered life.

Yet there was something more than that in his face, something that struck home to me and filled me with yearning. Was it the essential loneliness that I sensed in him, and wanted somehow to erase? I know only that I marched straighter,

64

that I was more alert, that I saluted with a snappier gesture and clicked my heels more sharply when I saw those ice-blue eyes upon me.

Those Friday afternoons were more valued by us boys at Black-Foxe than any other day in our school week, for if our deportment had been exemplary we all got to go home for the week end. Usually Syd and I spent one week end with Nana and Mother and the next with Dad on the hill, for now that we were in military school we were considered old enough to stay the whole week end with him.

Oh those wonderful week ends! That wonderful magical house on the hill, with the man who lived there, the man who was so many men in one. We were to see them all now: the strict disciplinarian, the priceless entertainer, the taciturn, moody dreamer, the wild man of Borneo with his flashes of volcanic temper. That beloved chameleon shape was to weave itself subtly through all my boyhood and was never to stop fascinating me.

10

And now it is time to speak of those nostalgic years in my father's home, where for almost two decades Syd and I were part of a domestic life heretofore unchronicled. I cannot go by the old house today without a feeling of loss over something good that has gone out of my life forever. Tim Durant, my father's closest friend in those years, tells me he, too, has this same depressing feeling. That house where my father, like royalty, used to entertain his guests when he was at the height of his popularity and power seems only a forlorn shell now, a symbol of the old days that have gone from the film capital and will not come back again. Modern picture making has lost much of the creative luster which characterized its beginnings; it has become less play and more a staid, respectable business.

The six and a half acres of my father's small estate in which he so delighted and which was so unassuming in comparison with those of our neighbors, Harold Lloyd's below, Pickfair above, are evaporating. Many of the trees my father planted on his hill slopes have been whacked away. Much of the ground has been leveled and subdivided and new building is in progress today. On the site of the tennis court which my father so loved and upon which he spent so many happy hours, stands an alien house.

Over this mutilated property broods our old home. The new owners are completely remodeling its interior, which has already passed through two epochs of alteration—one under Paulette and one under Oona O'Neill. The exterior has been repainted—shocking renovation! For as long as it was in my father's possession I can't remember his ever having the aged ochre stain rejuvenated, though he may have had the walls cleaned or washed occasionally. Capped by a tile roof, the great pile now stands there almost naked, like a staunch betrayed fortress, its walls stripped of their canopy of tall trees which my father had planted around it so that you could hear the sighing and the tapping of the branches at almost every window.

Looking at the place that today seems so melancholy to me, I seem to hear my father saying, "I love this house. I'd never live anywhere else but right here. What more do you want?"

My father's woods surrounded the house on three sides. Fir, hemlock, cedar, spruce and pine, they marched down the slopes of the hill. Narrow dirt paths lined by uneven stones and seemingly laid at random meandered among the trees. Dad especially loved to walk in his woods after a rain, when the odor of pine and fire was strong in the air.

On the fourth side the lawn slopes away in steep giant steps to the tennis court and swimming pool. Sometimes, after the pool had been drained, Dad enjoyed going down into it and turning on the water. This was one of the few domestic chores I have ever seen him perform, for he is not a handy man.

The front of the house faces a circular driveway so that cars can stop at the main entrance. Inside, you find yourself in a spacious hall, which extends down the full length of the house and which in those early days was two stories high for most of its length. It was as though my father wanted to keep the walls from ever crowding in on him again.

Toward the front of the hall a winding stairway mounts to the second floor, terminating in a balustered balcony that, before Oona's renovations, overlooked the hall. In the curve of the stairway below, Dad kept a suit of Oriental armor and a tremendous bowl-shaped brass gong with its black-handled knocker. There seemed to be a secret rapport between Dad and that gong. Sometimes when he was passing by deep in thought, he would turn and lightly tap it with one finger and then wait quietly to hear the muted tone come softly back to him as though in reply to some question he had asked.

To the left of the hall there is the spacious vestibule with its high ceiling arched like that of a cathedral. It was here that the pipe organ stood. Dad kept it until just a couple of years before he left for Vevey, when Oona persuaded him to have it taken out. I don't know how she managed it, for Dad loved it. Every now and then he would pick out something on it, usually one of his own compositions. But if a friend came in who knew how to play, he couldn't get by without first sitting down to that organ. It wasn't enough for my father to fill the vestibule with the mellifluous thunder of those swelling organ chords; he had amplifiers to carry the sound all over the house.

The vestibule also served as a small movie theater. The projection room was behind the stairwell in the hall, and there was a button to press to release the screen, which would drop down in front of the organ.

Down the hall from the vestibule was the living room, which in those days, before the study was added, opened on the terraced lawn behind the house. The room is elegant in shape, with broad windows and white-paneled walls. In the

68

center of the wall to the right as you go in is a broad fireplace, where instead of wood Dad always burned coal, in the English custom.

The fireplace was flanked by bookcases filled with volumes that covered a wide range of subjects and authors. On top of the bookcases my father kept his Oscar and his figurines, which he sometimes let us examine, though he hovered around us anxiously the whole time, cautioning us not to drop them because they were valuable. I remember some of them with special vividness, quaint little equestrians on their prancing horses, the whole figurine standing about a foot high, with every detail, even to the sabers, perfectly executed.

In the far left-hand corner of the living room stood the piano, a Steinway grand, and close by was the big Webster dictionary, which Dad consulted so often, and the table he used when he worked downstairs. To the near left of the door was the bright red lacquered Oriental cabinet decorated with a maze of dragons and other fanciful figures. In the cabinet my father kept the mementos of his trip to Japan, the kimonos and the ceremonial masks and the beautifully engraved samurai swords.

There were two of these swords with slightly curved, razor-sharp blades. Each was encased in a red, black and gold lacquered wooden sheath. The larger one was about three feet long and too formidable for my tastes. The small one was a foot and a half long, beautifully engraved with red and black figures and copiously decorated with gold braid. I loved that sword, but Dad would never let us handle it for long. He was always afraid we would hurt ourselves on the sharp blade.

In the days of my father's bachelorhood, the living room boasted an indiscriminate assortment of furniture, though most of it was in the heavy English style. Some of that furniture had served him in the small apartments where he first lived in Los Angeles. Other pieces had been bought for the houses he had rented. After he built his own place he just

69

moved everything he possessed into it. He never could bring himself to part with anything he owned.

Scattered around the room were the mementos of his trips abroad, the tasteful and the tasteless occupying equally important positions. Photographs stood in phalanxes on bookcases and table and piano. Like the mementos, they were there chiefly for personal reasons. It gave the room a somewhat cluttered but comfortable appearance.

Across the hall from the living room was the stately dining room with its wide windows, also opening out on the lawn. The dining room was really the most modern in the house. Above the fireplace, which was seldom used, a paneled mirror beautifully reflected the outside world opposite it and, on gala occasions, the elegant guests around the massive dining table. Now that Syd and I were young men in uniforms, we had a place at that table. Year by year our steady growth from boyhood into manhood was transiently recorded by the big mirror that looked down on so many fascinating scenes.

Next to the dining room was a small spare room which Paulette's maid occupied when she came to live with us. A narrow back hall separated both these rooms from the old-fashioned kitchen and pantry which were the scene of so many boyish memories. Behind the kitchen lay the servants' dining room, and their living quarters were on the floor below.

Upstairs there were three big bedrooms, each with a bathroom. There was the room where I was born and which came to be Syd's and mine when we stayed there. As soon as possible we would dash up to that friendly haven and strip off our uniforms like prisoners geting out of their stripes.

Down the hall from ours was the middle bedroom, where Syd was born and which was later to become Paulette's. Then came the master bathroom. That bathroom seemed to be always permeated with the odor of Mitsouko, my father's favorite cologne. He used to store bottles and bottles of it on his bathroom shelf. (My father kept himself well supplied in everything, as if he were always afflicted by a vague fear of running out.) For as long as I can remember he has used only Mitsouko. It has become so integral a part of his personality to me that I cannot smell that woodsy fragrance without turning around instinctively, expecting to see him there.

And now I come to another room, the most mysterious one in the whole house—for so my father made it appear to us. It was the organ room, which opened into the master bedroom. Every now and then Dad, Syd and I would make a solemn pilgrimage upstairs to this room. Dad would stand in front of the double doors which sealed it off and open one, causing a suction that would make the other fly out with a swish, as though released by an invisible hand. Then all three of us would go reverently into the big oblong room that housed the organ pipes. A shadowy stairstep army, they marched from the very small slender trebles at one end to the massive, dignified basses at the other.

"It took a lot of work to get them all in there. A lot of work!" Dad would say proudly. And he would lay his hands on the pipes in a caress, as though they were old friends.

Everything in that house seemed like an old friend to our father, but nowhere was this more apparent than in his bedroom. Before the study was built on downstairs, he did most of his work in that room, spending hours there writing and reading. It seemed to bear the imprint of his personality more plainly than any other place in the house. It is a spacious room full of wide windows and boasting a handsome fireplace which I cannot recall Dad's ever using. But it was austerely furnished—a writing table and chair, another big Webster, and twin beds, each with its night stand.

My father usually slept in the far bed, the one by the windows. I recall the pulp detective magazines that were always stacked by this bed. My father might read Spengler and Schopenhauer and Kant for edification, but for sheer relaxation he chose murder mysteries. Tired from a hard day's work, he liked to read them in bed for they put him to sleep.

In the drawer of the night stand beside his bed, my father kept a thirty-eight caliber automatic, with its bullets. He would sometimes show it to Syd and me, though we never saw him fire it.

"I practice with it," he would tell us. "I'm not a bad marksman." I could tell by the way he handled it that it gave him as much a sense of security as the samurai sword downstairs gave me.

In the alcove, where the windows which looked out on his stepped lawn commanded a fine view of the skies, of his neighbors' houses below and the whole town of Beverly Hills, my father kept another prized possession. It was the powerful telescope, mounted on a tripod, which he had owned ever since I could remember. Syd and I spent a great deal of time with Dad at that telescope, in which he found as much excitement as a boy, fiddling with the knobs, adjusting the lenses, trying to bring various objects into clear focus. At night we would study the moon, when it was up, and the starry heavens. Dad would point out the Big Dipper and a few of the main constellations, but actually he was no astronomer at heart. He much preferred training the telescope on his neighbors' homes below him, and under that powerful lens both the more distant and the very near were alike neighbors to him.

Sometimes he would train the telescope on a solitary man walking along the street. He would follow him, musing aloud and every now and then turning the glass over to us so we could get a look too.

"You see that man?" he would say. "He must be going home after a hard day's work. Look at his gait, so slow, so tired. His head's bent. Something's on his mind. What could it be?"

Yes, Dad with his lively curiosity was too close to humanity to go soaring off for long into the heavens. I guess it is not coincidence that his graceful pantomime expresses not the grandeur of the starry skies but the comic-pathetic foibles of his fellow man.

And speaking of foibles, I cannot close this chapter without talking of the most curious, even mysterious furnishing in my father's house. It was the Persian rug that completely covered the floor of his bedroom. That rug! It was reddish hued, with a flower design, and doubtless it had once been very expensive; but as far back as I can recall, it was old and shabby. My mother says it was there when I was born and was far from new then. From the door to the far windows a threadbare path ran through it where the nap had been completely worn down, exposing the warp and woof of the foundation weave. But my father would never part with it, despite the pleas— and there were many from all of us during the years that followed—to replace it with a new one.

"Oh, no, no, I have to leave it there," he would protest with a stubborn shake of his head. "I've had it such a long time and there's something connected with it. It brings me luck."

What that was, what very important incident out of his past, he would never divulge to anyone, but he always gave the impression that it was the memory of something very close to him. I don't know—I only remember my mother's telling me once, when I asked her about it, that it was along that route that my father had paced to and fro, timing her labor pains, the night I, his first living child, was born.

II

Eight years before, when Syd and I had lived in the house on the hill, we had been babies, indifferent to the routines of our home. Now as growing boys we suddenly found ourselves intruders in an establishment which had been formulated when my father first built the house and which had been running smoothly at the time my mother came there as a bride.

She, like us, had been an intruder, because although she was to all appearances the mistress, she had in reality no say in its running. She was very young and very inexperienced, without any notion of how to throw that smoothly running machine out of gear in order to set a new pace more to her liking, as Paulette Goddard was to do later. She could only kick out blindly at what she considered an injustice. But despite her protests, her despairing sense of outrage, the life of the house went on in the well-oiled grooves of habit. It was, I suppose, just about the only thing that remained stable during that stormy period of my parents' marriage. It survived the shipwreck of their union with its subsequent scandal, and during the ensuing years of my father's bachelorhood it settled into an even more rigid routine, the routine of a well-ordered English middle-class domesticity.

In all the reams of copy that have been issued about my father's alleged hedonistic activities and iconoclastic nature, I don't think one of his accusers has brought out his extreme, almost caricatured, bent toward domesticity—his love of a well-ordered home and a life in which surprise or chance, as such, piqued rather than pleased him. He was happiest, most comfortable, when things were the same, when you rose in the morning with the certainty of what you were going to do at four in the afternoon.

When he wasn't working, the day began for my father anywhere from eleven o'clock in the morning to one P.M., for he stayed up late at night. He read and wrote in his room until four in the afternoon, unless it was Saturday and he planned to take us on a jaunt with him somewhere. At four he had a quick game of tennis with friends, if any were there. If not, he would bat the ball around by himself down on the court. Tennis was followed by a quick dip in the pool and a shower or steam bath, after which he would either dress to go out for dinner or eat at home.

His home meals were always simple and seldom varied. They were essentially English—Dad has never cared for gravies or rich sauces. His main course almost always proved to be rare roast beef, roast chicken, roast lamb or lamb chops. There would be a vegetable, peas usually, and baked potatoes. My father seldom bothered with the menu but left everything up to the servants, who knew his tastes. If he went out he usually wound up at the Hollywood restaurant of his friend Henry Bergman. If he spent the evening at home he read or wrote. He seldom entertained in the days before his marriage to Paulette. And he always had tea and crumpets with marmalade served every Sunday afternoon at four. Tea and crumpets, the symbol of solid English comfort and security, was a little ritual with my father.

"It's four o'clock, boys," he would religiously inform us on the week ends we spent with him. "Time for tea and crumpets as it's done in England just at this hour."

This recitation of what made up my father's day during the stretches when a picture wasn't in production sounds very staid and dignified. Only life there was never like that. The staidness was just a shell, a veneer such as you find in the most riotous scenes of *Alice in Wonderland*. Indeed, a kind of Alice-in-Wonderland frenzy pervaded the house from top to bottom, and it was caused by my father's penchant for both perfectionism in service and split-second timing in action.

Dad couldn't have found better servants to fulfill his almost impossible dream of how a good house should be run than his small Japanese staff of three. (He employed Mexican gardeners to take care of the outside grounds.) I guess there never were any servants like those Japanese servants of his; they seemed to have an almost intuitive rapport with him.

Actually, there is a rapport between my father and the whole Japanese race. They understand and love his pantomime, which has so much in common with the tradition of their own Kabuki theater. My father, for his part, fell in love with the Kabuki style of acting, with its stress on pantomime, from the first time he saw a Japanese troupe performing in this country. He liked the Japanese on another score. They were perfectionists at heart, and perfectionism down to the slightest detail is my father's passion. If he ever showed any snobbery it was in this field. He wouldn't put up with an inefficient worker.

Dad was the unmistakable ruler of the house, though he left the entire running of it in the hands of his servants. At the head was Frank, who acted as butler, valet, housekeeper and all-round Man Friday. Square-shouldered, with an honest, homely face, Frank was almost a magician in being able to carry easily on his back a load of work that would have staggered Atlas. Among his other accomplishments he spoke English fluently, though with a colorful accent. He was always affable and friendly and Syd and I came to love him like a brother.

Kay, the chauffeur, was more along the line of what is considered the Japanese type. He had a set, impassive face, a brisk, almost martial gait, and a certain stiff formality of manner that, with his black uniform, his chauffeur's cap and boots, gave him the appearance of a manikin. I can't remember seeing Kay without that uniform and that deadpan face, except when now and then, in the servants' quarters away from his master, he would allow himself to relax in a smile. Kay spoke English but not fluently, and he did not talk nearly so much as Frank. He was a plodder, working methodically, efficiently and on course. I think that even in his dreams—if he had any —Kay was always on course.

George, the cook, had almost no command of English, and spoke it only in broken snatches. But when he talked in his pots and pans it was lyric poetry. There wasn't a dish of whatever kind or nationality that George couldn't cook better than anyone else in town. He was a small, wiry man, about fifty or fifty-five when I first knew him, and just as I can't recall ever seeing Kay without his uniform, I can't remember George without his white apron and tall chef's cap. He wore his apron even on his days off. I think he must have walked around the streets in it.

George was as animated as Kay was stolid. I never saw George when he didn't give the appearance of being tremendously busy at something. Even when he was sitting down he looked busy. It was his face, which was as expressive as Kay's was deadpan. Seamed and lined, with bright eyes that always sparkled as though over some inward humor, it seemed to have come straight out of some Japanese etching. It fascinated my father.

Syd and I came to know the servants well from the very first, just because we were strangers who hadn't yet been fitted in properly. For instance, there was no place to put us when our father dined out, so we were asked if we minded eating with the servants. Minded? In their cozy dining room where sometimes, to make things even more gay, their relatives would gather, everything was novel. We ate exotic Japanese dishes with chopsticks which Frank taught us how to use. And we never had to watch our manners.

But we didn't spend just mealtimes with the servants during those first week ends. Before we found outside friends and interests, Syd and I hung around them a good part of the day, and so we saw how things were run. Everything was peaceful enough in the mornings, before the hour Dad was accustomed to rise. The servants went calmly about their chores. Kay worked over the cars in the garage across the road. George puttered around in his kitchen. Frank did his housecleaning and checked over the household stock. He had charge of all restocking, from kitchen and linen supplies to items in my father's wardrobe—socks, shirts, even shoes. Dad just couldn't be bothered about such details.

Sometime before eleven o'clock Frank would go into the master bathroom and lay out Dad's shaving equipment. It had to be arranged in a special way, so that when Dad got up he could rush into the bathroom, grab up the lather tube, the brush and then the razor in quick succession and whip through the tiresome job in a minimum of time. Time! Dad always treated it as though it were some precious jewel.

When eleven o'clock came, the feeling in the kitchen was like that of soldiers on the eve of the big push. By this time George would have Dad's breakfast cooked and ready and now he would be hovering anxiously over it, coddling it along.

Sometimes earlier, sometimes later, you never knew when, that bell would ring. When it did, what action! You never saw anyone move so fast as those Japanese when the bell rang.

"Ah, golly, youh fathah ring," George would exclaim in his falsetto voice, flinging his hands over his head. It was a favorite gesture of his. Then with spatulas, spoons and ladles he would whip the breakfast onto a tray. Fascinated by his speed, I would watch him dishing up kippered herrings some mornings, on others flounder steamed in milk, or sand dabs, skate or shrimp—for Dad's breakfasts were as English as his dinners, though he left them also to the discretion of the cook. Sometimes George would have a dish of bacon and tomatoes instead, sometimes one of bacon and lamb kidneys. But Dad's favorite breakfast, the one he had most often, consisted of dollar-size sour-milk pancackes, sausage, marmalade, toast and eggs.

As soon as the tray was prepared, Frank, who had been hovering at George's shoulder, would snatch it up. Then with an affable grin at me he would say, "Come along, kid. He's your fathah, isn't he? Tell him good morning."

So Frank and I would fly with the tray to Dad's bedroom, where he usually had breakfast in those days. My father, waiting for us in his dressing gown, would greet me with a friendly smile.

"Your father had a restless night last night," he'd say to me. Even then I noticed how he always spoke of himself in the third person, as though he were two people—one just the commentator, the other the real person who did the things and won the applause, who was the Little Tramp.

Sometimes when George had prepared a special dish he would want to take the tray up himself to get Dad's reaction to it. And then I would go tagging along after him. George would set the tray down by Dad's bed.

"New dish," he would say. "You try, you likee."

Then Dad would sample it. He had a way of eating that made me feel like stuffing myself all over again just to watch him. Even seeing Dad chew on that old shoe in *The Gold*

Rush sequence makes me hungry. It's the way he cuts his meat so fastidiously, holding his knife English style, a tender, absorbed expression on his face. He lifts the morsel of meat to his mouth and slips it carefully in. He chews it slowly, savoring it with every taste bud—as though it were the most precious thing in the world.

When that rapt expression came over Dad's face as he sampled the meal, George would throw up his hands in delight and his whole face would beam.

"Oh, likee, likee," he would exclaim. "Good, hnh? Good!" No artist receiving praise for his work could have been more elated than George at those moments.

After the breakfast was taken to my father, quiet settled again on the house because he was holed up in his room working. Frank seldom disturbed him there. Once, long before, when he first came to work for Dad, he had made the mistake of announcing a visitor.

"Damn it," Dad ejaculated, lifting his head from his yellow, lined paper. "I don't want to see him. Tell him I'm out." And he went right back to his writing.

How could you possibly explain to someone that your master was out after you'd just gone in to announce him? Frank quickly learned to screen the visitors and decide for himself which ones Dad would want to see. There were very few of these. To the rest Frank lied blandly, because it was the kindest and easiest arrangement all around.

It was the same with the phone. Dad never could stand a phone, not the sight of it, not to talk over it, certainly not the sound of its ringing. Just to hear it would set him off on a tirade.

"Fatuous blockheads," he would say, "inventing that goddam thing. Goddam bloody racket! Shut it off! Shut it off!"

Dad loathed the phone with all the ardor of his conservative soul. But his favorite investment has always been A.T. & T.

When Dad had dinner at home, Frank served in his immaculate white jacket and prim bow tie. He was in charge of the big parties, and if the need arose doubled as a waiter. But his chores went far beyond these. He had charge of my father's appointments, and every morning he would go to his room to tell him the schedule of the day. When Dad went out of town, Frank usually accompanied him as his right-hand man. He was also custodian of my father's health, which, left to himself, Dad might have neglected. When Dad was indisposed—he suffered from an occasional nervous stomach and a tendency to colds—and a doctor wrote out a prescription for him, it was not only Frank who got it filled, but also Frank who saw that Dad took his medicine at the proper times. Frank was one of the few men who knew how to tell Dad what to do in a way that was pleasing to him.

Frank, of course, was in charge of the servants and had to hire and fire them, for though Dad has always hated inefficiency, he is also sensitive about dismissing the offending one himself. Dad seldom had to tell Frank outright that someone had to go. It was a kind of game between them.

"The food doesn't taste good," he would complain obliquely, and Frank would know that a new cook was in order. But once he found George he never had to look again. He didn't have to look again for a chauffeur, either, after Kay came to work at the house on the hill.

Kay treated the two cars—the black Cadillac limousine and the new Ford which Dad had just bought for his own use—like pieces of art. He would take them apart, polish and clean every piece and put it back in place again. Syd and I would watch him fascinated. But we could never get Kay to talk much.

"Oh, I have to fix cah for Mr. Chapilaine," he would say when we asked him what he was doing. "Must be velly puhfect foh youh fathah."

It seemed to me Kay was always polishing the limousine. When he drove around to the front door to pick Dad up, he would come fifteen minutes early and spend that time rubbing away on the car with his polishing cloth as if his life depended on it.

"Must shine, must shine," he would tell us. "Youh fathah always likes black, shiny cahs."

Kay was as dependable in his driving as in his care of the car. Dad had a great faith in his chauffeur's ability to make deadlines, no matter how pressed, but sometimes he felt that Kay wasn't doing his best.

"Why are you stopping, Kay?" he would demand anxiously. "Go on! Go on!"

"But, Mr. Chapilaine, the stop light," Kay would remonstrate plaintively, torn between loyalty to Dad and to the law. "The stop light is here."

For the most part, however, Kay had learned the knack of keeping the car moving at all times, to satisfy his employer. I recall with a vividness that still makes me laugh how one day he kept it moving practically without stopping the whole distance from Beverly Hills to Wilmington.

Dad and Tim Durant were planning a trip to Catalina on the yacht, and were already seated in the car when Dad suddenly remembered his tennis racket. He never went anywhere without that racket. He sent Kay on the run to the tennis house to get it.

"No, I think the racket's upstairs," Dad suddenly exclaimed after Kay had gone.

He jumped out of the car, Tim at his heels, and ran into the house to look for it. Not finding it upstairs, they came back down to see what luck Kay had had. The car was gone. Kay had found the racket in the tennis house, had come back with it posthaste, put it in the car and got in himself and driven off—all in double quick time and without once looking in the back.

Dad and Tim sat down to wait. They were sure that in a few minutes Kay would discover he had no passengers and return for them. But time went by and still no Kay. He drove all the way to Wilmington, a distance of some twenty-five miles, without looking back once, weaving in and out through traffic at breakneck speed in a desperate attempt to make up lost time. He did so, and more. He parked the car at the pier, leaped out and opened the back door in triumph. Dave Anderson, the captain of the *Panacea*, was there to record Kay's distracted cry when he gazed inside.

"Mr. Chapilaine! Mr. Chapilaine!" yelled Kay in anguish. "Someone kidnaped Mr. Chapilaine!"

The wholehearted devotion of those three Japanese servants to my father was something no Occidental could understand. Obediently they satisfied his every whim, even though it might be at great discomfort to themselves. When Dad asked George to go along on the *Panacea* as galley cook, George never thought of objecting, though he was a victim of seasickness, ghastly, uncompromising sickness that attacked him as soon as the yacht went into motion.

"No likee sea. No likee ocean. Ohhh," George would wail. But you would always see him there, often hovering near the rail pretending to be viewing the sky and water, for he was ashamed of his malady and didn't want others to know about it.

Frank, who was also a victim of seasickness, was spared the torture of going to sea on the *Panacea* because he wasn't needed and there wasn't room for him. But he, too, cheerfully made any sacrifice asked of him—such as the monumental one on the trip he took with Dad to New York one winter.

They moved into a suite high in the Waldorf Towers. It looked like a cozy haven to Frank, for it was sleety, subzero weather. But Dad stepped into the room, which was pleasantly warm, took one look at the radiator, sniffed disapprovingly and shook his head.

"We can't have this," he said firmly. "Turn off that gas at once."

It was steam heat, of course. But all radiators signify gas heat to Dad and he is convinced that gas gives him a headache.

Without a word Frank went through all the rooms turning off the radiators, though he was well aware of what the result would be. The room was soon down to freezing. Dad, who in spite of his convictions about gas heat is quite sensitive to cold, went to bed and piled on the covers. Frank sat shivering in his overcoat in the living room. Only at long last, when he was unable to take the cold any longer, did he retreat to his own room, shut the door and commit lese majesty by surreptitiously turning on his heat. He never complained then or later about that frigid visit in New York. His sole comment on the whole episode was a humorously triumphant, "But your father don't get a headache, that's for sure."

Frank found his greatest pleasure in keeping ahead of my father in everything. He devoted so much of his time to the job of making him comfortable that before it was all over he had become very intuitive where Dad was concerned. Instinctively he could feel when Dad was happy or sad or in an irritable mood, and he was always sympathetic.

It was to Frank that Dad poured out many of his troubles when he had had a hard day. And it was upon Frank that he showered much of his irrational anger when things weren't going right and he had to blow off at someone. My father would explode over the most minute omissions on Frank's part. The violence of his anger was always so out of proportion to the object that had stirred him that I couldn't help being frightened at it in those early days. That was what made Frank's imperturbability so amazing to me.

If Dad didn't find the shaving equipment laid out in just the proper way, he would storm at Frank. When he couldn't find a tennis racket he himself had misplaced, Frank would get it again. It was the same story if Frank set out the wrong pair of tennis shoes. As small a thing as moving a pencil from where he had left it the night before would irritate him. He would even take it out on Frank when people failed to show up for appointments, as if Frank, the wonderworker, were responsible for their dereliction. And then right in the midst of an explosion Dad would recall himself.

"I'm sorry, Frank. I didn't mean to raise my voice," he would apologize, though he seldom did so to outsiders. "I forgot myself a little bit there."

I remember a classic tirade one evening when Frank laid out the wrong suit for Dad. Often when Dad lost his temper with Frank it was because the latter had failed to read his mind aright. Dad had come to take Frank's intuitive care of him as the natural course of events.

"You're getting careless," Dad stormed. "Why don't you listen to me and follow orders? Remember, I'm paying your salary." When Dad was really angry he could never refrain from throwing in the bit about the salary.

Frank didn't say anything at all, much less remind Dad that he hadn't been told what suit was wanted. After all, he really felt he was to blame because his mind-reading act had failed. He came out into the hall and saw me standing there perplexed, unhappy, and he grinned.

"Oh, sure, your fathah gets mad now and then," he said. "But he's good—easy to work for. Something's on his mind— too many things. So he gets mad. But he don't carry it within his mind all the time. Gets rid of it quick. Next minute he's happy again."

Looking back from this vantage point, I don't know whether my father ever considered the servants as individuals in their own right, but I doubt if he did. They were far closer than that to him. They were like his heart, his liver, his spleen —so completely necessary to him that they had become a part of himself. He needed them as much as he did his vital organs and in the same way. He relied on them without question or even any conscious reflection. They were his servants, closer to him in some ways than I who was his son.

12

It was Frank who usually picked us up Friday afternoons at Black-Foxe. He would let us out in the circular drive at the front door and we would burst from the car and catapult into the house. But as we started down the wide hallway our footsteps would become slower and slower. We would be quite dignified by the time we entered the living room, because we knew this was expected of us. We always exchanged greetings with our father in the copybook way.

He would have wound up his work for the day preparatory to our arrival, and, if the weather were the least cool, would be waiting for us in front of the fireplace, a pair of bellows in his hands, a fire blazing in the grate.

"Hello, Father," we would say. When we were young we

always addressed him as Father. It was only as we grew older that we slipped into the more vernacular "Dad."

"Well, how are you, sons?" Dad would ask, looking around from the fire. "How's everything at the school these days?"

While we told him about school he would work with the bellows until he was satisfied. Then he would return them to their place and stand with his back to the fire, warming himself, nodding his head from time to time, and occasionally interrupting to tell us how he had been spending his week.

Behind him the glowing coal would sprout little blue flames, filling the room with a warmth that was pleasant if the outside air was nippy. But sometimes Dad would keep that fire stoked so high that Syd and I found the room a little too warm for comfort. Dad, however, never seemed to have enough of it. Perhaps those dismal London fogs that ate into his bones when he was a child made him shrink all his later life from the least chill.

At six thirty or seven, if Dad was eating at home, we would have dinner with him at the table in the dining room. Those dignified meals were most uncomfortable for Syd and me in our younger days, because it was here that our father's copybook disciplines came so painfully to the fore. We were supposed to mind our manners and remain quiet throughout the meal unless spoken to. We would sit straight as ramrods on our chairs, our short legs swinging nervously.

Sometimes our father spoke to us—he always called us Charles and Sydney, there were no nicknames with Dad. When he addressed us we answered. Otherwise we ate quietly while he sat absorbed in his thoughts, his face grave, his eyes faraway. We would have liked to bolt our food down and escape, but this too was denied us.

"Ah, ah, ah, ah," Dad would caution. "Not so fast. You mayn't leave till the grownups are through."

Often, though, Paulette would be a guest, and then we had a respite. Paulette took in the situation at once. From the very first we had a feeling she was our ally. She would talk to us,

87

draw us into the conversation, even get a little laughter out of us. And all the while her eyes would be twinkling encouragement.

It was different with Dr. Reynolds, the noted brain surgeon, psychiatrist and hypnotist, who was a frequent guest at our father's place too. We saw a great deal of the English-born Dr. Cecil Reynolds throughout the years, until in 1947 at the age of sixty-six he committed suicide to escape the constant agony of his last illness. He had testified at such notorious murder trials as those of Kid McCoy and William Edward Hickman, and had taken part in experiments in telepathy at the Pasadena Community Theatre. My mother tells me that when she first knew my father he and the doctor terrified her with their abracadabra over a ouija board.

To Syd and me there was an aura of the bizarre about Dr. Reynolds that extended even to his first wife, who, we learned, had been devoured by sharks off the coast of Maui while on her honeymoon with her second husband. Somehow that somber story seemed to agree with the atmosphere engendered by Dr. Reynold's personal appearance. He was a tall, cadaverous man with hollow cheeks, a rapidly balding head fringed with black hair, and deep-set, piercing eyes. Whenever his concentrated gaze fell upon me I couldn't help squirming, because my father had told me the doctor knew all about the mind and I was sure he was reading my every thought.

Dr. Reynolds and my father were drawn to each other by a mutual fascination. My father has always been attracted to the macabre, and as a surgeon, Dr. Reynolds had plenty of this kind of fare to serve him. The doctor, on his side, was lured by the footlights and had taken up acting as an avocation. In later years he retired from his proper field to devote much of his time to the theater arts. My father could never understand why the doctor, whom he considered a genius in his own field, should give up his profession to become a poor actor. But all this was to come later. At the time we first knew him, Dr. Reynolds had the discretion to indulge his yearning for the life of an actor only on the side. And in this Dad was humoring him by promising him a part in his next picture.

When Dr. Reynolds came to dinner he would launch into fascinating descriptions about the human brain and his delicate operations thereon. He spared no details, nor would my father permit him to, plying him with probing questions that kept him talking throughout most of the meal.

I remember one night listening to Dr. Reynold's dramatic description of how he had diagnosed an epileptic's trouble just by watching him when he was in convulsions.

"I knew at once we'd have to have a lower lobotomy done," Dr. Reynolds concluded.

"What's a lobotomy?" Syd and I burst out together. We had been following the doctor's account step by step, only to find ourselves baffled at the most exciting place by a medical term. But our interruption only brought us a rebuke from our father.

"Now you know better than to break in like that," he said sternly. "I've taught you better manners."

Syd and I fell back into an abashed silence, as we always did. He was the disciplinarian, the stern, grave father. And so when a few minutes later he changed chameleon-wise right before our eyes, it came as a delightful shock to us. Among other phobias, Dr. Reynolds had an obsessive one about cleanliness. He waged a constant war on imaginary germs. He never opened a door or touched a piece of furniture without carefully wiping his hands on his handkerchief. If he felt the pollution to be even more serious, he would hurry to the bathroom for hot water and soap. This evening he made the mistake of allowing his napkin to slip from his lap to the floor. He stooped down, recovered it and laid it aside.

"Excuse me," he muttered half under his breath, and jumping to his feet hurried from the room without a word of explanation.

Syd and I, who had no idea of the doctor's phobia, stared

after him in perplexity. Dad, seeing our bewilderment, proceeded to inform us of his destination, but not by word of mouth. His face assumed in a twinkling the doctor's lugubrious expression. He began to wring his hands as though under a faucet of water. The mimicry was so realistic that it was impossible not to guess at once what he was doing. Syd and I, like two conspirators in league with Dad, burst into suppressed laughter. Carefully Dad shook his hands in midair, pretended to dry them meticulously, then placed one to his mouth and burped discreetly two or three times as was the doctor's habit. It was all over in a twinkling. The next instant Dad's face had resumed its ordinary grave expression, so that all that had gone before seemed an illusion. But he put his finger to his lips.

"Shhh," he whispered warningly. "We can't hurt his feelings, you know."

He was the father again—stern, grave. But nothing was ever really the same after that evening, because from then on Syd and I were always on the lookout for these quick, irrepressible flashes of mimicry, which, we discovered, were a frequent punctuation of our father's existence.

Dad had a number of etiquette rules which he drilled us on during our visits to his home. Knock before entering. Sit quiet at table. Excuse yourself before leaving. Never interrupt conversations or shove ahead of others. Stand up when a lady enters the room. Help her with her wrap. Open the door for her when she goes out.

"Life is much more bearable if we all observe the little amenities," he used to explain.

I think the most important of all these rules to my father was the one about knocking on closed doors. Syd and I quickly discovered that opening a closed door without knocking could raise his hackles quicker than any other offense. Upstairs or downstairs, at home or at the studio, he could never bear to have anyone do it. And he would dress down not only his sons but his long-time associates, his closest friends and the servants for this infraction. That anger, at once so instantaneous and so desperate, could only have been bred in the humiliation of his childhood, when no closed doors of his were respected.

I remember the first time I ever opened a door without knocking. Full of some exciting news—I've long since forgotten what it was—I rushed to his bedroom and burst in. I didn't have a chance to tell what was on my mind. All at once my father exploded.

"Don't you have any better manners than not to knock?" he exclaimed, and I saw he was actually trembling. "Now go on, go on." Our father never once raised his hand to us in violence, yet we were in fear of him just the same when he was shaken with that anger. It seemed to express something dreadful, a very rage of loneliness.

All in all, Syd and I found our father a very good parent—more objective than most, perhaps, but concerned and watchful over our welfare. How earnestly he tried to curb his tongue in our presence! It was difficult for him because for so many years he had been free to vent himself in that picturesque language for which he has become famous. Dad's choice of swear words always served as an accurate barometer of the extent of his anger.

"Damn it" meant only mild irritation. "Goddam it" was stronger, but still everything was under control. "Goddam fatheads! Empty-headed blockheads! Fatuous sons of bitches!" All these phrases were an unmistakable sign that his ire was rising. But when he used the word "bloody," or, what was worse, "Goddam bloody bastards," then you knew his temper was at storm fury. Dad never used the expletive "bloody" unless he had lost his head completely.

Sometimes in the middle of a diatribe at someone he would turn to see Syd and me staring at him in open-mouthed admiration.

"Please, sons, your father forgot himself," he would say

to us apologetically in an aside. "I don't want you using those words."

Then he would turn back to the unlucky person he had been dressing down, and before long the words would start popping out again as if by themselves. And he would have to apologize to us all over again.

When Dad wasn't swamped with work he tried to provide entertainment for us on the week ends we spent with him. On occasion he would take us to a movie Saturday afternoons. Syd and I loved the Laurel and Hardy comedies and Dad could never get over that.

"Well, do you know about my sons?" he would say to friends. "They actually think other people are funnier than I am—their own father."

But Dad knew how much we enjoyed his pictures. Often he would give us and any friends we chose to invite a private screening of his films in the little theater in the vestibule of our home. Sometimes as many as twenty of us would be there.

Dad loved to join us in the theater, where sofas, divans and chairs from all over the house were brought in to accommodate the guests. He would take a chair at the side of the room and sit there with his arms folded, fully intending to be just another spectator. But the picture wasn't long in progress before he would get up from his seat and work his way across the room to stand beside us and our guests where he could watch our reactions. He was more interested in that than in the Little Tramp himself.

Dad, however, couldn't stay quietly watching for long. Presently he was providing a running commentary for us.

"There he is now, there comes the Little Fellow," he would say, rubbing his hands together gleefully.

"Yes, there he is, with the big fellow with the bandaged foot. That means trouble. Watch it, boys."

Our father's eager monologue seemed quite natural to

us. We never thought once, then, that we were the only children in the world to enjoy the privilege of Chaplin dialogue with silent Chaplin films.

Whenever the picture came to a high point and we would burst out laughing, Dad would laugh too. I can still hear that vibrant chuckle of his, which was not brought on by the Little Tramp's antics, but by our reactions to them. Sometimes we laughed until we cried. Then Dad was in seventh heaven.

"Do you really find it that funny?" he would ask, and add with satisfaction, "You know, kids are the toughest audience in the world to please."

Like most fathers, Dad used to play games with us, too. I remember our favorite one was the bogeyman routine. Syd and I loved that terrifying game in which our father would act out the bogeyman and come sneaking around corners after us, his face contorted into a truly maniacal expression.

Syd and I would back away from him until, half mesmerized with delicious terror, we could no longer move. Then we would begin screaming and Dad would realize he was going too far. He would stop short and his face would assume its familiar expression.

"Well, how'd you like that?" he would say, laughing. "Your father can be quite scary, too, can't he?"

Dad, like a good father, always told us bedtime stories. But what stories! Sometimes they would be ghost stories and Syd and I would lie there listening, feeling a thrill of delightful fear. Often his stories came from Dickens, but they were not, as you might expect, the sentimental or mildly satirical passages with which Dickens abounds. They were those which had a macabre cast to them. Oddly enough, my father and Dickens were alike in their predilection for the macabre.

I think *Oliver Twist* was a favorite of Dad's because young Oliver's experiences in the orphanage so closely approximated his own. The passage he usually chose to act out for us is the one that describes Oliver Twist's meeting with Fagin.

"How'd you like to be the little boy just waking up and you see this man with a beard standing there and the knife coming at you?" he would say in that soft, foreboding tone of voice that always ushered us into one of his characterizations. Then, contorting his face, he would begin playing the part of Fagin.

"What do you watch me for? Why are you awake? What have you seen? Speak out, boy! Quick—quick! For your life!" he would hiss.

Dad repeated the story often, but I don't recall his ever telling it in the same way. Each time he would add fresh embellishments from his own imagination, so that Syd and I never knew exactly what to expect. But we could always count on its being exciting.

Long after Dad had laughingly bidden us good night, we would lie in our twin beds discussing his performance. We talked, though, mostly to remind each other that we weren't alone, for his magic recital had penetrated our bones like ice. And there in the dark we would hear all around us the lonely tap, tap, tap of the tree branches against the windows and the melancholy sound of the night breeze.

13

Throughout my childhood and youth, life with my father was like life in an open boat on a sea with massive rollers. The rollers, spaced about five years apart, were the intense creative periods, each of which culminated in one of those pictures that made up his series of cinema masterpieces—*City Lights, Modern Times, The Great Dictator, Monsieur Verdoux* and finally *Limelight.* I do not know how my father brought *The King in New York* to completion in Europe, but I rather imagine it was with the same concentration and intensity that he did the others.

When Dad is working, all outside interests, family included, are ruthlessly sacrificed to that inexorable rush of creativity which rises to a wild crescendo before crashing over in a turbulent finale, leaving him drained. He himself has said that he usually has to go to bed for at least a day or two to restore his nerves after finishing a picture. My father was not the only one to be drained at such times. Everyone associated with him during these periods, either at the studio or at home, was drained too; drained, limp and more than ready to call it quits. Such is life with a creative perfectionist, but of course with a genius in the house you can't expect an atmosphere of sustained normalcy. Syd and I not only didn't expect it, we took our lives for granted until we got older.

The more or less tranquil home atmosphere which I have described in the preceding chapter took place in the trough between two waves—between *City Lights*, which had passed over us, and *Modern Times*, which was on the way. It was, comparatively speaking, a comfortable period, if you could dismiss from mind the uneasy agitation of the water below and the steady building of the heavy roller behind.

It took my father more than two years to complete the script of *Modern Times*, which he had begun immediately after his trip abroad in 1932. He always progressed slowly, at first in an almost leisurely fashion. He loved to write, anyway, much as Dickens, the writer, loved to act. Dad told me once that he tried to make a practice of putting down five hundred words a day on any subject, just to keep in practice. But by the time Syd and I first started going up to the house, *Modern Times* was heading for the home stretch. It was to go into actual production the next October.

As the press of ideas came faster and faster, and Dad's writing began to take up more and more of his time, Syd and I became familiar with that strange, inwardly directed concentration which had made life so difficult and lonely for Mildred Harris and my mother. Now when we came home from school Dad would be down in the living room ostensibly to greet us. But ten to one some idea would have caught him just before we came in and he would be sitting at his table working.

I remember the first time, one Friday afternoon, we burst in on him that way.

"Hi, Father, what's new?" we shouted, expecting him to reply cheerfully, as always.

He only looked up with an irritated frown and a dazed shake of his head.

"Don't bother me. Don't bother me," he said in a brusque monotone. "I'm in the middle of something. Go on, go on now. Play with your friends." And with a flourish of one hand he indicated the door.

Amazed and mortified, Syd and I stole off.

"What's the matter with Dad anyway?" we asked each other a little resentfully.

We wandered around outside and the resentment began to die away. Instead I kept thinking of him sitting at the table, his head bent, the brown-rimmed glasses perched on his nose, his hand racing with the pencil over the yellow, lined note-book paper. I stole back to the living room and peeked around the corner of the hall door.

Dad was still working. Once he stopped to stare into space, absent-mindedly caressing the top sheet of the pad between his fingers with the same tender, absorbed expression on his face that I saw when he was eating. He treated the pad as lovingly as though it were something precious, a rare old parchment perhaps.

I stood there in the doorway uncertainly but he didn't even look at me. I stole in quietly and sat down and waited. Dad had gone back to his writing. Then suddenly he finished with a flourish and jumped to his feet and saw me.

He grabbed up the paper and hurried over and stood before me just as though he had expected me to be there all the while, as though it were natural for me to be with him, waiting, just waiting silently and wishing him well.

97

"Now what do you think of this, Charles?" he exclaimed. "It'll be in the next picture."

And before I had a chance to say anything he launched into a description, reading his idea aloud, acting it out as he went along, as if I were a whole audience. "The birds will be singing . . . the woods will be calm and quiet . . . the Little Fellow . . ."

"How do you like it?" he asked anxiously when he had finished. And he added as if he were speaking of someone else's work, "Isn't that a lovely thing?"

"It's great," I answered him quickly. I could only think that Dad had read his work aloud to me. He had asked me my opinion of it. I had a place to fill—to listen.

After that, when Dad was working I would often sit quietly in the room with him. Sometimes he would go out and walk, with head bent, along the meandering paths of his hill, wrestling with his ideas. And I would tag along behind him, sometimes Syd with me, just waiting for that glorious moment when Dad would whirl round, his eyes sparkling, his voice jubilant.

"I've got it, boys. Just listen to this."

Another phenomenon of which Syd and I were made painfully aware during this period was our father's increasing absent-mindedness. We would get permission to engage in some venture. But when we started to carry out our plans, Dad, who always kept his word with us if possible, would suddenly explode without warning, and then, to his chagrin, discover that he had forgotten all about his promise. It added to the uncertainty of life around the house.

Syd and I quickly learned, for purposes of self-preservation, how to read the signs and govern our conduct accordingly. When Dad was happy he sang. How he would sing! Snatches from operas, from his favorite ditties, or stand-bys from his old music-hall days. One of his favorites ran, to the best of my recollection, something like this:

"Oh, ever since that fatal night
Me wife's gone mad,
Awfully queer, touched just here." (With this he
    would always point to his head.)
"Bad, bad, bad!
In the middle of the night
She'd sneak the sheets and walk round my bed post,
Singing 'Hamlet, Hamlet, Hamlet,
I am thy father's ghost.' "

He liked to sing his own tunes also. "Will You Buy My Pretty Flowers?" from *City Lights* was a favorite of his.

He would sing in the shower. He would sing while he was getting ready to go out of an evening. You could hear him all over the house—away downstairs, even outside. You could hear his voice all over the top of the hill. And Syd and I would relax. We knew it was going to be a wonderful week end.

Then there were those unhappy days when we would find our father plunged in one of his peculiar spells of moodiness, with which everyone who knows him well is familiar. Dad never had the habit of talking to himself unless he was reading some lines aloud which he had just written. When he was depressed he was usually just quiet—very quiet. Anything might bring on these spells—even the account of a tragedy in the newspaper could upset him—but they usually visited him when he felt deserted by the creative impulse, when he would wait in vain for ideas that wouldn't come. It was as though he were bound hand and foot in some dark dungeon of the mind. Then the pencil would lie motionless, the yellow pad unused. Sometimes he would walk over his paths, but there would be no spring to his step. He would drag himself along.

Sometimes he would be standing at the living-room window, perfectly motionless, staring out, with his hands behind his back, the fingers of one hand tap, tap, tapping upon the wrist of the other, or, if he were sitting, tapping his knees in the same abstracted manner. He would not see us when we came in, nor hear us when we went out.

Finally, when he had stewed within himself long enough, he would make a move to break the spell. The cure was simple. He would put in an urgent call to a friend to come up and have a game of tennis with him. I don't know what Dad's form is like now, but he was a delight to watch on the tennis courts in those early days. A left-handed player —Dad is left-handed in everything except writing—he played as gracefully, as effortlessly as he performed his most intricate pantomime routines.

Not only did Dad practice tennis every afternoon at home, but he made a point of fitting it into his life when he traveled. Dad went to New York about twice a year, usually accompanied by Tim Durant, whose former home is in the East. When they went by train they would sometimes go aboard in their tennis clothes. As soon as they hit Chicago, between trains, Dad would telephone and find a place where he could play. He'd play one game and then go back to the train. It was the same when he reached New York. He'd stay at the River Club, and as soon as he got there he'd be right out on the courts.

What liquor, sex, religion are to other men, tennis has always been to my father. He seems to find some kind of mystical release in it. I have seen him dragging himself down to the court, gloomy and depressed, and begin to play. But with the first lob of that ball over the net Dad would change. He would become alert, graceful, concentrated. It was impossible for him to focus his attention both on a tennis game outside and on the core of darkness within him. By the time the game was over that darkness would be completely dissipated and Dad would be his old self again—especially if he had won the game.

My father is egocentric, but only those closest to him realize on how sensitive a base that egocentricity rests. A word, a gesture can deflate him; a fear that his creative powers have forever deserted him can plunge him into the depths of gloom. At times like these, to win a game of tennis always bolstered him immeasurably, and his friends, who usually gave him a run for his money, would take care not to put up too much of a game, so that he would be sure to win.

As the bright spring days lengthened toward the hot California summer, Dad moved at a faster and faster tempo. His dark moods became more pronounced, his flashes of anger more frequent. The air of suspense and tension affected everyone in the house. We were all one in the great push ahead. It was as though our father, with us as his timorous army, were heading for Waterloo. Fear of failure, the perennial curse of the perfectionist, was plaguing him.

With the near-completion of his script, Dad took on another chore, coaching Paulette for the part she was to play. I remember those long hours he spent with her, either in the living room or down at the tennis courts. It was Paulette's first big part and she was grateful for the chance. And Dad was patient in his role of teacher.

But of course it was something far more fundamental than his pleasure in teaching that motivated my father. It was his almost ruthless determination for perfection. He and Paulette would go through the same scene over and over, Dad pounding and pounding away after the effect he wanted. Paulette was game. She would work until she was ready to drop with weariness. Dad never seemed to get tired. So far as I can recall, though he lost his temper on so many other occasions, he would never lose it or even raise his voice while coaching Paulette, no matter how many times they had to repeat the scene. But his nervous intensity was more wearing, perhaps, than a sudden explosion might have been. And he absolutely refused to be satisfied with second-best, even in the most minute gesture or facial expression.

"Try it again. Try it again. Try it again."

That phrase must have hounded Paulette even in her dreams. Sometimes she was reduced to tears at the sense of her own inadequacy.

"Oh, Charlie, Charlie, I'm not an actress," she would cry out. "I'm just not an actress."

And Syd and I, peeking from our hiding place at the tableau, would long to rush out and protect her, to snatch her away from Dad's ruthless coaching. For she was normally so gay, so young, almost like us, and we could not bear to see her unhappy. She really didn't need to be perfect, we told ourselves. She was pretty enough to make up for everything.

But Dad didn't share our view. He just went doggedly on, day after day, week after week, fashioning the beloved pixie gamin of *Modern Times*.

14

That summer of '34, Dad began to prepare for the actual production of *Modern Times*. He didn't need to reactivate his studio. He had his personnel intact, because during those past four years he had kept everyone on the payroll even when things were closed down completely.

I think it worthy of note that my father adhered to this ethical practice from the very first, when there were no unions and other studios were summarily dismissing their workers at the close of each production and rehiring them when necessary. His consideration accounts for the extraordinary loyalty his employees felt toward him, a loyalty which was noted by the whole town and commented on by the newspapers at the time.

My father was as loyal to those who had worked for him as they were to him. When Frank Antunez, Sr., head of his transportation department, was incapacitated with a heart attack, Dad dismissed him from work but went on paying his salary. I know he took care of many of his old associates, like Edna Purviance, his former leading lady, and Roland Totheroh, his cameraman from silent-film days. I can't tell you how many profited from his generosity because he was never ostentatious about it. But I do know that the rapport between employer and employee at Dad's studio made it seem almost like a family affair.

Since we were out of school and could visit our father during the week as well as on week ends, Syd and I had more opportunity to see the preparations going on at the studio, for Dad would take us along with him. Once inside the gates his attitude seemed to change. He became excited, exuberant. However it might be with him in the outside world, here he was the undisputed lord whose every word was law. Young as I was, I couldn't fail to notice how everyone from carpenters and prop men to the production managers greeted him deferentially. They seemed to be as much in awe of him as I.

There was just one man, really, who spoke up to Dad at his studio. That was his long-time associate Alf Reeves, business manager of the Chaplin studios. I remember Alf sitting behind his desk in a dark, paneled office that seemed to be lighted only by the gigantic diamond in the ring he wore. He would get provoked with Dad if he came snooping around there too much.

"Now, Charlie, get out, I'm busy," he would say in that broad Cockney accent which he never lost despite his years in America, and Dad would walk right out without an argument.

Alf's was the only office in his studio from which anyone could drive him. He was the head of all the others. He was the writer, the producer, the director, the chief designer, the composer, the film cutter, the makeup man. He was every· thing. Just look at the credits on a Chaplin film.

He had in his employ some of the best budget men in the country, and heaven knows he drove them relentlessly. But even then he couldn't refrain from putting in his two bits' worth of advice. He would haggle with his production managers by the hour over the expense of a nominally priced prop. And yet *Modern Times* cost him more than a million and a half dollars to produce, and that was an astronomical figure for budgets in those days.

Dad has always been an anomaly where money is concerned, so much so that legends along this line have sprung up about him in Hollywood. One of these is that when Dad signed with Mutual he demanded a thousand and twenty-five dollars as a weekly salary instead of the flat thousand offered him, explaining that he wanted the twenty-five extra to live on.

Whenever he went out to eat he would tip the waiter only ten percent of the meal, no matter how good the service was —especially if he thought it was due to his having been recognized. He was particular about that ten percent. Because he didn't trust his own arithmetic, he would hand the bill over to Paulette or Syd or me and have one of us figure out the right amount—to the last penny.

Then he might go right down the block and tip an unsuspecting barber five dollars for doing a good job without knowing who he was. He would go to all lengths to save odds and ends of things, even stubs of pencils. He would worry inordinately over the misplacement of one.

"Pencils cost money, you know."

He so imbued his *Modern Times* crew with his ideas of thrift that they kept a tense lookout during the shooting to save him dollars, even pennies. There's the story of how they haggled with the owner of a house they wanted to use for a location scene until they brought the rental fee down from the normal twenty-five dollars a day to five. But they carried the thrift even further by refusing to pay more than the initial five on the excuse that the first and second day's film hadn't turned out right and they were back on the third day only for retakes.

At the same time Dad could drop big sums with a shrug. It was as though when they became large enough he lost all concept of their reality. Joseph M. Schenck, the producer, who later had serious tax troubles himself, tells the story of how Dad reacted to the discovery that he was far in arrears on his taxes. There was some close dickering back and forth between his lawyers and Uncle Sam. Mr. Schenck remembers the outcome, for he was with Dad in his hotel room in New York when his lawyers finally brought the news.

"We've agreed to pay the million," they said a little fearfully, expecting Dad to hit the ceiling.

But my father only got up and walked over to the piano as though he didn't have a care in the world.

"Well, I'm glad that's over," he said. "Let's have some fun." And he sat down and began playing.

Dad was often so swamped with work now that he would sometimes telephone and ask Syd and me not to come up at all. We felt the banishment keenly. We had already made good friends with the neighborhood children. There were the three Krisel brothers across the street from us. Their father had been a judge in China in earlier days, and the whole family could speak Chinese. There were the Harold Lloyds, who lived down the hill and around the corner in a palatial mansion with grounds more spacious by far than ours. The Lloyds even had a nine-hole golf course, and a swimming pool which, with its stately tree-lined avenue and its fountains, looked like something that belonged to the Taj Mahal.

Syd and I liked to visit the Lloyd girls, Peggy and Gloria. From the very first I had a crush on Gloria, though I never dated her. Sometimes the girls would come up to see us with their small brother, Harold, Jr., tagging along behind. We and the Krisel brothers and the Lloyds and several others all had a lot of fun together over the week ends. So Syd and I would find the temerity to beg Dad to change his mind. He was not above compromise.

"Well, all right, if you keep to yourselves," he would say, relenting at last.

Syd and I knew that this partial reprieve didn't extend to our friends. We had long since learned never to ask them to the house without first getting Dad's permission, because when Dad was in one of his recluse moods and didn't want anyone around he could be embarrassing.

"How do you do?" he would say shortly, and then retreat hastily upstairs, not to be seen again until our guests left. Later he would rebuke us.

"You should have more respect for your father. You should let him know before you bring anyone up."

All through that summer Dad continued his relentless work with Paulette, both at home and at the studio, and Syd and I continued feeling sorry for her. And yet we needn't have, really. Paulette had her own bright ways. She knew how to wheedle in the most winning way.

"Oh, Charlie, you really should take time off," she would say. "Let's all have some fun today. It'll be wonderful for the boys too."

Paulette always brought us in, both because she had become very fond of us and because she had learned Dad could be touched by playing on his father instincts. The intimation that he was neglecting us would act like a charge to his energies. He would knock off work—the coaching, the conferences, the studio details—and he and Paulette and Syd and I would go on an all-day jaunt.

Usually we chose the Amusement Pier down at Ocean Park. During the long drive to the ocean Dad used to beguile us with Tarzan stories. I remember sitting in the back seat of the car while he spun them for us by the ream. They didn't come from the Edgar Rice Burroughs books, though. I doubt if Dad ever read one of those in his life. They were his own incredible, involved versions of the ape-man melodrama.

Inside the Amusement Pier gates, Syd and I would suddenly discover that Paulette and Dad weren't any older than we. Dad's eyes gleamed, and he walked along with a springy step as he looked from side to side. The honky-tonk, hurdy-gurdy air of the place always excited and delighted him.

Syd and I loved the roller coaster and sometimes Paulette joined us on the ride. But we could never persuade Dad to try it. He much preferred the Ferris wheel and he thought the chute-the-chute, which Syd and I considered tame, an exciting ride. But most of all he preferred the various concessions where marksmanship could be tested by throwing balls at milk bottles or rings over stakes. His favorite was the one with the little pig that, when the target was hit, would come walking across the ramp, slither down a child's slide and go back in again. Dad would laugh as hard as anyone at that little pig.

Dad had visited the Amusement Pier so often through the years that all the proprietors recognized him and knew his weakness.

"Hey, Charlie, come on over here. Try this one," they would call out as he went by.

"Charlie, come here! Charlie!"

Sometimes Dad was irritated by the clamor he stirred up. He would stare straight ahead as though he hadn't heard a thing.

"Now don't listen to them," he'd mutter to Syd and me conspiratorially. "We'll just play the ones we want."

Though Dad was left-handed he was an extremely accurate marksman. He religiously collected his tickets and in the end redeemed them in Kewpies or stuffed animals. When the concessionaires tried to palm off the smaller prizes on him, Dad would shake his head and doggedly count out his tickets again for them to see. Even in stuffed animals, which he always turned over to Syd and me anyway, he didn't like to have anyone trying to put something over on him.

Dad would come home from these jaunts beaming and refreshed. The next day he would plunge again into his work, just as though there were no beckoning Amusement Pier, no hurdy-gurdy music, gay lights and sounds of carnival to tempt him.

As the production date of *Modern Times* neared, Dad began to keep a watchful guard over his two chronic ailments —a nervous stomach and colds. He was a great one for home remedies when things hadn't got out of hand.

One of his favorite antidotes for a sour stomach was Alka-Seltzer. Every now and then, when he felt one was in the offing, he would take an Alka-Seltzer after dinner just to forestall it. Almost every night that summer Frank would bring in a tablet and a glass of water without being asked, and Dad would religiously drink it down.

To guard against colds, he would sleep with only one window slightly open, or if he felt the weather was very inclement, with all his windows closed. He looked upon drafts as extremely dangerous, even in the warmest weather. He would be working and absorbed in something when a stirring of air would bring him suddenly to attention. He would glance all around for the offending breeze, find a window barely open and get it closed in a trice. Sometimes I would find him bundled up not only in his sweater but in a robe as well.

"I have them on because I'm perspiring now and I don't want to catch cold," he would explain to me.

His concern over his health was no indication of hypochondria, however. He would beat himself unmercifully during production, sometimes missing both meals and sleep. He was afraid of illness for only one reason—the amount of production money it would cost if he had to stop work, as had happened on *City Lights*.

15

As he had with *City Lights,* my father pondered long over whether to make *Modern Times* a silent picture or a talkie. He was still of the opinion that silent pictures alone represented true cinema art and that artistic values were lessened in proportion to every decrease in the use of the imagination. He felt that talkies were concerned too little with art, too much with commercialism.

At the time the movie-going public was being fed massive doses of very voluble comics. There were the new men like Wheeler and Woolsey, and Joe E. Brown. There were the old silent-picture comedians who had successfully crossed over to talkies, men like Buster Keaton, Laurel and Hardy, and Harold Lloyd. Harold Lloyd's meteoric rise to success on situation-type comedy gave Dad special cause for concern. He had to ask himself whether the public had been completely weaned away from his own kind of tragicomic pantomime.

On the other hand, he was worried about taking the plunge into talkies, not only because he still felt that his Little Fellow had no place in them, but also because he wasn't sure whether his voice would go over on the screen. In the end his solid conservatism, mixed with his reticence about tackling the unfamiliar, made Dad shy away from direct competition with Lloyd and the other talking comics. He handed his Little Tramp one more reprieve and decided to make *Modern Times* a silent movie.

Everyone in Hollywood thought my father was crazy. While other producers like Jesse Lasky, David O. Selznick and Cecil B. De Mille were studying new ways of improving talkies, Dad was stubbornly clinging to the passé era of silent film. People began to think of him somewhat patronizingly as a former Hollywood great who was now a has-been, unable to adjust himself to the new techniques. He was finished in pictures—you heard that all over town.

Fall came. Our mother went back East to fulfill her singing engagements. Syd and I returned unhappily to our cramped military existence at Black-Foxe. At Dad's orders Paulette changed her hair back to its natural brunette coloring. And in October the production of *Modern Times* began.

Gone were Dad's days even of semileisure now, days he could arrange for himself. He might be late for other appointments or social engagements, but he was never late to work—he usually got there at seven in the morning—and neither was anyone who ever worked for him. Lateness in a studio costs money and one person can keep a whole crew idle.

Usually Kay would drive Dad to the studio, sometimes Dad would drive himself. Often Frank would go with him to help with his costumes and act as general liaison man.

Syd and I were once more restricted to week ends with

Dad. But in those days, unions had not yet established a forty-hour week and there was no such thing as a Saturday off when my father was working. So Syd and I had the opportunity on week ends of accompanying him to the studio.

Dad's mood for the day was always conditioned by what he had seen in the rushes the night before. If they had been good he would come to work buoyant, and the day would go forward smoothly. If not, he would drive himself and the whole cast and crew relentlessly, and everyone would have a difficult time of it.

I remember tagging along with Dad, feeling very important as his son while he checked the sets and went over the production chart for the day's shooting. Finally we would move on to makeup. Once again, as in our younger days, we had the delight of watching Dad transform himself into the Little Tramp before our eyes.

As soon as he had become the Little Tramp, Dad stayed that way until he drove out of the studio gates at night and was finally relinquished by his alter ego. He never stepped out of character even when he became upset about something, but would go shuffling around in those oversize shoes, grimacing and gesticulating with all the Little Tramp mannerisms. It was an odd thing to Syd and me to see the whimsical character who was always so ebullient on the screen acting short-tempered and brusque.

As soon as Dad had his makeup on, we would follow him once again out on the set, the stage that had been closed and idle for almost five years. Once more we were in that magical revivified fairyland. But now we were older and better able to appreciate the sets in themselves. Not only that, but now the chief set at the studio was far more elaborate than anything in *City Lights* had been. Detail in background was my father's one concession to the new world of picture making. The set represented the interior of a factory. But no one in a thousand years could have guessed what was being manufactured there. It looked like something out of a nightmare, with its gigantic gadgets, wheels and whirring assembly lines.

How Syd and I loved that assembly-line sequence, with Dad trying desperately to keep up the pace and shaking uncontrollably and automatically whenever there was a lull in production! And how we howled over the ridiculous exhibition of Dad being fed nuts and bolts and a corn cob by an automatic feeding machine gone wrong. We screamed hilariously when the board above the door of the little shack kept falling down and hitting him on the head every time he went through. And it almost proved too much for us when finally, after performing all kinds of gyrations, he took a big somersault into the water and landed in about two inches of it—a concealed mattress underneath breaking his fall.

In later years Dad was to explain to me the secret of his success in comedy—of the success of most comedy, actually.

"You can use the unexpected to some extent to get a laugh," he used to say. "But the gag that is sure to go over is the one where the audience has been tipped off in advance. That's why I like to use old gags. Like the diving scene—it's been done so many times everyone is already familiar with what is going to happen. All you have to worry about is your interpretation."

My father's interpretations are always unique. He has the ability to pull funny pieces of business right out of the air, so that with his clever innovations the hoariest gags look brand-new.

Watching the play-acting from the sidelines was just fun for Syd and me, but it was real work for the actors and the crew. Though Dad was the Little Fellow now, nice but ineffectual against the powers of the world, he was at the same time the famous, awe-inspiring director who literally held the destinies of that company in his hands. I've talked to many people who have said to me, "Oh, I was terrified the whole time I was working for your father."

It wasn't just his fame that intimidated them. It was the magnetic intensity of his perfectionist drive that kept them all on edge. If props were out of line by so much as a couple of inches, if the lights weren't in place, or even if he were handed a dull pencil he was likely to blow his top.

"Damn it, do I have to do all this myself?" he would explode. And at this point he would seldom fail to remind the culprit, as he did Frank, "Remember, I'm paying you to do a good job."

Dad might allow a green crew member a few mistakes, but if he made too many too early in the game he would be peremptorily fired. The actual firing would be taken care of by Alf Reeves in the outer office, because, just as at home, Dad couldn't bear to dismiss anyone, no matter how inefficient. Nor would he ever rehire anyone so fired, though he might contribute money to the man's family if he learned it was destitute. To him inefficiency was a major crime. On the other hand, if a man proved himself in my father's employ he could count on a permanent job. Dad was scrupulously loyal with his employees that way.

With actors who couldn't get a scene he was more patient than with inefficient stagehands, but in that seething, nervous way that could upset them more than an outright explosion. Sometimes, to get the exact effect he wanted, he would demonstrate a piece of business, showing them how to cross the room, how to sit down, how to make the gestures. He was impatient with the actors when they couldn't seem to catch on the first time. He would repeat the gestures with lightning speed, as he did so explaining what he wanted in a low, fast monotone. But the actor, upset to begin with, couldn't understand the monologue and still couldn't mimic Dad's gestures.

"Look, look, look! No, no, no!" my father would exclaim. "Try it again! Try it again! Try it again!" And at last, when he was in the final throes of desperation, he would get what he wanted.

While taking in the overall scene to see that it was exactly how he had pictured it when writing the script, Dad's quick eye would concern itself with such insignificant details as the position of an actor's hand or the tilt of his head. Nothing seemed to escape him. I've wondered occasionally if, when Dad is directing, he even sees actors as flesh-and-blood people. I feel that sometimes he treats them more like dolls, or statues to be arranged to achieve the pictorial scene he has in mind. And I think it is this quality that gives his pictures their air of almost symbolic fantasy.

When Dad was engrossed, he lost all conception of time. Lunch hour might come and go without a break, especially as no one could find the temerity to interrupt and tell him that it was twelve noon. Sometimes it would be as late as two o'clock before he would come to his senses and dismiss the company for an hour. Syd and I always took lunch with Dad in his dressing room.

"Well, how'd you like what we did this morning, eh?" he'd say, if he were pleased. But he knew already, for his eye had been quick to take in our responses even while he was working. I was more aware now than when I was younger of how Dad was always watching to see how his comedy business went over with the workmen around the set—the prop men, the cameramen, the grips, the gaffers, the carpenters. Dad used to tell me that he learned from the beginning to please only himself in his acting, because he found that when he tried too hard to be funny just to satisfy others, everything fell flat. But I have noticed that although he feels pleasing oneself is the only sure way of putting over comedy, he needs the laughter of those around him to bolster his ego and keep him going.

After lunch Dad would go back to work again, driving the company all afternoon and sometimes late into the evening. He seemed to be tireless, bounding everywhere, showing the same alert attention for every detail as in the morning. By late afternoon, when the rest of the company would be drooping and listless, Dad's energy stood out in even stronger contrast.

"My God, that Chaplin!" you could hear the people around muttering, "He never gets tired."

Only Syd and I knew the truth about that, because only Syd and I saw him after work. On Friday afternoons when school let out and we went to the house on the hill we would find it empty. Even though the servants were there it seemed empty to us without Dad. He alone seemed to fill it and to make it come alive. It was as though it, too, like the servants, like Syd and me, felt itself to be a part of him—just an extension of him in space.

Syd and I would play with our friends awhile, but as the afternoon lengthened we would keep thinking of Dad, what he was doing, when he would be back. When the time drew near for his return, we would usually be sitting on the front steps with our elbows on our knees, our chins in our hands, keeping a vigil for him.

At last the long black limousine with Kay at the wheel would pull round the circular drive, and Syd and I would dash down the steps to greet it. Kay would stop in front, come around and open the door. And we would see the Little Fellow sitting inside, still in makeup, still wearing his silly mustache, his head against the back of the seat, relaxed and half asleep.

"Mr. Chapilaine, we are home," Kay would say deferentially.

The Little Fellow, still in his baggy trousers because he had been too tired to change, but minus the tight-fitting jacket, the too-big shoes and the too-small derby, would suddenly rouse himself and peer out.

"Hello, boys," he would say in a half-dazed way, seeing us. "Oh, we had a day today! We had a day!"

Kay would help him out of the car.

"Let us help you too, Dad," Syd and I would say eagerly.

Kay would take one arm, and Syd or I would take the other, to help him up the steps. He would walk slowly into the house, looking and acting more lifeless than anyone I've ever seen. We would go inside, climb the circular staircase and pass on down the hall to the master bedroom. There Dad would flop on his bed. Syd and I would sit beside him talking, until Frank arrived to help him undress.

"Dad, may we stick around?" I would ask when Frank

showed up. Dad was always so drowsy I thought we might irritate him being there. But he seemed to welcome our company.

"Sure, sure, stick around, boys," he'd say. And then he'd add, not so much as an afterthought but more as an apology, "I'm so tired . . . very tired."

He would lie there while Frank removed his shoes and socks, his shirt and baggy pants. Stripped to his underwear, he would remain sprawled on the bed. Presently, however, the sight of Syd and me sitting there watching him became more than he could resist. After he'd relaxed a little he would get off the bed and go over to the mirror and start hamming it up for us. First he would make a few faces at himself, and then at Syd and me. Then he would begin to pull the mustache off, pulling it in sections as he had done when I was a baby, and making the most horrible grimaces all the while.

"These are the pitfalls to becoming an actor," Dad would say with a scowl, and a savage yank. "Ninety-nine percent sweat"—another yank—"and one percent talent. . . Oh," he would add after a pause and a quick look at us, "and that one percent better be good.

"There! Now!" he would exclaim with a last jerk. "Do I look like your father again?" Then he'd sponge off his upper lip with alcohol and give us another grimace.

Next Dad would put on his terrycloth robe and head for the bathroom and his steam room. The steam room, which was about five feet across and perhaps eight or nine in length, had a marble slab along one side. When Dad turned on a faucet the steam would come gushing out of a vent. Dad would lie down on the slab in his terrycloth robe and stay there for perhaps as long as three-quarters of an hour, though it was so hot that I could scarcely stand it, completely naked.

That steam bath seemed to revive him amazingly. Often he would be refreshed enough to go out to dinner, though he would always make a point of returning home early, since he had to get up the next morning for work. Sometimes, however, Dad was too tired to be revived by the steam bath, and then he would go to bed for the evening and have his dinner sent up to him.

Though Dad gave himself a physical beating every day of work, I'm sure much of his weariness came from emotional stress, for I saw that it was most noticeable when everything at the studio had been at sixes and sevens.

"You know, it's so hard trying to be funny when you have to be and you don't feel like it," he used to confide in Syd and me sometimes as we sat sympathetically by his bed.

He was the greatest comedian in the world. What could eight- and nine-year-old boys say to comfort the greatest comedian in the world when he feels washed out, deserted, abandoned by the comic muse?

"I just didn't get over," Dad would go on. "I couldn't make anyone laugh. I had a very bad day. Very bad. Tsh tsh tsh."

Some days the mood of depression would strike Dad before he even left home. "Golly, I don't want to go to that studio," he'd say.

He would drag himself down, resigned from the start to a drab day. But sometimes right at the beginning of shooting, a prat fall or some other piece of business he hadn't thought so funny might cause a wave of merriment. Buoyed up by the unexpected applause, Dad's mood would change. He would get so interested in what he was doing that he would work until late in the evening.

Sometimes, though, the depression would persist. Then Dad would shoot only until one o'clock or so, dismiss the company and relax the rest of the afternoon.

The next morning would see him on the set again. He seldom took time off like this, but when he did he would usually try to make it up. If the mood was with him he might stick to it till eleven o'clock at night, driving his company and crew along with him in that relentless way he had. Though Dad's pictures took longer than most to complete, he worked on a much more rigid schedule than most studios in town. It

118

was just that, being such a perfectionist, he had to do many things over and over again—especially over and over again where *Modern Times* was concerned.

Every day he was forcefully reminded of how he was sticking his neck out. His silent-picture making was the gossip of the town. There were lugubrious headshakes from his fellow producers and friends and tongue-in-cheek speculations by columnists. Sometimes he must have been appalled himself at his own conservatism.

16

That fall of 1934, while in the midst of producing *Modern Times*, my father was troubled by another kidnaping threat against us. A studio workman reported that he had overheard a conversation that sounded suspiciously like a plot to abduct us. Dad would have dismissed that as mere barroom talk if a few days later he hadn't received an anonymous threatening note.

He acted at once with his usual flamboyant thoroughness. He hired bodyguards for us—or at least he issued a statement to the press that he was doing so, for I don't remember ever seeing these stalwart protectors of ours in person. He also announced that he had converted both the studio and his hill estate into arsenals with guns trained on every approach.

I know Dad was genuinely worried. Even long after the incident he continued to be troubled every time he read of a kidnaping in the papers. And when sometimes in our carelessness we would go off visiting with friends and fail to return on time, we would find him waiting for us in a state of high tension.

"Where were you? Where were you?" he would demand, turning on us sternly. "I was afraid you might have been kidnaped. Don't you realize you're worrying your father to death? He's getting grayer than he is gray." And with this Dad would run his fingers nervously through his handsome hair—hair that had actually started graying in his early youth.

From Thanksgiving to Christmas of that year my father was completely tied up in production, which among many other things included a hurried business trip to New York. But fortunately Syd and I had Paulette, who managed to squeeze in time for us. She took us to football games and the zoo and often to lunch at the Brown Derby. It was Paulette who planned Christmas for us that year, buying us our presents from Dad.

Her principal contribution was as impractical as it was delightful. It was a motor glide, a little gasoline-powered cart. I'm sure when she bought it Paulette didn't stop to consider that our house was at the top of a steep hill, with cars coming fast around the curving street on which our private road opened. Syd and I had fun with that glide from the first. It was an object of pleasure and curiosity to the whole house. Even Frank and Dad tried it out. Dad rode it around sedately, pleased as we were with the daring putt-putt of the motor. Syd and I couldn't help slyly poking a little condescending fun at his cautious rate of speed.

We were different. We would fly down that hill and burst out on the highway below, often just missing passing cars. Sometimes we would hit an obstruction in the road and be flung from the glide into the middle of the street. I came home once with a bump as big as a goose egg on my forehead, and Dad surveyed it with horror, his fancy, as usual, picturing dreadful scenes of carnage in which Syd's and my battered and bloody corpses were the principal feature. He pleaded with us to be more careful, but he never once threatened to deprive us of the glide. There is a peculiar integrity of conviction in my father that, coupled with his stubbornness, has caused him a lot of trouble in his life. The glide was ours, and I don't think it ever entered his mind that he had the right as a father to take it away from us.

There were others besides Dad who were concerned about the motor glide, but for a different reason. They were our neighbors, the David O. Selznicks, who dearly loved their morning sleep. The raucous motor of the glide shattered the quiet day completely for them. They complained fruitlessly about the noise, as they were to do later when Big Bill Tilden gave tennis lessons on Dad's court at seven in the morning. After Dad married Paulette, I believe she got a little fun now and then out of teasing the Selznicks by encouraging us to get at our demon driving as early in the morning as possible.

Christmas that year was a red-letter day. Just before it arrived, Mother turned down all professional engagements and flew in from New York to spend the holidays with us. She took a suite at the Ambassador Hotel in Los Angeles, where she gave a party for Syd and me and our friends on Christmas Eve. I vaguely remember that party. I recall far more clearly the following Christmas morning, for it proved to be one of those rare occasions that brought our parents together.

Dad came to see us at our mother's invitation. Suddenly there he was at the door of Mother's suite, putting out his hand to her.

"Hello," he said, just as though they had parted yesterday. "How are you? You're looking well."

"So are you, Charlie," Mother replied.

Syd and I ran up and kissed Dad and went back to our

game, which was a kind of boisterous tag, while Mother and Dad chatted together. But Dad had been there only a little while when suddenly he got to his feet.

"I don't think I should stay too long because I have Paulette in the car," he said diffidently. "She might be miffed if I just leave her sitting there."

"Why don't you ask her up?" Mother said.

So Dad called down to the bell captain and asked him to invite Paulette in.

Paulette came up, and she and Mother met for the first and last time there in the parlor of the Ambassador Hotel suite. Mother was as captivated by Paulette as Dad and Syd and I had been.

"She was so disarming," Mother says, recalling that day. "A wonderful, wonderful girl with a good sense of humor. I'll never forget how beautiful she looked in her black velvet dress with her dark soft shoulder-length hair."

Though Paulette never saw Mother again, she kept in touch with her throughout the years, sending her friendly little notes to show she was remembered. After Mother's first breakdown, when she was hospitalized with an operation, it was Paulette who sent her a bottle of wine in a basket and a note which read, "Get well quickly, Lita, we wish you the best."

Was Paulette trying to thank Mother in this way for the loan of her two sons? I don't know. But Mother has often told close friends, "I was so happy Charlie married Paulette, because she cared so much about my children. She was wonderful to them. She used to take a lot of time out of her own life and her own interests just to spend with them."

Yes, Paulette gave us a lot of her time. That January, after Mother had returned East to fulfill the rest of her engagements, Paulette took us to the mountains for a long week end, driving us herself to Lake Arrowhead. How wonderful that holiday was in the white, quiet land of snow, so different from the warm lowlands. Paulette might have been our older sister up there. We played in the snow together. We went sledding. All day long we kept busy and we were ready for bed—all three of us—when night fell.

But we hated to tell Paulette good night. It was cold and lonely. The wind had a sighing sound and a biting edge to it. We went to her room shivering in our pajamas.

"Let us stay here with you," we begged.

Paulette laughed.

"Okay, ten minutes," she answered. And Syd and I jumped into bed with her. It was restful lying there with her arms around us, listening to her tell us a fairy tale. Soon we were drifting off to sleep.

Then from a long distance away we heard Paulette saying, "Okay, come on now, back to bed you go."

And she shook us gently and shoved us out, and Syd and I wandered off to bed.

There never was a nicer winter holiday, but of course it couldn't last. We had to come back to the lowlands to mundane things—Syd and I to school and Paulette to work and the gossip of the newspapers that were speculating loudly about what it meant when a man's best girl took his sons on an out-of-town holiday. Paulette loved it.

That year, on the eve of my tenth birthday, I experienced one of the biggest disappointments of my childhood. It was the year I first did an imitation of my father for the public. Around the house Syd and I had always done imitations of movie personalities—Lloyd, Gable, Garbo, even our father. Dad was amused by us and encouraged us on occasion to show off for his guests. But this was different. This was on a stage in front of a real audience, at the Ebell Theatre in Los Angeles.

Syd and I attended a dancing school, and the children put on a show in which dolls that represented different fictional characters came to life. I did one on Dad as the Little Tramp. Everyone said afterwards that I was good but I wanted to hear that praise from only one person—the Little Tramp himself. I wonder if anyone in the cast or audience guessed how I scanned that shadowy sea of faces below for one familiar face, or how I strained my ears to hear that infectious laugh, rather high-pitched yet resonant. But I neither saw nor heard my father.

I learned later that Dad, who had told me he planned to come, was held up by a last-minute rush of work. He was amused to learn of my imitation of him and pleased with the praise I had received. But it wasn't the same as if he had been there to see with his own eyes. I couldn't hold back my feeling of disappointment, though I understood how it was with Dad when he was working.

By this time he was spending nights as well as days at the studio. He solved the problem by moving to the studio altogether, with his cook, George. Finally, after ten months of cyclonic activity, the production work on *Modern Times* was completed, and Dad came out of his spell to find himself surrounded with broken, or at least soured, personal relationships.

Hardest hit was Paulette. She had submitted to my father's perfectionist drive in every detail, and so the gamin of *Modern Times* had been charmingly created. But Paulette, the real woman, had been ignored. Terribly weary from the long ordeal, she must have felt a desire to escape her relentless mentor and enjoy herself. At least newspapers began to report that she was being seen around town with other men. This naturally led to talk of a breakup. But breakup of what? Even now, when it appeared that everything might be over, the reporters were still speculating on whether it was to be the breakup of a marriage, an engagement or just a romance.

Fortunately for Syd and me, we didn't hear of the newspaper gossip. By this time Paulette had come to mean a great deal to us. One week end while the papers were reporting her estrangement from Dad, she took us to Palm Springs with her. And when she came back she and Dad were once again seen everywhere together.

It was Paulette who, at Dad's request, went to meet H. G.

Wells, who arrived on November 29 at Grand Central Air Terminal in Glendale. Dad had been Wells's guest in England and now Wells was returning the visit. He spent two or three weeks at Dad's home. I remember him as a man with a walrus mustache and a decidedly British manner of acting and speaking. Syd and I weren't too impressed with him at our age; to us he was just another of Dad's writer friends, and a nuisance in our lives because, during his stay with Dad, he was given our room. So long as he remained we couldn't spend any nights at the house on the hill.

Though the filming of the picture was over, Dad still had his musical score to complete. Music combined with a few spoken words allegedly coming out of loud-speakers, and a final nonsense song by Dad, were to be his concession to the world of sound. He told me the nonsense song was primarily to test his own voice for screen projection.

My father didn't have a music department of his own and had to go over to United Artists to make use of their musicians and recording rooms. If the people in his own studio had suffered from Dad's perfectionist drive, the musicians who now began working with him endured pure torture.

Dad can't read a note of music himself, but he knew what he wanted, and when he wasn't getting it, and he wouldn't give up until it sounded right to him. He had some of the industry's top musical talent to help him. Alfred Newman, who has won several Oscars and who at the time was under contract to Sam Goldwyn, was assigned to do the score and direct the music. David Raksin, the talented young composer who was later to make musical history with his tune "Laura," was hired, with Edward Powell, to take down and orchestrate Dad's music.

Dad wore them all out. Edward Powell concentrated so hard writing the music down that he almost lost his eyesight and had to go to a specialist to save it. David Raksin, working an average of twenty hours a day, lost twenty-five pounds and sometimes was so exhausted he couldn't find strength to go home but would sleep on the studio floor. Al Newman saw him one day in the studio street walking along with tears running down his cheeks.

But David still had plenty of resilience in him, enough to play an occasional prank on Dad by way of lightening the pressure.

Dad had a recording machine similar to a Dictaphone, into which he would hum his tunes. This enabled him to work longer hours and have his ideas canned, ready for presentation when he and Raksin got together. One day as a joke David recorded snatches of Prokofiev's Third Concerto and Shostakovich's First Symphony to give my father a proper start when he turned on the machine. What David hadn't expected was that that afternoon Dad would be showing off his studio to a party of distinguished visitors—Alexander Woollcott, H. G. Wells and King Vidor among them. He stepped proudly over to the recording machine.

"This is how I compose my music," he said and turned it on.

He jumped about two feet when Shostakovich came blasting out. Then he looked at David Raksin for a long, meaningful minute and shook his finger at him. It was his only acknowledgment of the gag.

It was Al Newman who finally broke under the pressure. With only two hundred feet more of sound track to go, and after endless changes and grueling work night and day for weeks, his nerves were as taut as though they had been subjected to the Chinese water torture. He just exploded one day and called my father every name he could think of, throwing his baton all the way across the stage to emphasize what he was saying. Then he stalked out, went to his suite in the building across from the sound stage, tossed down a half pint of whiskey to calm his nerves and phoned Goldwyn to tell him he was through. Nor would be go back, despite pleas and pressure. They had to bring in another man to take Newman's place.

But at last they made it through all obstacles and got the music of *Modern Times* recorded. Then my father entered the final phase of picture making, the most difficult of all, as any producer will tell you. It is that period of uncertainty between the completion of a picture and its presentation to the public. It is the same anxiety that an actor feels on opening night, but only in part, because until the last curtain falls an actor has an opportunity to wake up a difficult audience.

A picture, however, is a canned product. It is no longer possible to play up a scene or to improve on a bit of business when audience interest seems to flag. You have to stand or fall on what has been completed in preceding months, and you are at the mercy of an audience with whom you have no physical contact.

Dad once told me the story of how such an audience put him through an excruciating evening. It was a sneak preview of one of his most popular silent pictures, *Gold Rush* or *City Lights*, and it was being shown at the old Belasco Theater, which stood in a Mexican section of Los Angeles. I don't know why the Belasco was selected for the test unless it was assumed its audiences were made up of people in ordinary walks of life who would provide a good cross section of public reaction. At the beginning of the show, post cards were handed out to each patron with a request for an opinion of the picture.

Dad couldn't wait for those cards. He decided to go to the theater incognito and find out for himself.

"I got a seat behind three burly Mexicans," he told me. "They were all sitting with their arms folded. I thought they would limber up when the picture started. But they didn't. They just sat there like rocks. I got a feeling of panic and I looked round at the rest of the audience. There wasn't a peep out of any of them either. My stomach began turning upside down. I had to get up and go to the rest room and throw up.

"I told myself in the rest room it just couldn't be true. And I went back. The audience still seemed about as noisy as a tomb. I found the three Mexicans just as I had left them, motionless, with their arms crossed. They fascinated me. Why, there wasn't so much as a twitch out of them at any time. I had to go back to the rest room. I must have gone four or five times to throw up during the course of that picture. Each time I came back hopeful I would find those Mexicans laughing, the audience in an uproar. But I didn't. Throughout the whole picture I didn't hear a single belly laugh, just a few discreet chuckles now and then.

"To cap everything, three fourths of the way through the picture the three Mexicans in front of me got to their feet as one man, stretched, yawned and walked out. I couldn't stand it any longer. I followed right behind them. I went home a nervous wreck. All I could do was pray that there might be at least some people who would like it. After all, I'd spent well over a million dollars on the production. I *had* to pray."

When the cards came in, my father was astonished at the high praise most of the audience expressed for his picture. He could only assume that Mexicans as a nationality don't roar with laughter when they're amused. They just chuckle.

Dad worried the same way over *Modern Times*. I guess he drank his glass of Alka-Seltzer fizz water practically every night until the picture was launched. Critics were not as enthusiastic as they had been about his earlier films, but the audiences seemed to like it. In this country alone it grossed almost two million dollars, which was a healthy figure in the wake of the depression. It was sure proof that even in the world of sound the Little Fellow could hold his own. And now the critics who had been predicting a dismal failure for the film began conjecturing learnedly about the causes for its success. Producers and directors started to study its techniques to see if any could be used to improve their own pictures. Dad was no longer looked on as a has-been. He was still the King of Comedy.

But for my father, everything about *Modern Times* was now passé. He didn't want to discuss it or even think about it again. His churning mind began to grope for something new and exciting upon which to fasten itself. And he settled upon a visit to the Orient, which had so impressed him when he went there on his trip around the world. But this time he did not plan to travel alone. Paulette, accompanied by her mother, Mrs. Alta Goddard, was to accompany him. Dad was never niggardly where praise was deserved, and out of appreciation for the wonderful job Paulette had done in the picture he had presented her with a piece of expensive jewelry. But the trip was to be an additional reward, and Paulette was as excited about it as a child.

Syd and I told them good-by one day in February, and accompanied by good, honest Frank, they sailed away on the *President Coolidge,* bound for Honolulu. What envy filled us as we thought of all the exotic places they were going to see! We felt a kind of emptiness, too, at being left behind in our barracks-like school. But who wants children along on what is very likely to turn out to be a honeymoon trip? At least this was what all the papers were predicting. And Dad and Paulette, as usual, were neither denying nor affirming it.

17

For more than three months our father toured the Orient with Paulette. Not once in all that time did we have a letter from him, though I'm sure he thought of us. But it has always taken an earth-shaking event for Dad to sit down and write.

Though we never heard from him, Syd and I could follow his odyssey in the daily papers. His ports of call had strange, exotic names—Yokohama, Shanghai, Hong Kong, Singapore, Batavia, Java, Sumatra, Bali. At each stop he made, the newspapers were speculating about whether he and Paulette were secretly married.

But all these speculations made little impression on Syd and me. We thought only of how long a time it had been since the house on the hill had been open to us. We missed it, we missed

Dad and Paulette and our friends. It wasn't a happy spring for us that year anyway; we were making our first acquaintance with tragedy.

That Easter Sunday, in the middle of a successful singing tour in Scotland, Mother collapsed with her first nervous breakdown. Except for her faithful maid, Gladys, she was all alone in a foreign country. A cablegram came for Nana, urging her to come to Mother at once. But at the time Nana herself was gravely ill with double pneumonia and couldn't leave her bed. Gladys had to get Mother back to the United States unaided and place her in a sanitarium. It wasn't until early May that Nana, barely well enough to travel, was able to leave her sickbed and go East to bring Mother home.

When they returned, Nana bought a five-acre ranch in the San Fernando Valley for us all. It was just over the hills from Hollywood, and at that time far removed from the bustle of the city, from people in general and old acquaintances who might have had a disturbing influence on Mother. And there Nana started the heartbreaking task of nursing Mother back to health. Mother's mental turmoil was greatly aggravated by a glandular imbalance. She needed an operation but she was so run-down the doctor didn't dare risk it. It turned into a vicious round robin, with the physical condition aggravating the mental and that in turn operating to tear down the physical. It was an agonizing period for all of us, but especially for Mother, who had to make the long and lonely fight back to normalcy and health.

How different Syd and I found her this time. She was no longer the glamorous, vivacious girl we had known, who had always been ready for a laugh and some fun. Now she was quiet and hysterical by turns, and she could be upset by the smallest things. I had only to tune in to classical music on the radio to send her into hysterics. Her frantic terror at those times frightened and bewildered me.

She spent most of the time in bed. I remember how she lay there hour after hour in a daze, though I did not know that the doctors were giving her sedatives to keep her quiet.

I felt bad about it, as a child feels toward an illness he cannot understand, but I didn't take it too seriously at first. I just accepted Nana's explanation that Mother had worked hard and was run-down and needed lots of rest.

I remember the day in early June when Dad phoned the school and said he was back and would like to see us. Syd and I were jubilant. On Friday, just as though no months had intervened, a smiling Frank showed up in the car to take us to the house on the hill.

"Your fathah," Frank told us on the way home, "he got married down at Hong Kong on the boat."

When we asked for details, he shook his head.

"I didn't see 'em get married," he said with a laugh. "I don't hang around them all the time. They have their things to do. I have mine. But they tell me so."

At last we were back in our father's familiar home again. Dad and Paulette were waiting for us. They looked happy— Dad especially. He always enjoyed his excursions abroad, but each time he was thoroughly glad to get home. He really wasn't much of a traveler, and the feeling of being rooted had become so strong in him by this time that he was to stay in the United States for sixteen years after this trip.

Syd and I ran up and kissed first Dad and then Paulette. Paulette stooped and hugged us both while Dad laughingly confirmed Frank's piece of information. But though Dad told us flatly that he had married Paulette, it was to remain a family secret for years, because neither one of them bothered to tip off the reporters. Throughout the long period they were together the newspapers continued to speculate as to "when" and "if" and "where."

June! It brought so many things that year. It brought my mother an anguish of remorse that was to haunt her for years, though she was really not responsible for what happened. How can you hold a tragically ill person responsible for anything? And it brought me in the end a deeper understanding of life. My mother has agreed that I should tell this story because it gives a clearer insight into my relations with my father at the time.

Up until June of 1936, Syd and I had not considered ourselves any different from the children of other divorced couples. We knew our parents hadn't been able to get along and had separated when we were very small, but we had been carefully shielded from the ugliness that accompanied the divorce. And there had been nothing really shocking in the two subsequent court battles over us—just unpleasantness. Both our father and our mother had taken care to stress respect for the other.

"Don't bring any tales back to me about your father or take any tales to him from our place," Mother would caution when she was staying with us. "We live our own lives and have our separate ways of doing things." For his part, Dad never asked what went on in Mother's home. His inquiries about her were always polite. "How is your mother? I hope she's well. What's she doing these days? Touring?"

At school, too, no one talked about divorce. There were other children of divorced couples and everyone took it for granted. There were also a lot of children with parents in show business as Dad and Mother were—writer Ken Englund's son George, Buster Keaton's sons, Paul Whiteman, Jr., Max Factor's son. When we discussed our parents it was mostly in terms of their accomplishments in the theater or in pictures.

"You lucky fellows," our friends would say to Syd and me. "Your father's a famous comedian. Your mother's a beautiful singer. Is your father going to marry Paulette? She's a doll."

Listening to our friends' envious remarks, Syd and I had the feeling that, all in all, life had been very kind to us. It never occurred to us there was a darker side to the story until I learned it from my mother on June 28, my eleventh birthday—or at least the day they had always celebrated as my birthday.

Syd and I were home from school now, dividing our time between our father's place and our mother's house on Ventura Boulevard. That day I walked into the bedroom where Mother was lying. I was always wandering in there, vaguely worried about her and hoping each time to see that she had improved. But this day I had a special purpose in mind. It was my birthday and Mother had been asleep all morning and hadn't yet congratulated me. I was hoping I would find her awake and she would remember, but she was still lying there very quietly. I was about to leave when suddenly she sat bolt upright.

"I have something very important to tell you, Charles," she said with a mysterious air. "Very important! It may mean life or death."

I didn't pay much attention at first to what she was saying. Mother had such a strange way of talking those days. What I did notice plainly for the first time were her pitifully thin arms. They were like pipes. It came to me that I could circle them with one hand. I saw, too, how large and black her eyes were in her thin face. They had a wild, haunted look.

"Charles," she insisted, seeing my wandering gaze. "You *must* listen."

Then all at once she began talking in a rush of words, giving vent to the fears and resentments that had piled up inside her during her marriage to Dad. I was the one to hear them because I had walked into the room at that particular time and because, since it was my birthday, I was the focal point.

After her recovery Mother could remember that ordeal only with remorse. She told me that all the while she was talking she knew she shouldn't be. But she was powerless to stop. The sedatives had destroyed all volition and she had no control over her tongue. It was as though another person had borrowed it and was talking through her.

She launched into a wild description of my father as she was convinced he really was. But the man she described, the man she saw in her phantasmagoria, had little connection with the flesh-and-blood human being I knew as my father. He was a monster, huge as a myth, with unbelievable powers of destruction. And all this power, my mother told me, was focused on her to destroy her and had been for years. His spies had even followed her to far-off Scotland and caused her to fall ill. And now they were all around her. And they had in their possession dreadful potions with which they were poisoning the air. She could smell it plainly. (Later the doctors were able to explain to her that her sensitized nostrils had picked up the internal odors that came from the secretions of her own overworked glands.) So far, she explained, she had managed to evade death, but she did not know how long this would go on.

Her vivid words wove a spell around me. I stood rooted to the spot, while Mother kept repeating over and over her conviction of my father's malignant power.

"He has so much money," she said. "He can hire anybody to do what he wants. It's almost impossible to fight him."

Malignant, malevolent, the phantom Mother had created from her disordered fantasy seemed to tower between us in the shadowy room like a horrible genie released from a lamp. Mother leaned toward me now, speaking confidentially.

"I have to warn you, Charlie," she said. "You have his name and he didn't want you to have it. He wanted to keep it all to himself, so that there would be just one Charlie Chaplin. Now there are two. So he intends to destroy you too."

Mother began crying. Trembling all over, she went on through her sobs. "No, he never wanted you, Charlie. He had to marry me because of you and so he never loved you from the first. I have to tell you about your birthday, Charlie. It's not today, the twenty-eighth of June. It's really back on the fifth of May. The records were changed. He has all this power, you see. You can't fight him. You can't fight him."

Mother's voice had risen to a hysterical wail and suddenly Nana came running in.

I slipped quietly out of the room and walked all about the house, too dazed even to reason about what Mother had just told me. She had made it seem so real I couldn't be sure of anything. I had to talk to someone about it. I remembered Syd. I looked around until I found him and I told him everything, just as Mother had told me.

Syd was able to look at the whole thing more objectively than I because he hadn't been caught in the spell of Mother's terrible conviction.

"Don't pay any attention to Mother, Chuck," he said. "She's sick, she's awfully sick. You can tell. Sometimes here lately she doesn't even know what she's saying. She just makes things up."

Syd's words were like a prick in a giant balloon. The fantastic picture Mother had drawn with such clarity collapsed under his common-sense words. Later Nana verified what he had said.

"She's delirious, Charlie," she tried to comfort me, half crying herself. "Just forget everything she told you."

At first I believed Syd and Nana implicitly, because it made everything better that way. But after a while a doubt began to nag at me. I kept returning to one point. The more I thought of it, the more I was convinced that one point, anyway, wasn't fantasy. It was the one about my birthday. It stood out clearly just because it looked so rational in the midst of all the rest of it. And it put everything concerning me and my parents in a different light.

It wasn't any longer just a case of their having been incompatible after their marriage. They had never wanted to marry each other in the first place. And I had forced them into it. That made me the cause of all their unhappiness, perhaps even of my mother's illness. The logic of a child is terrible, and once he gets started there is no limit to the burden of guilt he will take on his own shoulders.

18

What is an eleven-year-old boy's reaction to the information that his father does not love him, and never did? Now when I went up to the hill I began studying Dad surreptitiously, his words and gestures, the expression on his face, to see if I could detect his true feelings toward me, whether of coldness or warmth. I never could be sure because he was the same father he had always been. It was I who had changed. Without realizing it I began to be quite formal, even deferential, toward him. It was as though I had become a stranger in my own home.

It came to me one day that I could settle everything by a forthright question to my father about the circumstances of my birth. But I was afraid to make the move. Afraid of what? Afraid of discovering it was all true? Afraid of a rebuff?

It was especially wonderful then to have Paulette around. She wasn't just pretty. She was warm and enthusiastic about everything. And she loved to joke with Dad.

Paulette was such a good audience that Dad must have pulled a hundred gags a day on her, some of them so corny you couldn't believe it. Out of a clear sky he would jump up from the couch or chair on which he was sitting, pull his hair down on his forehead and, with his hand in his coat, strut around the house looking exactly like Napoleon Bonaparte, who fascinated him.

Sometimes, when the evening had proved long enough for him, he would get gravely to his feet.

"I'm ready for bed," he would announce solemnly. "Good night, honey buns," and he would go behind the couch and start walking along it, crouching lower and lower with each step so that it looked exactly as though he were going down an imaginary flight of stairs. He always wore the silliest expression on his face. The last you would see of him would be his head with that silly expression.

Now that Paulette had come to live with us, we began to do many more things together. Dad had meant well toward us before, but often, caught up in the press of work or a sudden rush of ideas, he had forgotten about us. Paulette saw that we were included in the plans for the week end. She would get Dad away from his writing table to go to a movie with us or go on an outing to the Amusement Pier or the zoo. The monkeys at the zoo reminded Dad of the gorillas he had seen in Sumatra. (He was always recalling one or another fantastic thing from his trips to the Orient.) He spoke in awe of those Sumatra gorillas, with their tremendous heads and massive bodies. But strangely enough, though he mimicked almost everybody and everything, including vultures, which he considered among the most graceful of living creatures, I can't recall ever seeing him mimic a monkey.

Often we would end the day with dinner at a small restaurant in Chinatown or some other out-of-the-way spot. Sometimes Paulette's mother would come along too. Mrs. Goddard was just like Paulette in so many ways. They laughed alike, had the same sparkling eyes and effervescent sense of humor. Dad got along with Mrs. Goddard. Perhaps he could give some valuable pointers on how to keep peace with one's mothers-in-law, because he was on good terms with all of his. Even after the bitter divorce trial between him and my mother, he resumed a warm friendship with Nana. And he is very fond of Mrs. Agnes O'Neill, Oona's mother.

But Paulette wasn't the only one to suggest entertainment for us that summer. Sometimes Dad would get a bug in his head about taking us all on a little drive, the sort of ordinary outing a lot of families enjoy, if you could call Dad's kind of driving ordinary. He always used the Ford, a black four-door sedan. He kept that Ford for years because he was confused by the strange gadgets on later models. He'd learned to drive when he was thirty-five and he was proud of his accomplishment. For driving he wore what I considered a regular outfit —his brown-rimmed glasses, a tweed jacket and a brown felt hat which he kept tilted at a cocky angle.

We would all set out for the car. Dad would help Paulette into the front seat while Syd and I climbed in the back. Then he would get in himself. When he stuck the key into the ignition he would straighten himself, throw back his shoulders, cock his head, thrust out his chin and grasp the wheel in a masterful fashion. And off we'd go.

Dad would start at a moderate pace, but then he would get interested in the scenery and his foot would automatically press down on the accelerator. Suddenly he would recollect himself and relax on the gas. We drove in spurts like that most of the time, while Dad rubbernecked. I think he seldom looked at the road ahead.

Dad enjoyed pretending we were tourists driving around taking in the homes of Hollywood stars. There were a lot right in our neighborhood. Besides Pickfair just above us and the Lloyds below, Kay Francis, Ronald Colman, Fred Astaire and Tom Mix all lived nearby. When we passed Mix's house

Syd and I would crane our heads out the window, hoping to catch a glimpse of him in his cowboy outfit, but we never did.

As we came to the outskirts of Dad's place he always had to point it out to us with an extra flourish. And when Syd and I greeted his effusive ballyhoo with laughter he would look grieved.

"They just about fall out of the car trying to get a look at Tom Mix," he would complain to Paulette. "And here I am considered the greatest comedian in the world by a lot of people and they just take me for granted."

Sometimes, instead of sightseeing around town, Dad would get it into his head to take us on long drives into the country. Oh, what drives! Beautiful lawns, bright flowers, stately trees, any of these were enough to distract Dad from the task at hand. Sometimes he would sail right through a stop light.

"Charlie, Charlie," Paulette would cry, "the light's red!"

But by that time Dad had left it far behind.

"What light?" he wanted to know.

"Do be careful, Charlie," Paulette, who is a very good driver herself, would say.

But Dad was incorrigible. He'd go right back to viewing the scenery on either side of the road and forgetting his foot was on the gas.

"My God, Charlie!" Paulette would suddenly scream. "Look at the road!"

And Dad would get his eyes back and his wheel turned in time to keep from colliding with an oncoming car.

"Oh, what a terrible driver," Paulette would sigh, and then she would burst out laughing, because it was really very funny, and Syd and I would join her.

Dad always passed off Paulette's barbs about his terrible driving as a joke. I think he took a lot more from her than from anyone else, because he could never stand a back-seat driver. He couldn't stand to be passed on the road, either, because it seemed to him this was a reflection on his rate of speed. And the toot of a horn—which was usually to get him back on his side of the white line—could send him into a tizzy.

"Oh, those fools," he would exclaim, jumping as if he'd been shot. "Why are they honking at me like that? I know how to drive."

Another thing Dad couldn't bear when he was driving was to have the route pointed out to him. It seemed to him to be an aspersion on his sense of direction, which is very poor despite his firm faith in it. His complete disregard of all advice reached a climax one day when he was driving with Tim Durant down Sunset Boulevard in a thick fog. Tim, peering anxiously out of the window, suddenly glimpsed a landmark that told him they had come to the road which leads to Dad's house.

"Here you are, we'd better turn here," he exclaimed.

Dad shook his head.

"Not yet, not yet," he said brusquely.

"But it *is* the road," Tim remonstrated.

For answer Dad kept driving doggedly along.

"Look, Charlie," Tim suddenly exclaimed in horror. "We're not on Sunset Boulevard at all. We're on the bridle path now. There's the hedge that lines it."

Dad gave a cursory glance out the window.

"Nonsense," he replied with all the nonchalance of near-sighted Mr. Magoo. "It's the edge of someone's lawn. We'll come to the turn soon."

And he kept on down the bridle path that bisects Sunset Boulevard, past the hedges that even he must have seen were hedges by this time. Only he wouldn't admit his mistake. He never did. After about a mile or more he came to the end of the bridle path and rolled out on Sunset Boulevard again, and just kept on going as if it were the most natural thing in the world.

Of course our adventures led us farther afield than those drives around town. We saw a great deal of the yacht that summer, and sometimes we would all go up to the mountains for a few days, where Paulette taught us to ice skate.

She was a good skater herself. Dad was too, though I never saw him do much skating. Often when Dad was busy Paulette would take Syd and me alone to Lake Arrowhead or Big Bear. It became a ritual with us never to go to bed up there without first joining Paulette for a bedtime story.

Fun—we had a lot of it that summer. But if you have a problem, fun has a way of making it stand out even more plainly. For weeks I had tried to dismiss from my mind what Mother had told me and enter into the activities around me. But every once in a while the thought that perhaps I was there at my father's house only on sufferance would come up to nag at me. Was he just tolerating me? It was a terrible question because I loved him, and because I so much wanted him to love me. But I couldn't be sure of that any more. I couldn't really be sure of anything about him. At last I knew I couldn't go on like that any longer.

I remember the day. Paulette had left for a dancing or singing lesson. Syd and I were playing with the Krisel brothers down by the swimming pool. Suddenly, as so often happened in my boyhood, I felt drawn to the house and my father. I kept wondering what he was doing. I left the pool and came up to the house and looked into the living room. He was sitting at his table writing. Since he had married Paulette I noticed he worked much more downstairs in the front room.

I went in and stood there quietly watching him, feeling both warmth and loneliness, a sensation which had become painfully familiar to me of late. He was only the length of the room away and yet he seemed completely cut off from me.

Finally he came to the end of what he was writing, lifted his head and saw me for the first time.

"Charles," he said, "is there something you want, son?"

"Dad," I answered. I went into the room. I stood before his table, groping. Then all at once the words came stammering out.

"I wanted to ask you, Dad, I'm sorry to bother you. But

Mother's been talking a lot of things about the marriage. I mean yours and hers. I wanted to know."

Dad looked intently at me, and an expression of surprise came over his face.

"There were a lot of unhappy things about it, son," he said gravely after a pause. "There was a big stink in court. It was nobody's fault, really. I was so much older than your mother and we were so unlike. It was a bad thing for all of us."

"But, Dad, my birthday," I insisted. "Mother told me it's not in June. It was May fifth. You had to get married because of me."

"Well," Dad said, and all at once he smiled, "you weren't exactly planned, son, if that's what you mean. But that's just one of the things of life."

He got to his feet, came over and put his arm around my shoulder. It was a warm, spontaneous gesture, surprising in Dad, who is not given to affectionate displays.

"It's all right, Charles," he said, and I knew he was distressed at my obvious unhappiness and uncertainty and was trying to comfort me. "You're here. You're my son, I'm your father. Birthdays aren't really important."

As Dad talked, the last of Mother's weird fantasy fell to pieces in my mind.

"But, Dad," I went on hurriedly, wanting to get the final confirmation from him and afraid I would lose my courage. "She said you hated her. You were after her. You had spies all around."

Dad shook his head. "Even though we had our troubles once, it isn't true, of course," he said. "You know that, son. The mind is a strange thing. When you get hurt deeply, when your problems get too big for you, it plays tricks on you. You believe things that aren't true, you say things that aren't true. Your mother is a very sick woman, Charles. You must remember that."

He spoke gently of her, plainly disturbed and unhappy by

the thought of her illness—as he was always disturbed by suffering of any kind.

"I'd like to see her. Maybe I could help her. If I could talk to her . . ."

As I listened to my father's hesitant, anxious voice it came to me that whatever had happened between him and Mother later, there had been a time, perhaps just a little time, when they were dear to each other, and I was the child of that time. Throughout my boyhood I clung to that assumption because it was so important to my sense of security. But it was to be verified for me only in later years, when my mother was suffering her second breakdown.

19

I had my answer from my father. I could relax and enjoy myself with him now. The trouble was that a single answer is seldom enough for a child. I found myself wondering later if Dad had really meant what he said, or if he had just said it to make me feel better. But I never found enough courage to revive the subject again, and Dad never brought it up with me.

All summer our mother had been improving steadily, though she was not nearly so well as she appeared to be. When she met Henry Aguirre, Jr., a dancer, it took only about two weeks of whirlwind courtship to convince her he was the right man.

That September of 1936 she and Mr. Aguirre eloped to San Francisco without telling even Nana. When they returned they rented a small house on Beachwood Drive, where we visited them several week ends. But Nana had stayed at the ranch and when we weren't with Dad we usually went out to her. So my recollection of Aguirre is a shadowy one. I remember him as a pleasant, mild-mannered man who now and then advised us how to behave. After about three months he and my mother separated and I never saw him again.

To Syd and me there was an air of transience and unreality about our relations with our mother throughout this whole tragic period. Because we hadn't seen her for so long and because when she came home she had been so ill, she was virtually a stranger to us. And now that she was living separately from Nana we were torn between three homes—hers, Nana's and our father's. So it came to be that the most stable place to us those days was the house on the hill, where Paulette and Dad were always ready to welcome us, to laugh and joke with us and to take turns telling us bedtime stories.

Sometimes in the middle of the night I would waken with a childish longing to get closer to them. I would steal out of our room and down the hall to try their doors. But they were always locked. There in the quiet hall under the dim night light that Dad kept burning I wondered what they were afraid of, and I would feel shut out from their circle of safety. Then I would hear the creak and pop of the floor boards as the wood contracted under the sudden chill of the night. It is a common sound in California, where there is such a great variation in the temperature between the day and the dark. But it seemed to me when I heard those tentative noises that the house lived a mysterious and even sinister life of its own when we were all abed.

My father, too, was alert to the sly noises of the night. With his vivid imagination he had at times the uncanny feeling that something was about. At least he would occasionally leave his room and prowl through the bowels of the house, investigating. The first time I heard him in the hall, I opened our door and went out to see what he was doing. By the night light I saw him in his dressing gown. He had his pistol in one hand and he was stealing quietly toward the stairway.

"What's wrong, Father?" I whispered.

"Shhh, son," Dad whispered back. "I thought I heard someone. I'm checking. Go back to bed."

But I didn't. I stood rooted in terror to the hall floor. I heard my father moving around below, going from room to room, turning on lights, opening up doors, closing doors, turning off lights. Just with my ears I followed him around. Then he was coming up again. He saw me waiting.

"It's no one, son. Go back to bed," he said. And he went to his room.

I heard the door shut and the key click in the lock. I felt very lonely and frightened. I ran back to our room and shut our door quickly and turned our key in its lock too. I felt better then. I groped my way to my bed and climbed in. Sydney hadn't even wakened. I could hear him breathing evenly in the other bed. Suddenly I felt safe, and a wave of strong, warm feeling for my brother came up in me. How wonderful it was to have him there. How wonderful it was for Sydney and me to be brothers. We belonged together. We were the Chaplin boys.

20

With Paulette's arrival in the house on the hill, a subtle battle line was almost immediately drawn between my father's heretofore comfortable bachelorhood and her determination to mold him into the ways of a husband. In every room her feminine touch was at once apparent, softening the casual masculinity. There were flowers on the dining-room table, flowers on the piano by the picture of Syd and me, flowers, lots of flowers, in Paulette's bedroom upstairs. There were no flowers in Dad's bedroom, however, because though he loved flowers he had heard they used up oxygen.

But there was more than the odor of flowers to remind us men that there was a woman in the house. There was perfume, exciting, exotic, that now impregnated the middle bedroom, which had become Paulette's. It left its faint telltale aroma throughout the house, vying with Dad's very masculine Mitsouko scent.

The all-male servant staff was breached, too, for Paulette brought her own maid along, a Scandinavian girl whom I recall only as Jenny. And then there was Puddles, the first dog to come to the house on the hill, though she wasn't to be the last by far. During Paulette's time, dogs usually came to our house in pairs. Whenever Paulette thought of gifts for us, her mind gravitated to dogs.

Now Dad likes all small creatures, but I suspect his fondness for them is more in the abstract than the concrete. I've never seen him act really comfortable around dogs, though he has written charmingly about the little female bitch and her five pups which he took on tour with him when he traveled in his teens with the Sherlock Holmes Company. He must have really changed from those early days when he kept the six dogs with him in the small apartments he rented, for ever since I've known him he hasn't approved of dogs in the house. He is sure their fur is a carrier of germs. Their drooling is distasteful to him and he intensely dislikes the rough feel of their tongues licking his hands. Occasionally he pets them, but in gingerly fashion. And he always washes his hands afterwards.

My father feels differently toward cats.

"A cat," he told me once when I was a child, "is proud and independent. You don't find that in a dog. If a cat is hungry it'll drink the milk you give it. But it won't for a minute think it owes you anything in return. It never sells its liberty. And just look at its grace and beauty!"

As Dad grew eloquent on the merits of a cat he jumped to his feet and started being a cat on the prowl for me. His hands became paws. He put each one before the other with a liquid grace. Now and then he flicked one hand behind him and twitched it, and it became a tail. He craned his head forward, peering through slit eyes, a sly inward smile on his face. He was exactly like a cat. He was a cat.

United Press International photo.

Charlie Chaplin, Charles, Jr., and Lita Grey Chaplin. "Though my father didn't know quite what to do with me, still, he was proud that he had a son . . ."

Above: Charles, Jr., and Sydney (1933). "Boarding school was our father's idea. He felt we were surrounded by too many women. Mother and Nana decided on Black-Foxe Military Institute."

Below: Lita Grey (1946). " 'I always thought your mother was the most beautiful girl I've ever known,' Dad said."

Left: Charles, Jr., aged six, and Sydney, aged five (1931). "There must have been about twenty photographers with shutters clicking and flash bulbs popping, recording the momentous fact that the Chaplin boys were going to Europe."

"I seem to hear my father saying, 'I love this house. I'd never live anywhere else but right here. What more do you want?' . . . It was the first real home he had ever known. It seemed impregnable, solid as the old hill itself, looking down on the small town of Beverly Hills that lay scattered out below it."

Opposite: "As Hollywood personalities go, Dad didn't have a lavish wardrobe . . . the riding clothes must have come from that period of Dad's life when Doug Fairbanks talked him into joining a riding set."

United Press International ph

Charles, Jr., Paulette Goddard, Charlie Chaplin (about 1940). "Syd and I lost our hearts to Paulette at once, never to regain them through all the golden years of our childhood."

Above: Alf Reeves, Randolph Churchill, Captain John Churchill, Captain Churchill's son, Charlie Chaplin, American Ambassador Alexander Moore and Winston Churchill at the Chaplin Studios (about 1930). "My father was a celebrated person upon whom great men, many of them geniuses in their own right, came to call."

Below: Frank, the Chaplin household's "butler, valet, housekeeper and all-around Man Friday," with Paulette and Charlie.

United Press International photo.

Above: During the second trial of Joan Barry's paternity suit against Charlie Chaplin (1945), Miss Barry holds up her daughter so the jury can note any facial resemblance. "I think the saddest victim of all was the little plaintiff of the case, eighteen-month-old Carol Ann, who was brought needlessly into the courtroom every day, exposed to the stares of the curious and made an object of notoriety."

Opposite: Above: Jack Oakie with Chaplin on the set of *The Great Dictator.* "One of the pleasantest things about the new film was the affable relationship between Dad and Jack Oakie . . . Dad has always had a great admiration for Jack." *Below:* Oakie and Chaplin in a scene from the film.

Martha Raye and Chaplin in *Monsieur Verdoux*. " 'I was honored,' she told me seriously. 'I would have done it for nothing—just to have the opportunity of working with him . . . I tell everyone that I look on it as the greatest experience in my life, next to having my daughter.' "

Above: Both Charles, Jr., and Sydney appeared in *Limelight*. Sydney, seated, is shown with his father. "Toward Syd and me he was, I believe, even more exacting than toward the others . . . He was especially tough on Syd as the young romantic lead . . ."

Below: Jackie Coogan with Charles, Jr. "I asked Jackie what it was like working under my father's direction. 'Whenever he wanted me to cry for the camera,' Jackie said, 'he would tell me sad stories until the tears started rolling down my cheeks . . . Your mother and I used to play together on the set. She was always so gay.'"

Charlie Chaplin, Oona O'Neill Chaplin and Tim Durant. "From the first, Oona had some magical touch about her where my father was concerned . . . 'If only I had known Oona or a girl like her long ago,' he said, and there was a tinge of wistfulness in his voice . . . 'All my life I have been waiting for her without even realizing it until I met her.' "

Puddles, a little black cocker spaniel, was a puppy when Paulette first brought her to our home, and as her name implies, she wasn't yet housebroken. But Paulette persisted in keeping the little dog with her in the living room during the evening, and sooner or later Puddles would live up to her name. At those moments Dad didn't see any humor in the dog's doing what he had got his biggest laugh for imitating as a child on a London stage.

"Look what that goddam bitch did," he would shout aghast. "Get her out of here!"

Paulette would meekly comply, but the next night it would be the same thing all over again.

Dad was discovering that things weren't nearly so easy to handle as they had been in his bachelor days, when his every word had been law. The servants were beginning to notice the difference too. George was no longer left alone to turn out his delicious but unvaried English meals. Now Paulette would give orders for delicacies that would send Frank flying to the store on short notice, and George would apply his masterly touch to exotic new dishes for the table. Every day it would be something different and exciting to spice up the meal.

To spice up life in general—that was Paulette. The house began to blossom out of its former quiet into a gayer social life, though even then it was more staid than most homes of its kind in Hollywood. Paulette loved to entertain. Dad, who hadn't entertained much before because he couldn't be bothered with domestic details, now discovered he could leave all these tiresome arrangements to Paulette. And he entered wholeheartedly into the spirit of the thing.

Everyone in Hollywood considered him a marvelous host. Playing host, I believe, was a kind of drama with him. His manners were those of English royalty, the upper class, formal and yet gracious. He went out of his way to make his guests feel at home, young and old alike. But Dad wasn't just an ordinary gracious host, never would be, because first and foremost he's an entertainer. He could seldom pass up an opportunity to play a prank, either in his own home or in those of his friends.

When he and Paulette first came back from China, they were given a welcome party by Doug Fairbanks and his new bride, Lady Sylvia Ashley. Upon Dad's arrival he was let in by Doug Fairbanks' Chinese houseboy.

"I'm going to talk Chinese to you," Dad whispered to the boy. "Even if you don't understand what I'm saying answer me."

The boy caught on. All that evening he answered my father's gibberish with straight Chinese, and everything sounded so genuine that the guests went around whispering in awed tones that Dad must be a true genius, because though he had been in China just two or three weeks he could speak the language like a native.

At his own parties my father was even more daring. One night at a very stiff affair he found himself seated next to a wealthy English lady who kept droning on and on in a high intellectual vein. Monotony is the torture my father can least endure.

"Excuse me a minute, please," he said politely when the waiter came by with the salad bowl. He gravely dipped his hand into the bowl, lifted out a fistful of salad and put it on his plate. He wiped his hands meticulously on his napkin.

"Now, what were you saying, Mrs. . . . ." he asked conversationally.

But she wasn't saying anything. She was laughing hysterically. It was the end of formality at that party.

In many ways Dad's and Paulette's personalities complemented each other. Dad liked a quiet life; he enjoyed spending his evenings reading or writing. Paulette was fond of reading, too, and she liked to spend some evenings working on petit point. But she couldn't take night after night of quiet, and when she'd had enough of it she would talk Dad into taking her out for some fun.

Paulette seemed possessed of a steadfast gaiety that was seldom fazed by Dad's sudden spells of taciturn moodiness. Until he was ready to come out of his shell and join her again, Paulette would cheerfully occupy herself with her dancing and music lessons and with Syd and me.

Even in dress there was a great disparity between the two. Dad was very conservative; Paulette was flashy and extravagant. She loved expensive jewelry. Necklaces, bracelets, rings set with precious stones were all for Paulette. Dad couldn't bear to be weighted down by anything. He never carried much money on him—usually not more than twenty-five dollars. He signed tabs for everything. For as long as I've known him he never wore a ring or a wrist watch. He always told me it bothered him to have something on his hands. He carried his watch in his vest pocket as long as vests were fashionable.

Paulette's closets were a swirl of color. Her evening gowns were modish and expensive. Dad had, as I recall, three dinner jackets—one double-breasted and the other two shawl-collared—and he had had them for a long while. He also kept two old-fashioned tails which I never saw him wear, and a riding habit and pair of brown leather boots. The riding clothes must have come from that period of his life when Doug Fairbanks talked him into joining a riding set, though Dad never cared for horses and always maintained they had a tendency to run away with him. As Hollywood personalities go, Dad didn't have a lavish wardrobe. His suits were conservative in style and color, grays and browns and blue serges. He would keep them for three or four years, then give them away and have some more made—why I don't know, since the new ones always looked exactly like the old.

Though Dad was conservative in dress, he did follow the fashions except for one detail, the high, button-top shoes he used to wear on special occasions, either afternoon or evening. The shoes had patent-leather bottoms and gray suede tops, so that it looked as if he were wearing spats.

My father's addiction to those shoes was a sentimental one. "When I was just a boy doing bit parts in the music halls I would see all the great actors and the important managers, men like Sir Henry Irving, going around in shoes like this," he told me once. "All through my boyhood I dreamed of wearing them myself after I'd made it."

Unfortunately, by the time Dad felt he had "made it"— around the period of the First World War—button tops were well on their way out. That didn't make any difference to him. He began to wear the shoes he had dreamed about. He wore them for years, even into the Second World War, and to the amazement of a whole generation who had never even heard of the fashion. He always kept three pairs of them at a time, for he had to have them specially made for him in England. Whenever a pair began to show wear, he would have Frank ship leather back to England and order another pair, so that he would never be without them. The shoes were very expensive, of course, but though Dad is economical in many ways, it never once occurred to him to eliminate this extravagance.

I always thought Dad looked interesting, even distinctive, with his graying hair, his conservative blue serge suit and those button-top shoes. But Paulette couldn't bear the sight of them. To her they represented something completely archaic, and she made up her mind they had to go. First she threw out hints about their being so old-fashioned. But Dad ignored this. Then she began to be more open about it.

"Honey bun," she would beg, "please, just for me, wear your other shoes tonight."

Paulette had a way about her. She could wheedle a lot of things out of Dad. But she wasn't successful with the shoes. So one day she took a more daring action. She hid them—all three pairs. That night Dad went to put on his shoes and they were gone. We heard him in his room muttering to himself and moving things around. Then he rang his bell and Frank came flying up. Dad confronted him in the hallway.

"Where are my shoes, Frank?" he demanded in shocked disbelief.

"Aren't they there, Mr. Chaplin?" Frank asked, surprised, and he went in to see for himself. Dad followed him and came right out again. He had a dazed look on his face, and when he saw Syd and me standing there he appealed to us.

"Charles! Sydney!" he said pleadingly. "Have you seen my shoes? . . . Oh, of course not," he added with complete impatience, not waiting for our answer. "Damn it, where are they?"

He called to Paulette; but Paulette, busy with her own preparations, gave him a vague answer.

"Damn it, they must be somewhere!" Dad said, and dashed for the stairway. Syd and I tagged along after him, as perplexed as he, and Frank came striding out of the room and joined us, shaking his head.

Followed by all three of us, Dad went like a cyclone through the lower part of the house, looking for those shoes. He turned everything topsy-turvy, scouring cupboards, closets and cabinets. He moved furniture and looked behind the piano and the organ. As he became progressively more desperate, every unlikely as well as likely place was investigated.

"Damn it! Goddam it!" Dad kept muttering. "Where could they have gone?" He spoke as though the shoes had a mind of their own and had made off by themselves. "Where are they, Frank?"

If Frank had any idea he didn't voice it. With true Oriental imperturbability he just went on helping Dad look.

Paulette was dressed by this time. Looking as composed as a Reynolds portrait, she came breezing out of her room.

"Come on, Charlie," she said. "Aren't you ready yet? We're going to be late."

"My shoes!" Dad shouted, reaching the boiling point at last. "Some goddam bloody bastard has stolen my shoes. I can't go without my shoes."

"They'll turn up tomorrow somewhere," Paulette said placatingly. "Put your others on now, Charlie, and let's go. Come on! It's getting late."

Paulette could never bear to be late to parties, but her pleading didn't do any good.

"I can't go without my shoes," Dad reiterated, and he went on turning everything upside down in his desperate search. At last Paulette realized she wasn't getting anywhere with her plot, and conveniently located the shoes—all three pairs of them. Dad put on a pair without a word and he and Paulette left.

Dad had won that little fray, but there was a glint in Paulette's eyes that said she hadn't given up—not on the shoes, not on anything. She would continue pressuring Dad out of the quiet groove of his ultraconservatism, of which those shoes were a fitting symbol.

She had that same gleam in her eyes whenever she surveyed the living room. "Oh, Charlie," she said one day, "you know we ought to get rid of a lot of the stuff in here. It's too cluttered."

Dad was reading at the time, but his head came up fast. "Why, what's wrong with it?" he said. "I don't see a thing wrong." And he cast a loving look around at his mementos, his photographs and whatnots that had been there so long they had almost taken root.

"Oh, but, Charlie," Paulette went on wheedling, "it's such a beautiful room—with the proper drapes and a new carpet and up-to-date furniture. I can just picture it!"

"Damn it, Paulette!" Dad snapped. "The room is perfectly all right."

Paulette appeared not to have heard Dad's last remark. "Yes, Charlie, we should really redo the whole house," she expanded ambitiously. "It needs repapering, repainting, recarpeting. We could make a show place out of it."

"Show place!" Dad suddenly stormed, completely stirred

156

up now. "Goddam it, Paulette, are you trying to break me with your extravagance?"

But it really wasn't so much the idea of spending money that was painful to Dad. He had built the house, but the interior had grown up around him and was part of him. He felt uneasy at having a single thing shifted from its rightful place, let alone completely removed. He could never bear drastic changes in his personal habitat.

Paulette didn't pursue the subject further that day, but you could see she hadn't given up. She kept looking around the living room as though she were thinking things over to herself. Dad, preparing to immerse himself once more in his book, saw the expression in her eyes. He had won the victory, he had put Paulette in her place. He had banished once and for all the threatening ogre of change. Still, he stirred uneasily in his chair.

21

Paulette didn't get very far with her renovation of the house that fall, except for the removal of some of the more prosaic bric-a-brac in the front room. Dad continued stubbornly to reject all ideas of change. And Paulette herself was not just a typical housewife with a new husband to domesticate. She was also an actress with a career to further, and this was foremost in her mind all through that fall of '36.

Her success in *Modern Times* had been instantaneous, and she knew as well as anyone that she ought to follow it up at once with another picture. Dad himself could see the logic in her reasoning. During their trip abroad he had spent most of his time aboard ship in his cabin working on something in which to star her—a talkie he planned to produce but not appear in. But though he expected to return with a finished script, nothing had come of it.

All through the summer and fall he continued his search, making start after false start on ideas which looked promising to begin with but which he discarded almost immediately, like a miner whose promising lode peters out on him. Despite Paulette's pleas to get her before the public again while she was still remembered, it was to be almost three years before he was ready to shoot a picture, a picture that was to shock and stir audiences around the world both then and after the Second World War under the title of *The Great Dictator*. It has always been the irony of my father's genius that, whatever his good intentions, it could never be rushed but visited him with a creative idea only in its own good time.

Dad was still hunting for that story for Paulette when Christmas came that year. Christmases at my father's home form a composite picture in my mind, for every one of them was almost identical in style and texture. Even the weather was the same. As far back as I can remember, the Christmas days of my boyhood were sunshiny and mild.

Accompanied by Nana, Syd and I arrived at Dad's house around eleven—brunch was always at twelve. To walk into his home on that day was like going between the leaves of a Dickens novel, because Christmas for Dad was a typically British institution. As we came in the front door we could see the Christmas tree standing at the far end of the hall. It was always a stately white tree, tall enough just to miss the ceiling. It had been decorated the week before by the Japanese servants under the supervision of Frank. Christmas was just as much a day of celebration to them as to us, for Dad never omitted a generous bonus to each.

Though the tree was beautiful, Syd and I seldom gave it more than a quick appraisal. We were far more interested in the stacks of presents underneath it. As we walked down the hall, Dad came forward to greet us, a jovial father, all vexations completely erased from his mind. Christmas represented drama to him, and every year of our boyhood he played that drama with little variation.

"Well, boys," he would say, seeing our eyes on the packages, "I'm sorry but you don't have so much this Christmas. Just a few little things. It's been an expensive year."

Syd and I would recognize our cue. "That's all right, Dad," we would answer, getting just the right tone of disappointment in our voices.

"Well," Dad would reply philosophically, rubbing his hands together with delight over his unfolding drama but carefully keeping the pleasure out of his voice, "we can't have a big Christmas every year, can we, boys?"

"Don't worry about it, Dad," Syd and I would answer, and as we grew more proficient at playing the game we learned to release an involuntary sigh.

All morning friends and relatives had been gathering for brunch. There was our actor half-uncle, Wheeler Dryden, who had by this time followed Dad to California. His son, Spencer, was younger than we and yet he could recite pages of Shakespeare, because his father had pounded it into him. He pounded so hard that when Spencer grew up he chucked the whole thing; the culture went down the drain fast, and Spencer became a jazz musician instead. Today he plays the drums most efficiently.

Our father was always amused by Spencer's knowledge of Shakespeare and sometimes he would brag about his accomplishments. Perhaps he had the hope of inciting us to do on our own what Spencer's father had forced upon him, but if so he wasn't successful. Syd and I couldn't be jealous of Spencer, who was such a nice, mannerly little boy. And besides, we knew we had the better deal, a father who never made us learn a single line of anything.

Uncle Sydney Chaplin was there, too, as was our macabre dinner guest, Dr. Reynolds, and Dad's oldest friends, Amy and Alf Reeves. Tim Durant, whom Dad had just met that year through Director King Vidor, came with his daughter, Marjorie. Constance Collier, Anita Loos, King Vidor and, until his death in 1939, Doug Fairbanks and his wife, Lady Sylvia Ashley, were all Christmas Day visitors. Each of the guests brought Syd and me a gift—a sweater, a billfold, a book—depositing it under the tree with the other packages.

At twelve we sat down at the big table in the dining room. Christmas brunch was a carefree occasion. Gone was Dad's strict insistence on manners that day. Syd and I might talk as we pleased, interrupt as we chose, laugh as much as we liked. Every year the menu was the same. It started with roast beef and ended with Yorkshire pudding—a plum pudding with rum on it which was set alight when it was time for dessert—and champagne for everyone. After brunch Dad always gave Syd and me a taste of the holiday champagne.

Then we gathered around the tree to open our presents, and once again Syd and I found ourselves in the very center of the drama. Assuming resigned expressions, we began looking in the pile for the presents marked for us. One by one we sorted them out and opened them. As our piles grew we allowed our faces to put on more and more astonishment.

"All these for us, Father?" we gasped.

Dad chuckled at our perplexed delight.

"Yes, they're yours, boys."

"But you said . . ." we let our words trail off in a bewildered way. We were truly happy about the presents, which were always lavish. But we were almost as happy playing the little drama with Dad.

Two gifts stand out in my mind from that Christmas of '36. One was an album of Tschaikovsky's Concerto No. 1 in B-Flat Minor for piano and orchestra. One night at Dad's house I had tuned the radio in on that concerto and, unable to tear myself away, had fallen asleep listening to it. Dad and Paulette had remembered and bought me the album. The other gift, as might have been expected, was from Paulette, and Syd and I didn't find it under the Christmas tree. She slipped out of the room and came back with a puppy under each arm—Bedlington terriers, one for each of us. And now Dad found himself once more confronted with the problem of dogs, three instead of one, for Puddles, house-trained at last but with a very definite mind of her own, was still around.

Dad thought the Bedlington terriers were cute, with their long ears and their pert sheep faces; however, he didn't want them in the house either. But with surreptitious aid from Syd and me they learned how to slip in, and we would all romp through the rooms together until Dad would become aware of what was going on.

"Get those filthy things out of here," he would order sternly, and Syd and I and the Bedlington terriers, whom we had dubbed Punch and Judy, would fly for the outside door in a flurry of fur and heels.

Once Christmas was over Dad went immediately back to the grind. He didn't even take time out to accompany Paulette on a gay holiday house party given by King Vidor at his lodge in the San Bernardino mountains. When Paulette returned after six days she found Dad working away at white heat on his latest story. In the past year he had already run through one with an Oriental background and another one to be laid in the South Sea Islands, and toyed with heaven knows how many others. But he was convinced that this one, which was based on *Regency*, a novel by D. L. Murray, was the real thing. Dad's enthusiasm, as always, was so whole-hearted that, listening to him talk, Paulette was sure she was on her way at last.

Then that spring something else came up which really set her head spinning. David O. Selznick was searching for someone to play Scarlett O'Hara in his multimillion-dollar production, *Gone with the Wind*, and he approached Paulette to make a test for him. It was small wonder Paulette was excited. She had come to Hollywood an obscure little chorus girl, and the only role she had had since was the one of the gamin in *Modern Times*, a silent picture. And now Mr. Selznick was interested in her for one of the biggest starring parts in the history of the movies.

But Dad didn't share Paulette's excitement. She was his wife and she was also under contract to him. He didn't want her to be working for someone else. He kept doggedly on with his script.

That was how Easter came to the Chaplins, and once more Dad put everything aside to celebrate a holiday. Up until this year Syd and I had not participated in the coloring of the eggs. But that Easter Eve we were allowed to help Paulette, all three of us working away in the living room. Dad reserved for himself the hiding of the eggs, a chore he loved because of its conspiratorial nature. I have never ceased to be amazed at the simplicity of the things in which my father found so much pleasure. I can remember him with that sly expression on his face, packing us off to bed early so he would have freedom to work. He hid the eggs in the chairs and the sofa of the living room, in the dining room, out on the lawn.

Easter morning we had a late breakfast together on the porch, and the relaxed atmosphere was like a burst of sunshine after Dad's tension of the past months. A little later Syd's and my friends gathered for the hunt. Soon there were children all over the place, squealing and yelling and tearing everything apart in their exuberant search. And there was Dad following right behind us with his hands clasped behind his back, as though to keep from rooting out the eggs himself. "Now you're hot! Now you're cold! Lukewarm now!" his steady monologue guided us like manikins on a string until we had found them all.

After Easter Dad went back to his *Regency* script, Paulette to waiting. But with a sinking heart she began to realize it was to be the same thing all over again. Dad was showing less and less enthusiasm for his story. It was petering out like the others.

A feeling of desperation took hold of Paulette. It was now

well over a year since the première of *Modern Times*, which had introduced her to the public. She was afraid that if she waited much longer she would be forgotten. And she began to turn an even more eager eye to the role of Scarlett O'Hara which Mr. Selznick was still dangling before her. Dad, however, was as adamant as ever against her testing for the part.

All this didn't make for harmony in the Chaplin home, and the papers began to gossip about trouble between my father and Paulette. But we boys never were aware of any real friction between them. They were always careful to keep their dissensions from us.

22

Syd and I were too entranced by the shifting vagaries of childhood at this juncture to be troubled about anything in the adult world. We were at an age to enter wholeheartedly into the macabre world introduced to us through our father's ghost stories, and we couldn't get enough of blood and violence and ghoulish horrors of all descriptions.

The Japanese servants soon realized it would take more than their jokes and mild folk tales to keep us amused now, and when we took our meals with them they began to describe for us the life of the knights of Japan. They vied with each other in bloodthirsty descriptions of executions in which the samurai sword played a principal role.

"Take that biggest sword," Frank would say. "One swipe

like this and the head is chopped off. Out in the streets, head after head. Blood everywhere. It's a public execution in Japan. That's how they used to do it."

"Yes, yes," George would agree, making a chopping motion and then flinging both hands into the air as usual. "Off with head! Like that!"

Then Frank would launch into further details of the gory scene, with Kay and George and whatever relatives might be present putting in their excited interpolations. From descriptions of the executions they went on to tell us other bloodcurdling tales. Syd and I pumped them mercilessly, and greedily sopped up everything from ghosts to the agile sport of Sumo wrestling.

Later we would tell these stories to Dad. We could always count on his being a fascinated listener, and he showed great pleasure in what he chose to regard as our interest in the customs and tales of another race. But when we came to the stories of the Sumo wrestlers he couldn't keep still.

"Yes, I've seen them," he would say. "They're big, six feet tall, with huge bellies—powerful men."

Then Dad, who is only five feet, six and a half inches tall and slight of build, would suddenly become a Sumo wrestler. He would go through the motions of rubbing his hands in salt. He would crouch and try to lift himself by the belt. He would go around in a circle, stalking in the ceremonial way that Sumo wrestling begins. Then he would suddenly make a feint at an imaginary enemy, his eyes glittering with such a deadly expression that a chill would run through us. Dad is a small man, but when he was a Sumo wrestler he became frighteningly big. He seemed to fill the whole room.

After Dad had depicted Sumo wrestling for us he would go on to describe the wrestling he had seen in Siam.

"They box with their feet, too," he said.

All at once he became a boxer from Siam, only he was burlesquing it so that it was a kind of dance, with Dad jumping into the air and thrusting out his feet with an *oomph* every so often. Each movement seemed so incredibly simple when Dad made it that we had to experiment for ourselves to realize how difficult, almost impossible, it really was.

We never could top Dad. Whatever stories we told him he always managed to have one a little bit better than ours. Not that we didn't try. We began to buy horror magazines by the stack from the drug store across the street from our school. We read every science-fiction and weird tale we could lay our hands on in search of a gem that would best him.

At last one week end we thought we had one. It sent real shivers down our backs and we were sure it would do the same to Dad. We could hardly wait to tell it to him. You could always count on his attention when you had something macabre to offer.

"Oh, it's very good," Dad said when we had finished, and he seemed impressed with it, though, strangely enough, I can't remember a single bit of the involved plot today. "Now," he continued, rubbing his hands together in anticipation, "let me tell you about something Dr. Reynolds and I did once."

Dad had only to name the doctor to send an anticipatory shiver down our spines.

"One evening while you boys were at school, the doctor gave a very interesting anatomy lesson to some guests of mine," Dad began.

All at once, through the magic of his description, Syd and I were plunged into the event. In our imaginations we suddenly find ourselves in the dining room, which is dimly lighted with a couple of candles. Around the table sit a group of queasy guests. The doctor and my father are at the head of the table. Beside the doctor Something is lying on a great board supported by sawhorses. The Something is, of course, a human cadaver.

From this point on Dad acts the entire story out for us, changing from part to part in a second. Now he is the doctor, solemn, efficient, dipping his fingers into an imaginary finger bowl. He flicks them in the air and wipes them fastidiously on a napkin, equally imaginary. He picks up an imaginary scalpel and cuts into the invisible cadaver beside him, making careful incisions. One by one he brings out the heart, brain, kidneys, lungs, liver, stomach and tongue. Holding each carefully, as though under the candlelight, he gives a brief matter-of-fact discourse about its functions. (Dad had picked up as much medical lore from Dr. Reynolds as the doctor had pried loose the secrets of acting from him.)

After the brief lecture, Dad, as Dr. Reynolds, passes each imaginary organ on. Then suddenly becoming himself he accepts it, examines it with that familiar tender expression on his face, and hands it to the next person. As it runs the length of the table Dad becomes every guest in turn. He is curious. He displays bravado. He becomes a fainthearted woman. At last the imaginary object returns to Dr. Reynolds, who lays it carefully aside, building up an invisible heap of discarded organs before our eyes.

By the time Dad came to the end of his little tableau, Syd and I were popeyed.

"Now," Dad concluded, pretending to rinse his fingers for the last time, "Charles, you and Sydney and the doctor and I are all going to have a dinner just like that one night. Would you like it?"

Syd and I only stared at him tongue-tied. Seeing our dubious expressions, Dad laughed aloud.

"It's only make-believe," he said. "Just a horror story to match yours."

Despite Dad's admission that everything he had told was fantasy, that macabre dinner scene continued to live in my imagination. For a long while I couldn't even pass through the dining room without a shiver when I came to the spot where he had placed his imaginary corpse.

Everything was so wonderfully fascinating at the house on the hill that Syd and I hated to be sent packing back to prosaic Black-Foxe on Sunday evenings. As the hour approached for our return, we would become gloomier and gloomier. Then Dad would give us a pep talk to put us in the right mood.

"Oh, you boys are fortunate," he would say. "Look at me. When I was your age I was out in the streets, hungry, cold. You don't have to worry about any of those things. You have a steady income, a home, three meals a day. Schooling! I never had a chance to go beyond the fourth grade. Consider yourselves lucky."

When Dad talked about his childhood like that I would go back to school with my mind made up to appreciate my life, to study hard, and to take advantage of all the wonderful opportunities I had that my father had missed. I would fall asleep pitying the boy my father had been. And the next day, with all my firm resolutions floating around in my head, I would find myself bounced back almost immediately into the hard reality of military life. The pathetic image of the little boy in Kennington would fade from my mind. I would, ironically, discover myself envying instead the freedom he had known, finding his own food, later making his own way in the music halls, his own master, with no one to tell him what to do.

Blue Monday! That was what all the boys called it at school, because it was so difficult to endure after the freedom of the week end. You couldn't feel grateful for anything on Blue Monday, and I don't know whether Syd even tried. We were still as different in personality as we could be and still as close to each other as any brothers have ever been.

We had chosen different modes of behavior at school. I governed my deportment primarily to keep from spending my week ends there and in doing so earned the reputation for being a model pupil. But I had to pay a heavy price for my exemplary behavior. I was tense and nervous throughout my whole stay at Black-Foxe.

Syd never bothered about being exemplary. He was just

happy-go-lucky Syd who still continued to challenge the grownups. I don't think Syd could help himself. He automatically rebelled, turning everything into a big joke at the same time. When a teacher went to ferule his hand, instead of holding it quietly out, taking his medicine and forgetting about it, Syd would shamelessly fling himself on the floor, groaning and writhing.

"Don't hit me! I'll confess. I'll confess," he'd moan.

The instructor couldn't help laughing, but Syd got the feruling, and demerits besides. He'd start with a clear slate on Monday and by Friday he'd have enough demerits to hold him at school for the week end. Sometimes it seemed to me Syd spent more week ends at school than he did at home. Though Dad never discussed his feelings with us openly for fear of undermining authority, you could see he was put out about Syd's detention, for he liked to have us visit him together.

I missed Syd most at bedtime, alone in my bedroom with only my vivid imagination to keep me company.

I remember the first night the idea came to me. It was an especially lonely night, with a gusty California wind blowing outside. You could hear the intermittent scraping of the tree branches against the windows. I thought of Syd there in his bed at Black-Foxe. I thought of Paulette and Dad behind their locked doors, and the servants in their quarters in the basement. I felt completely shut off from everyone.

Then I remembered Dad's pistol in the night stand by his bed, and the wonderful samurai swords in the cabinet in the living room. I thought of them lying there side by side, curved and sharp in their lacquered sheaths.

"Don't touch them, don't ever play with them," Dad had told us so often. "Why, you might cut off your hand."

I thought of his order and how he disliked disobedience; I thought again of the samurai swords. Cautiously I went to my door and opened it and looked down the hall. Everything was quiet. I hurried down the hall and the stairs. I was alone on the ground floor of the dark, mysterious house. I found the light switch and turned it on. There was light now in the lower hall. I flew down it barefoot to the living room, past the gaping mouth of the dining-room door—the dark room where Dr. Reynolds' fanciful cadaver had lain, perhaps was lying still, a ghost to rise up and stop me.

I reached the living room, turned on a light and ran to the cabinet. I was terrified. My breath was coming in gasps. I flung open the cabinet door. In the hands of a giant samurai the big sword might prove very serviceable for executions, but it was too unwieldy for me. My fingers closed on the handle of the smaller one. I took it out of its sheath and left that in its customary place on the cabinet shelf, so no one would notice the sword was gone.

I shut the cabinet door and gingerly tested the razor-sharp edge with my finger. Then I flashed the sword over my head several times. Suddenly I felt safe. Who could overpower me with a weapon like this? I turned off the living-room light, and my heart sank a little with the sudden darkness. I waved my sword in the direction of the dining room, at the ghost of the cadaver lurking there, and then sped down the hall for the stairway. How shocked Dad would have been to see me flying along with that naked sword in my hand!

I turned off the lower-hall light and crept upstairs and down the upper hall to my own room. I shut my door and locked it. I climbed into my bed, laying the sword on the night table beside me, and almost at once I fell into a deep, dreamless sleep.

I woke with the dawn and got the sword back in its cabinet before anyone discovered it was gone. No one ever found out about it, though it wasn't the last night by far that it kept me company.

23

Though our father didn't guess it at the time, he was to be harassed that summer and fall of 1937 by more than the difficulty of finding a suitable script for Paulette. Without Dad's noticing it, Syd and I had reached "that age," as it is despairingly called by parents. That is, we were eleven and twelve years old and so full of bravado we were ready to attempt anything and everything despite our father's cautious counsel. That Fourth of July we even dared flout his ban against firecrackers.

Dad never celebrated the Fourth of July himself, any more than he did Guy Fawkes Day, the traditional patriotic English holiday. He was never a flag waver for any country, and his complete lack of concern about an individual's politics was to prove a major cause of trouble to him after the Second World War. But he loved to watch fireworks, and one year he even endured the press of crowds to take us to the Los Angeles Coliseum to see the display. Firecrackers were a different matter, though. He hated them because their sharp explosions shattered his nerves, but he translated his apprehension in terms of danger to us.

"Don't shoot firecrackers," he warned us sternly. "Why you can get your hand blown off. You might be blinded for life." Always the Chaplinesque hyperbole! But Syd and I were no longer impressed. We just took care he was not around to hear us when we fired them.

We were no longer affected by his disapproval of violence in general, either. We came home bragging about the fights we'd won. I remember one week end telling him of a set-to I'd had with Bobby Keaton, Buster Keaton's son.

"You should never fight," Dad told me reprovingly.

But when I started to describe my fight, Dad became so interested he seemed to forget everything he'd said about violence, and when I finished my story he nodded and said, "That's in the old Chaplin tradition. You know your father was in a fight once, too." And he launched into a graphic description.

He was, he said, in a restaurant in New York City with several friends when he was spotted by a big man across the room. The man, according to Dad, was at least six feet tall and built to match. He'd been drinking. He came over to Dad with a martini in his hand.

"Are you Charlie Chaplin?" he asked, and as Dad told it he became the man.

"Yes," Dad answered politely, becoming Dad again.

"Well, I don't like your face," the man said belligerently.

"Then why don't you just go back to your table?" Dad suggested.

"I ought to hit you in the teeth," the man growled, and with that splashed his martini in Dad's face.

Dad was furious. Without thinking he jumped to his feet; his head came below the other man's chin.

"That wasn't very nice," Dad said, and he grabbed the fellow by the necktie and in a flash jumped up and hit him right in the face with his big head. As Dad told me the story he jumped to his feet and showed me how it had been done. Dad can move like lightning and he has a lot of power in his movement, too. He broke the man's nose, knocked out two of his front teeth and floored him. Then Dad saw the man's friends, all big men, too, moving ominously toward him. Fortunately the police intervened before Dad had to use his head for a battering ram again. He dusted off his hands, which hadn't even been involved, and returned to his dinner.

Dad was carried away while he was telling the story, but afterwards he recollected himself.

"You see," he concluded, "your father knows how these things are. And it's a good thing you won. But remember, no more fighting. Fighting is silly. Why take the chance of marring your features?"

But it wasn't only daredeviltry or pugnaciousness with Syd and me. Surprising, even outlandish things just began to happen to us—especially to Syd. There was the time he actually managed to get lost on the yacht while it was in the middle of the Catalina Channel one boisterous day. He was tucked away comfortably between two life boats while everyone, frantic for fear he'd gone overboard, was running all over the ship searching for him. Dad lost his head completely and even began pulling open drawers to see if he was inside.

But it must not be supposed that Syd was always just a victim of circumstance. He was a boy with ideas, too. Most of those ideas centered on ways to augment our weekly allowance of fifty cents which Mother or Nana gave us. Sometimes Dad came to our rescue. On birthdays he could always be counted on for a monetary gift that ranged anywhere from fifty to five hundred dollars. And every now and then, out of the blue, he would reach for his wallet and hand us a five- or ten-dollar bill, cautioning us to spend it wisely. But we couldn't depend on these unpredictable spurts of generosity. Sometimes to replenish our supply we tried to conduct tourist tours through our grounds at twenty-five cents a head. But tourists on Summit Drive were few and far between. Then one day Syd got an even better idea.

"Let's set up a stand like kids do with lemonade," he said when we arrived that Friday.

"Who'll buy lemonade from us up here, Syd?" I asked.

"Not lemonade," Syd said. "Liquor, Chuck. Come on, I'll show you," and he led the way to the kitchen.

It must have been the servants' day off, because no one was around. Syd found the key to Dad's liquor closet and opened it. There stood the rows of bottles Dad had been collecting for years.

"All the adults drink this stuff," Syd said. "We can set up a stand right down at the end of the driveway. We'll sell it to them as they come by. Fifty cents a bottle. We'll be rich, Chuck."

The idea of the money sounded good to me.

"But, Syd," I said, ". . . Dad . . ."

Syd waved his hand.

"He's got so much he probably won't even notice. He's rich, Chuck. Come on."

Swept away by Syd's argument, I helped him with the bottles. We took out about forty of them and carried them down to a little stand we set up at the end of our driveway. There we waited for our first customer. He wasn't long in coming. Fittingly enough, who should it be but David O. Selznick, whose sleep we had so often interrupted with our motor glide. He backed out of his driveway across the street and saw our stand with the bottles on it and us waiting. He brought the car to our side of the street and parked and got out and examined the bottles. His eyes shone.

"How much you boys selling these for?" he asked.

"Fifty cents a bottle," Syd and I piped up.

"I'll buy the lot," Mr. Selznick said. And he did. We got about twenty dollars out of the deal. We helped Mr. Selznick load his purchase into his car—well over two hundred dollars' worth of expensive Scotch and bourbon and fancy liqueurs. He seemed in a great hurry about it. He drove back across the street and into his driveway and got all the liquor into his house posthaste.

Shortly afterwards Dad came home. He wasn't around long before he called for Sydney and me. We went in and his ice-blue eyes bored into us.

"Have you boys been drinking?" he demanded. "Come over here. Let me smell your breath."

He thought a minute and decided the question was ridiculous. "Well, no, I didn't mean that," he amended quickly. "But what did you boys do with the liquor that was in the closet?"

If we had been thinking before that it wasn't so hard to pull the wool over our father's eyes, we knew better now. There wasn't much that went on around his house he didn't know about. He had discovered almost at once that the bottles were missing.

"Well," we said, stammering, "we sold it to make some money."

"What?" Dad exploded. He was furious. "Goddam it," he exclaimed, "it just isn't done—to take your own parents' things and sell them." He choked, aghast at our perfidy against a father who had always so carefully restrained himself from interfering with any of our possessions.

"Do you know what people bought them?" he said when he regained his voice.

"Oh, just one person," we told him, trembling. "Mr. Selznick across the street."

"Did he buy all of them?"

"Yes, sir, he bought all of them."

Detesting the telephone as he does, Dad nevertheless picked up the phone that day and called Mr. Selznick. He explained that we had taken the bottles without authorization.

"So will you please return them?" he asked. "They're very rare. A lot of them are imports and I had a hard time getting them."

But Mr. Selznick was enjoying the joke too much to give up the bottles so readily. I don't know how he and Dad finally settled the matter between them, or if it was ever settled, but I do know that Syd and I had now to pay the piper for our unfortunate get-rich-quick scheme. Dad turned back to us and began a lengthy discourse, much on the order of a prosecutor at court. The more he talked the smaller we shrank, and when he began listing all the fitting punishments we deserved, we truly felt like criminals.

"I could keep you in bed all week end. That's what I'll do. I'll lock you up. Yes, they lock thieves up in jail. I'll have my own jail here for you, because that was stealing, boys." He ran on and on.

He was very angry, and we were scared, of course, but it was more than that. We could feel obscurely that he was hurt, too, that we had betrayed him. That was what made the whole thing so terrible.

Finally Dad talked himself out and came down to leveling the penalty. As Syd and I were expecting by this time, it was a stiff one. Bed right now, this afternoon, and bed Saturday and Sunday at six o'clock promptly. No dinner for any of those nights, no home movies, no playing with our friends. It sounded like a very dismal week end.

Syd and I went upstairs quietly. Quietly we got into our pajamas and into bed. Perhaps we cried a little, I don't remember. We were very subdued, and it came to us lying there that our transgression had been so flagrant that not even Paulette, though she was around, had been moved to come to our defense or to say a word in our behalf. The day lengthened, finally turned into twilight. Night came and with it hunger. We were soon very hungry, and it didn't help to know that downstairs they were eating now. It was a lonely, melancholy feeling away up there in the dark.

Then suddenly the door opened. Someone felt for the light

switch and turned it on. It was Paulette. She carried a tray and on the tray were steaming dishes of George's food, filling the room with their wonderful aroma. Paulette quietly shut the door.

"Shhh," she said. "Your father doesn't know. I just felt sorry for you boys."

She brought the tray over and set it on the night stand.

"But of course," she added, "it was wrong to sell the liquor like that. Your father's very upset."

What could we say to Paulette except to let her see the gratitude in our eyes and to pitch into that dinner?

Every one of those three nights Paulette stole up with a tray of food for us. Every night she came in softly whispering, "Shhh, your father doesn't know. But I thought you boys ought to have something to eat."

Goodhearted Paulette, braving our father's wrath, faithful ally, loyal pal. It was only later, after we were much older, that we came to realize the truth. Dad, whose eagle eyes never missed much, must have known what Paulette was doing every night—mitigating a punishment he had made too harsh. He had known and hadn't stopped her.

24

I don't know how many ideas my father mulled over in his long search for a story for Paulette, but I do recall some interesting details about one of them. It came to him by way of a curious little item which someone clipped from a newspaper and mailed him. The item concerned an edict by Adolf Hitler banning Chaplin films from Germany because Dad looked so much like him.

Something clicked in my father's mind when he read it. In the Little Tramp getup, with the silly mustache, he plainly did resemble Hitler. And when he looked further he saw other points of similarity between himself and the German dictator. They had been born in the same year, in the same month, just four days apart, and both had known extreme poverty in their childhood. But their destinies were poles apart. One was to make millions weep, while the other was to set the whole world laughing. Dad could never think of Hitler without a shudder, half of horror, half of fascination.

"Just think," he would say uneasily, "he's the madman, I'm the comic. But it could have been the other way around." And he couldn't resist concluding with the quote, "There but for the grace of God go I."

The more Dad thought of the dictator's ban against his pictures and his own resemblance to Hitler, the more intrigued he became by the idea as a whole. He began casting about in his mind for a plot and incidents with which to fill it out.

About this time he met Konrad Bercovici. Bercovici's boast of having Gypsy blood was enough to recommend him to Dad, and for a while he was a constant visitor at the house. He too commented on Dad's resemblance to Hitler. One thing led to another, and before long Dad and Bercovici were tossing ideas back and forth. Dad often used his friends and acquaintances as sounding boards in this fashion.

But long before he began doing any serious work on the Hitler idea, his enthusiasm for Bercovici had died out. This has happened to a number of people. Dad has an incurable enthusiasm and expresses it so wholeheartedly that they get the impression they're indispensable to him, but for Dad it is often a temporary emotion. Once they are out of sight he forgets them completely, or else he just wearies of them and withdraws himself from their company.

So it was with Bercovici. Dad stopped seeing him altogether and at the same time he threw the idea of doing something about Hitler into the discard. Hitler, he decided, was too grim a figure to provide good material for a comedy.

The year 1938 found Dad still with no script for Paulette. To complicate matters further, Mr. Selznick continued to be very interested in having her work for him. In fact, I think it was her signing of a long-term contract with him that fore-shadowed the end of her marriage to Dad. But of course it went deeper than the Selznick episode. The root of the whole trouble was that perennial Hollywood plaint between married players: career. Dad was satisfied with things as they were, but Paulette had a need to establish herself in her own right, to prove to the world that she could be something more than just the protégée and wife of a world-renowned star.

The dissension between Dad and Paulette had become so strong by February that Dad quietly left town one week end to get a respite from it. Inviting Tim Durant to join him he went up north for a holiday at Pebble Beach. Tim, whom Dad was later to appoint his personal representative at United Artists, was his logical choice for a companion. My father admired his honesty and his staunch New England conventionality. I remember how he used to refer to him affectionately as the "irreconcilable Yankee." He liked his companionship because he was not only easy to get along with but superb at bouncing both ideas and tennis balls. It isn't surprising that in the years ahead Tim came to be regarded by Hollywood as Dad's closest and most loyal friend.

Before it was all over, Dad's week end of flight had stretched into five long months. Through Tim Durant my father rented a house overlooking the ocean from Mrs. Estelle Monteagle, a Pebble Beach socialite. He sent for George and Kay and just struck roots there, severing himself completely from Paulette, from us, from the whole world of Hollywood.

Syd and I missed him, and we missed the house on the hill with its aura of magic and excitement. But we had compensations. Paulette still came around to take us places occasionally, and our mother had become her old cheerful self, so that we had the freedom of the ranch where she lived. And we also had a father substitute—well, not exactly a substitute, for we never looked at him that way. I'm speaking of Arthur Day, the Los Angeles salesman whom our mother married the following summer. He was a friendly, cheerful man who took us to ball games and on outings. We thought of him as a pal then, and even after he had married our mother he remained in the same category. But that spring he helped fill the vacuum left by our father's departure.

And so we come to Dad's interlude at Pebble Beach, which is just outside Carmel, the famous artist colony. Pebble Beach is the Gold Coast of Northern California. Its twenty-six-mile drive is lined by the magnificent homes of San Francisco millionaires whose fortunes, the accumulation of generations, were amassed in days when taxes were low. Capitalists in every sense of the word, born and bred to their life of luxury, none of them have ever had to cope with any economic problem at the level of dire need.

Among these people Dad at first lived the life of a recluse, concentrating all his attention on the troublesome script for Paulette and refusing to see anyone. But after a couple of weeks Tim Durant ran into an old friend, the former Peggy Brokaw, a New York society girl who had married into the socially prominent Crocker family and was out west on her honeymoon. Through her, Dad gradually became acquainted with Pebble Beach society and was presently drawn into the round of entertainment that was a large part of the life thére. He became so popular with the denizens of Pebble Beach that presently no one thought of giving a party without inviting him. They even asked him up to their homes in San Francisco.

During their stay at Pebble Beach, Dad and Tim Durant repaid their social obligations by taking over the Pebble Beach Lodge and giving a mammoth dinner, with a band, a couple of imported movies and champagne in rivers. Everyone came. It was a high point of the social season. Even today, twenty years later, it is still remembered there as a memorable event.

Champagne and caviar—Dad loved it all and what it represented: luxury, leisure, the opportunity to cultivate and indulge good taste. It was a case of mutual attraction between him and the millionaires of Pebble Beach. Dad always got along well with millionaires anyway, either in California or New York. After all, he's a multimillionaire in his own right and he takes great pride in referring to himself as a capitalist. The difference between him and most of the millionaires with whom he associated was that he had intimately known the other side of the scale. He was both amazed and highly amused by the social set's conception of what constitutes poverty. One of his favorite stories highlights this view and concerns the Harrison Williams family, with whom he and Tim Durant once spent a week end on Long Island. They were discussing the stock market crash of 1929, an event which Tim, who was a member of the Stock Exchange in those days, had witnessed first hand. During the course of the conversation Mrs. Williams recalled how her husband broke the news to her. What was funny to Dad was that she told the story factually, without in the least seeing the humor in it. Her husband, she said, came home one day in a very gloomy frame of mind. "Something terrible has happened," he told his wife. "The market has collapsed. We lost thirty million dollars. We only have seventy million left."

Dad could never get over that "only."

My father had lost money in the crash himself, but he wasn't cleaned out because he had been shrewd enough to buy his stocks outright, so that he was able to hang on to them when the values went down and he still had them when they started going up again. I think he got burned once on a phony Mexican deal. After that swindle, in which he lost heavily, Dad never bought on margin again, and he always picked established stock like A.T.&T. He has a good business head for an artist.

But an artist he primarily is. His role among the society people of Pebble Beach was that of an observer, a commentator on life. He was quick to see that though his new friends had no real economic worries, they had as many emotional problems as anyone else. And this intrigued Dad, with his sense of the dramatic. He studied them all, tucked them away for future reference and, of course, pantomimed them superbly whenever the opportunity arose.

My father didn't confine himself to the social set at Pebble Beach. He was just as interested in the Bohemian colony at nearby Carmel. Here, too, he judged people by what they were. Wealth alone doesn't make a person stuffy any more than having artistic inclinations makes him interesting. Dad noted just as many stuffy people among the Bohemians at Carmel as anywhere else. He thought many of them im-mature—they did a lot of talking but not much getting down to business. Dad has never had any patience with a dilettante attitude toward creative work. He's a slave to his own muse and he expects anyone else in that field to be as sincere as he.

He found this sincerity in California's great poet, Robinson Jeffers, who lives in a big stone house on Point Sur. Dad made the acquaintance of the poet through a mutual friend who invited them both out to dinner, and he visited Jeffers several times after that. He admired the poet's maturity and honesty of purpose, but I think, all in all, Jeffers was a little too dour for Dad's fun-loving spirits.

My father also admired the very real acting talents of an unknown whom he saw perform in the theater at Carmel. She was the ill-fated Dorothy Comingore, who was to achieve movie fame in several years by playing the leading female role in Orson Welles' *Citizen Kane*. In later years Dad was to be impressed in the same way by another red-haired girl with similar latent talents and a similar unbalanced personality, Joan Barry.

A name with which Dad's was romantically linked at Pebble Beach was that of Geraldine Spreckels, the sugar heiress. Though Dad was supposed to be married to Paulette, neither he nor she had yet confirmed their status—a public confirmation was to come, ironically, just before their separa-tion—and this indefiniteness set the reporters like blood-hounds on the trail of Miss Spreckels.

"We've never exactly discussed marriage," Miss Spreckels

responded in a rather tongue-in-cheek interview. "A tea here, a luncheon there, a little time aboard a yacht or on the beach at Carmel . . . that's all I've seen of him recently . . . Yes, I like Mr. Chaplin very much. I think it would be nice for anyone to be Mrs. Chaplin."

During his stay up north, Dad didn't confine himself to Pebble Beach and its environs. He was a great admirer of another hard worker, John Steinbeck, and visited him at his home in Los Gatos. Dad was fascinated by Steinbeck's books and used to drive around the countryside where his stories were laid, trying to place the characters in the books in their proper locations.

But Dad didn't spend all his time sightseeing or visiting or being entertained. The giant part of the day went to work. He spent hours bouncing ideas back and forth with Tim, and writing. He was still angry with Paulette, so angry he wouldn't even answer the phone when she called, begging to speak to him.

"Oh, to hell with it," he would say, though he was writing the female lead for her.

It was the story of a young millionaire who takes a cruise to China and meets and falls in love with a beautiful White Russian employed in a dance hall. The picture was to be a comedy with social implications. Dad was writing it with Gary Cooper in mind for the male lead. He was a great fan of Cooper's, not because he thought him a fine actor, but because Cooper didn't even try to act. He was always himself and thus completely believable. Dad was excited about this script.

But at the same time, perversely, ideas about the discarded Hitler script kept coming into his head and clustering around the central nucleus of his resemblance to the dictator. He discussed these ideas with Tim, too, perhaps more as a form of amusement, bouncing them off him as before he'd bounced them off Bercovici. Presently, for no logical reason, he brought out of the mothballs the plot of an old story he had

had for a long while, but hadn't yet done. It was built around an impostor who took the place of Napoleon.

From as far back as I can remember, Dad had wanted to do this story of Napoleon, which would have been a biting satire on the Little Corporal. For a while he thought of playing the lead himself, and once he considered James Cagney for the role, but Cagney didn't seem interested. After *The Great Dictator* had been brought to the screen, Dad talked of doing the Napoleon story with Greta Garbo in the female lead, himself in the male lead, Jean Renoir directing and the late Dudley Nichols writing the screenplay. I can't help thinking what a picture it would have been with Garbo and my father co-starred. But though several conferences were held, nothing came of that, either. I think the reason Dad never did his Napoleon story is because he had already done it in *The Great Dictator*, with Hitler taking the place of Napoleon.

About the time my father's interest in the Hitler story was reviving, Bercovici came up with Melvyn Douglas for a week end at Pebble Beach, and he and Dad talked generally about *The Great Dictator* again. It was this exchange of ideas, both in Beverly Hills and that night in Pebble Beach, which Bercovici made the grounds for a plagiarism suit against Dad in 1947, seven years after *The Great Dictator* was released. Perhaps something more than plagiarism was involved. In his exuberance Dad may have made some vague suggestion that Bercovici do the screenplay. But suggestions like this come a dime a dozen in Hollywood, and there was no definite commitment. On the other hand, Hitler was common property and Dad could prove by his scrapbook that he had been seriously considering the idea before he ever met Bercovici. Tim Durant, who testified for my father, told me he thought Bercovici would have had a hard time winning the case if Dad had fought it through to the end. But by that time Dad had had enough of trials, having been dragged through the courts on the Mann Act charge and the two paternity suits Joan Barry brought against him. He decided to settle by paying Bercovici ninety-five thousand dollars with the stipulation that Bercovici drop all claim to coauthorship of *The Great Dictator.*

At the end of June, Paulette came up to Pebble Beach to see Dad, bringing us along with her, perhaps as a peace offering. At that time he had an almost completed screenplay to show her. But he was also still playing around with his Hitler ideas, which, like the jagged bits of a jigsaw puzzle, kept fitting themselves together. Impostor . . . little Jewish barber . . . young Jewish girl . . . things were clicking into place at a faster and faster rate of speed.

With our arrival, however, Dad forgot everything from Cooper to Hitler and threw himself into the business of entertaining us. Almost immediately he and Paulette were back in the same close relationship. Paulette was accepted by Pebble Beach society as his wife and it was dutifully noted by the ever vigilant reporters that when she entered a golf tournament at the club she signed her name Mrs. Chaplin. It was newsworthy because it was one of the rare times she used that title instead of her own name.

As for Syd and me, we found our Pebble Beach interlude delightful. We did some yachting, and went on several drives through the countryside. Dad went horseback riding with us a couple of times, though he had no real fondness for the sport. And then there was the house, the haunted house that stands out in my mind as the highlight of the whole trip.

It was a vacant house not far from where we lived. Dad and Tim must have spent hours planning the spook show they put on for us there.

Around dusk of the day before Syd and I were to go back to Hollywood by train, Dad began to talk to us about this house and the weird things that went on in it. We believed every word he said. It wasn't that, as boys, we were especially gullible, Dad just has a knack about him that way. Even Tim couldn't withstand his graphic descriptions. After twenty years he still remembers the verbal picture Dad painted for him of a certain man at Pebble Beach who, Dad was always convinced, would one day be murdered by his nagging wife. "We will go in that house," Dad used to say to Tim each time they went up the front walk to ring the bell, "and there we will find his severed head in the very center of the marble floor, waiting to greet us. Sooner or later it's bound to happen."

So it was with Syd and me and the ghosts which Dad described so vividly. We didn't notice that while he was talking Tim had slipped out. With a length of heavy chain, he made off for the house and ensconced himself on the top floor.

"If you don't believe me, come along and see for yourselves," Dad said to Syd and me after he'd given Tim enough time to get in position.

So we went with Dad to the house and he let us into the living room. There in the semidarkness he resumed his macabre ghost story. Suddenly he was interrupted by a "Whoooo," like the wind, floating down from the top floor.

"Hear that?" Dad whispered.

Syd and I shivered.

Dad resumed his story. Suddenly there was another "Whoooo." Then followed a soft, dismal groan and a muffled cry and another groan. Syd and I were already teetering on our heels when the climax came. *Clink, clank, clank*, a chain was rattling across the floor. It was enough. We fled from the house, Dad right at our heels, acting as frightened as we were.

Syd and I talked about that haunted house until we fell asleep. We dreamed about it that night, and the next morning at breakfast, to Dad's and Tim's amusement, we were still discussing it.

By chance the grownups had an appointment that morning and couldn't see us to the train. But the railroad depot was within easy walking distance, so they told us good-by and left.

We had time on our hands, and our thoughts kept going back to the house with the ghosts.

"Let's go see it in daylight," Syd suggested presently, and I agreed.

We walked to the house and strolled around it. It was obviously vacant, haunted; its broad bay windows seemed to glitter in the sunlight with a sinister reflection.

"Let's knock the ghosts out," Syd suddenly cried energetically.

"Yes, let's get rid of them," I said.

Self-appointed exorcisers, we picked up rocks and began hurling them at the big plate-glass windows. It was fun, and we did a thorough job. We broke practically every window in the house before we hurried off to catch our train.

It was only during that long ride back to Hollywood, when we were freed of the magical spell our father had cast over us, that we began to think of the house realistically. It had been vacant, but it hadn't looked like a deserted place—too well kept for that. And the windows, the big plate-glass windows—expensive!

"Do you suppose there really were ghosts, Chuck?" Syd ventured at last.

"I don't know," I faltered. "Maybe we shouldn't have . . ."

"I don't think we should have, Chuck."

A stab of horror went through us, as we remembered the elegant house standing gaunt and mutilated with all its windows broken.

"Dad'll be mad, real mad," I summed up the situation.

"I don't think we'd better go see him when he comes back," Syd said. "That is, if we know what's good for us."

I nodded. It was the prudent course to follow, but at the thought I felt a sinking feeling in my stomach. All spring we had been exiled from the house on the hill, and now, after a wonderful reunion with our father at Pebble Beach, we would have to be exiled from him again.

25

My father came home from Pebble Beach toward the end of July. We knew from the papers that he and Paulette were back, but we didn't phone him. Much as we wanted to, we didn't dare. He didn't phone us, either, though always before he'd made a point of getting in touch with us. So we were sure he was angry with us. Perhaps he thought we had turned into a couple of young gangsters and didn't want to have anything more to do with us.

The rest of the summer went by and Syd and I were back in school before the fascination of the house on the hill became too much for us and we decided to get in touch with Dad whatever the consequences. Frank, of course, answered the phone.

"Where you been?" his jovial voice came over. "Sure, come up and see him. He's your fathah, isn't he?"

So that Friday Syd and I went back.

"I haven't seen you for a long while," Dad said. He spoke in a mild voice. But from the way he looked at us Syd and I knew he was thinking of the broken windows in the house at Pebble Beach. We didn't say anything, but it wasn't necessary.

"You know," Dad was going on, "kids can go to reform school for breaking windows in houses. It's an outrageous thing to do. And besides, your poor father here working so hard while you boys are having fun maliciously destroying property."

"We didn't mean to, Dad," we tried to put in. "We just thought we'd scare the ghosts away."

"I don't care what you thought, you were destroying property," Dad went on. "Now suppose I didn't pay for it, what would happen to you? Well, you would be arrested by the police . . ."

On and on the lecture ran. It was just as it had been when we sold the bottles of liquor to Mr. Selznick. Just as then, we knew the verdict in the end could only be "Guilty!" And we waited with sinking hearts for the sentence.

"Boys, it cost me a lot of money, over fifteen hundred dollars," the voice of the prosecution was concluding. "Now never do that again. If you do, I'll really punish you."

That was all—no sentence, no penalty, just that stern but calm lecture. This was something new, and Syd and I went away dazed. But after we'd talked it over we realized we had just discovered a valuable clue to our father's personality. If you could escape the moment of his first wrath you were safe. His angers might be quick and intense, but apparently he didn't carry a grudge.

We were back in the house on the hill, back with Dad and Paulette. The rift between them had narrowed again without its existence ever having been apparent to Syd and me. The marriage still looked as durable as rock to us.

Paulette, who was sure her career was on the move at last, was happy. She had played a small role in *The Young in Heart*, and audience reaction to her had been good. She had been signed by MGM for an important role in *Dramatic School*, with Luise Rainer, which would keep her busy that fall. And she was still being seriously considered for the Scarlett O'Hara role. Even more promising was the fact that Dad had come up at last with a completed script, the script in which he planned to star Paulette and Gary Cooper. It was ready for production, the first time such a thing had happened in the past two years. Dad even went so far as to have an interview with Cooper for the role.

Where my father was concerned, however, things still weren't going to move as fast as Paulette imagined. Up at Pebble Beach he had isolated himself from newspapers and radio, and when he came back and saw what was happening in the world he was shocked. Hitler, his double, was spreading monstrous tentacles beyond the bounds of Germany, and within Germany there were terrible persecutions of the Jews. Suddenly Dad saw a purpose for his comedy beyond the mere art of making people laugh. It could also, through the medium of satire, waken people to the horror of dictatorship. It became his mission to hold up the mirror of ridicule to his alter ego, the mad Hitler, and show him for what he was—an evil buffoon. Dad put aside the script he had worked on so laboriously for the past six months and once more flung himself into the Hitler idea, which he was then calling *The Dictator*.

For three years now he had been caught up on successive waves of enthusiasm. But the difference between that steady writing and what he was now doing was that in the previous ventures he had been decidedly the master. In *The Great Dictator*, however, his genius was in the driver's seat and Dad was only carried along.

We were all in the surge of the mounting roller with him. Just as when I was younger, I wanted to be a part of it, to help my father in any way I could. And so it made me feel important to have him search all through the house calling, "Charles, where are you? Charles, listen to this!" I was just a boy of thirteen, and yet he had come to depend on me. But I knew it wasn't my opinion he wanted. What he needed always was encouragement.

As I grew older my father had lost the mythical qualities with which he was surrounded in my childhood, but he was now even more awe-inspiring to me as an international figure. He was a celebrated person upon whom great men, many of them geniuses in their own right, came to call, and who, when he went abroad, was invited to their homes. Men like Lion Feuchtwanger, H.G. Wells and Jean Cocteau all had been his guests. He was always showing us new awards he had received from cinema groups and other organizations around the world.

He had been honored by various nations, too, and sometimes he brought out these trophies for Syd and me to see. He showed us the documents, the medals and ribbons among which was the French Legion of Honor decoration.

Once Dad told us a funny story about his medals. During his trip to England in 1931 he had become good friends with the Prince of Wales, now the Duke of Windsor. He used to see a great deal of the Duke, who one day invited him to a ball.

"Wear your medals," he said offhandedly. "Everyone who has any will."

Dad had about five of these big medals. He pinned them all on and went to the ball, sounding like a medieval knight in armor—*clink, clink, clinking* around with the medals flopping all over his breast. He looked about and saw with consternation that the other guests were just wearing the ribbons that go with the medals. He stole out as inconspicuously as possible—which wasn't easy, considering the racket the flashy medals were making—and exchanged them for the ribbons. He had learned the hard way what royalty meant when it said, "Wear your medals." It was one of Dad's most embarrassing moments, but afterwards, such is the caliber of his humor, he loved to tell that joke on himself.

Dad also told us that he had been approached for a possible knighthood in England but had turned down the suggestion. He didn't believe in titles but only in the achievements of the individual. Syd and I were proud that our father had been considered for a knighthood, and I guess there were times we couldn't help wishing he had overcome his odd kind of inverted snobbery, which is based on the nobility of creativeness, and accepted it. It would have given us a thrill to refer to him as Sir Charles. That was then. At a later age we were openly to take him to task for another omission, that of not becoming a citizen of the United States.

When he showed us all his honors Dad would impress us with the fact that these things had been won without benefit of a formal education, that he had had to pull himself up by the proverbial bootstraps. And it would all end in a grave lecture to us to take advantage of our opportunities and be good students.

Studying was in some ways hard for me. I had been, like my father, left-handed, but I had been broken of the trait at a preschool age and it had affected both my studies and my speech, so the school nurse surmised. I did not stammer as a child; when I got excited I simply was not able to talk at all. The words would stick in my throat. I was also slower at learning than many of the other pupils, so that it took me longer to achieve what seemed to come to them with enviable ease.

But I found compensation for my hard work in the interest Dad showed in my progress at school. Now that Syd and I were in junior high, we were taking our studies seriously. Sometimes when I came home from school with my books,

Dad would lay aside his writing to look at them. He was especially interested in grammar and rhetoric.

"Let's see what you've learned this week," he would say, in his role of a father checking up on his son's progress. "What is this now, son?" And he would ask me a question about some point of grammar. I would give him the answer and sometimes he would shake his head and correct me. At other times he'd nod approvingly.

"Well, that's very good, son."

Then just for fun I would pop a question at him. Sometimes we'd have a friendly argument over who was right and, in the end, go to the grammar for verification. Sometimes Dad would catch himself up with a quick flustered shake of his head.

"No, no, no, that's wrong, of course. Now let me see. The subjunctive is like this."

And we'd study English together for a couple of hours. Even as a child I realized that, under the cloak of seeing how much I knew, Dad was brushing up on his own English. It seemed strange to me that a grown man who no longer needed to trouble himself with such things should show so much avidity for what I considered a tedious chore, but for years Dad had been trying to make up for his lack of formal schooling. He had an old dog-eared grammar which he studied and which he kept about him for reference. He wanted to speak perfect, not just passable, English. Nana recalls how when they were living at the house, she and Mother would sometimes correct Dad's grammar.

"Well, who invented the language and who has the right to make these rules anyway?" Dad would laugh. But he never took exception and he seldom made the same mistake twice. Today nobody has cause to correct his grammar, for it's impeccable.

Though my father admits to not being very good at spelling, his vocabulary has always seemed tremendous to me. As a child I thought he knew every word in the dictionary as well as its derivation. I used to carry a pocket dictionary around with me to check up on him privately. But much as I tried I could never catch him in an error.

Another thing that impressed me about my father was his habit of reading. It became almost an obsession with me to catch up with him. Now and then Mother, who had suffered so much ill health herself, became fearful I might hurt mine, and would separate me from my books and literally drive me outdoors to play.

In those days Dad's store of knowledge seemed bottomless to me. He knew the classics—the Bible, Shakespeare, Plutarch's *Lives*, Burton's *The Anatomy of Melancholy* and Boswell's *Life of Samuel Johnson*. One of his favorite stories, which illustrates Dad's interest in the meticulous use of words, concerns Dr. Johnson and a modish young matron with whom he was sharing a carriage. Dr. Johnson was most slovenly in his person and the young lady felt called upon to take him to task for it.

"Dr. Johnson, you smell," she said bluntly.

"I beg your pardon, madam," Dr. Johnson gravely replied. "I stink. You smell."

Among the fiction writers, Dad's favorites were Charles Dickens and Maupassant, perhaps because of the peculiar combination of the humorous and the macabre in their works. He also liked Edgar Allan Poe, Oscar Wilde and Mark Twain. The philosophers he read included Nietzsche, Emerson, Robert Ingersoll (whom he got through when he was seventeen), Schopenhauer and Spengler. I remember how one day when I was older my father took down a volume of Schopenhauer and handed it to me.

"You ought to read him, son," he said. "You don't need to take him too seriously, though—especially what he says about women. He's bitter, a great pessimist, but he's amusing."

Dad was fascinated by Spengler's *Decline of the West*. He

set great store by the writings of Aldous Huxley and Will Durant, both of whom were visitors at his home.

Some people have called Dad an intellectual, and others a dilettante. Some even claim he mimics intellectuality with such superb skill that it is only after you leave him that you realize it was all just a brilliant façade. But whatever my father's actual accomplishments in the field of learning, I have always appraised him as an earnest thirster after knowledge with a jealous determination to make up for all the advantages he missed when he was young.

Low marks on our report cards always distressed Dad. Once when I flunked in math he tried to jack me up by bringing in Dr. Einstein. "He's one of the few men on the face of this earth who knows the theory of relativity," Dad, who was never much good at figures himself, told me. "And I know him. He comes right up here to this house to play the violin with me."

I met Dr. Einstein only once. I remember him as a small man of mild appearance with a great shock of unruly gray hair. Yet I was much in awe of him, for he understood the intricacies of mathematics, a mystery which neither my father nor I could master.

In the field of music my father and I were on more certain ground. By this time I had discovered that the teachers at Black-Foxe were not such ogres after all. I had become especially fond of the one who had seemed the most formidable of them all, the physical education instructor, Mr. Douglas (Oleg) Mourat, who played the part of a father substitute to all the boys at school. He met with us in small groups to instruct us bluntly on the facts of life. He reprimanded us, paddled us when necessary, told us entertaining stories about his flight from Russia, showed an interest in our social affairs and encouraged us to develop our talents. He endeared himself to me by teaching me how to become an expert horseman, Cossack style. It was he who discovered my aptitude for music and suggested that I take lessons.

I started studying piano under the famous Russian pianist, the late Raissa Kaufman. She was also the teacher of a beautiful young girl named Dolly Loehr who, as Diana Lynn, was later to make a place for herself in Hollywood. I used to see Dolly sometimes when I went for my lessons. I was quite attracted to her but I never found the courage to ask her for a date.

My father was proud of my new accomplishment at the piano. "Sit down, play something for me," he would beg, and when I did he would stand by my shoulder with his hands behind his back listening attentively. "Oh, if you would only practice, Charles, you would be a great concert pianist," he would say longingly.

It was only later that I learned from an old newspaper clipping that even when I was a baby my father had proclaimed me a musical prodigy who would one day make my mark in the world.

All my life I had been hunting for a way to make my father proud of me, and suddenly I had found it. Music was the magic "Open sesame." But after six months of practice I discovered I could not keep up both it and my studies. My school curriculum was tough and I was a slow student. I couldn't find the extra time to put in the amount of practice I needed to be expert at the piano. And though my fingers were nimble enough and I could play a little by ear, I was slow at reading music. So my lessons were dropped altogether, which was a source of great disappointment to my father, though he never tried to coerce me into resuming them.

I compensated for my inability to keep up the lessons by taking all the music-appreciation courses I could cram into my curriculum throughout my years in high school. I studied the lives of composers, their styles and habits, everything about them I could lay my hands on. I learned to recognize a composer by the phraseology of a composition even though I didn't know the piece in question. And in this manner at least I was still able to hold my father's admiration.

"Oh, my son Charles, here, knows all about the classics," he would sometimes boast to his friends. "All the composers. Play something, Charles."

I was always afraid that Dad, who spoke with the air of one offering an entertainer with an expansive repertoire, would ask me to play one of my three pieces in front of the wrong person. Artur Rubinstein and Igor Stravinsky were visitors at the house. Rachmaninoff came once, but I missed seeing the latter because he visited my father on a week end when I wasn't there. Dad told me about it the next time I came up and I was almost inconsolable. Imagine it! Rachmaninoff at my father's house! Rachmaninoff, who was brilliant not just in one but in three fields, composer, pianist and conductor, and who had studied under Tschaikovsky, my first guide into the beautiful world of classical music!

I plied my father with questions about Rachmaninoff. What was he like? What had they talked about? How had he looked?

My father was amused by all my questions. He described Rachmaninoff for me—a tired old man with piercing eyes who spoke such broken English he had had to converse with Dad through an interpreter. Then suddenly, to make things plainer, Dad began to pantomime Rachmaninoff—the slow, shuffling gait across the floor, the sudden change to animation when he sat down and became immersed in subjects dear to him.

Later I went with Nana to hear Rachmaninoff playing at the Philharmonic auditorium. When I saw his tired old shuffle across the stage, his sudden metamorphosis to brilliance and youth as he took his place at the piano, I thought of my father. So well had Dad pantomimed the great artist that I saw not only Rachmaninoff that night, but my father in him.

Another visitor to our home was Vladimir Horowitz. When I was around sixteen I met Horowitz with his wife, Wanda, Toscanini's daughter, and their little girl Sonia, who was about eight at the time. Horowitz got her to play the piano for us. She played like the wind, but Horowitz shook his head.

"I must apologize for my daughter," he said in his thick Russian accent. "She hasn't practiced much lately. Practice, young lady!" Not practiced! My God, she was playing like a genius! I was perspiring for fear Dad would bring me up, me and my three pieces, and I would have to compete with her.

Dad could never have enough of Horowitz's playing.

"It's like a whole orchestra in the room," he would say admiringly. "He lifts the roof off."

Dad loved all his music loud. When he turned on the radio you could hear it blasting through the whole house; but he would sit there almost on top of it, entranced. He began to listen to his combination phonograph-radio more when I started taking an interest in music. The music was a bond that seemed to draw us close together. Now and then we would exchange comments about it. My father was especially enthralled by the Good Friday Spell from the third act of Wagner's *Parsifal*. I believe it was his favorite of all musical passages.

"Just listen to this, just listen to it," he would say, shaking his head, enthralled. "How could such a bastard write this beautiful music? Why, it's not mortal, it's heavenly, and he was such a son of a bitch in his personal life! Look what he did to Franz Liszt's daughter, and how he skipped town owing debts."

Sometimes, with the music swelling like golden thunder around him, Dad wouldn't be able to stay seated any longer. He'd jump to his feet, walking around, shaking his head, praising Wagner for what he had composed, and in the next breath excoriating him for his private life. I found it a bitter irony when, after the Joan Barry scandal and the accusations of being a Communist which were hurled against my father, I began to hear the the public condemning him in much the same way he had spoken of Wagner in earlier days.

26

That December of 1938, Dad finished the script of *The Great Dictator*. All the characters were clearly defined in it now. The female lead, that of the winsome Jewish girl, had been written around Paulette. Dad was to play both Hitler and the little Jewish barber. But he didn't completely discard his Little Tramp. In his baggy pants and oversize shoes he shuffles out of the picture as the barber at the end. Dad told me he kept the Little Tramp in as a talisman, because throughout his life he had brought him luck, wealth and fame. Dad had had a lot of laughs out of him, too, Dad and millions of people the world around.

They went to his pictures. They flocked to see him when he traveled. They held countless Charlie Chaplin contests. Dad told me about one of these that had taken place before I was born. It was at Grauman's Chinese Theatre in Hollywood, and there were thirty or forty people on the stage doing their best to imitate Dad. Dad was one of them. He'd gone up incognito to see how he would fare. He came in third. Dad always thought this one of the funniest jokes imaginable—whether on him or the judges or both, I don't know.

It is understandable why my father felt the need of keeping the cheerful Little Tramp as a good-luck symbol in *The Great Dictator*. He knew as well as anyone that he was taking a risk in making the picture at that time. Neville Chamberlain, with his famous umbrella, had visited Hitler at Munich. The Sudetenland had then been annexed and Hitler's greedy eyes were at the time fixed on Czechoslovakia. His intentions were obvious, but equally obvious was the fact that no Western power—not England, not France, certainly not the United States so much farther away—cared to interfere.

Dad was planning to do what others were afraid of doing —hold the little monster of Europe up to public ridicule. He was far ahead of his day in this, as he had been when he made *Modern Times*, which was an outcry against the standardization of man. The only reason events caught up with him in the case of *The Great Dictator* was that Dad progressed slowly, while his counterpart in Europe, encouraged by appeasement, was moving with unbelievable speed.

Because *The Great Dictator* was to be a talkie, Dad's first talkie, he brought in writers to help him with the screenplay. I can remember those story conferences, many of which he held at home. The writers Dad hired were professionals who knew their business, but it was still a one-man show where he was concerned. He would listen to an opinion, but if he didn't agree with it, it wouldn't be used. If anyone put up an argument—and I heard more than one heated discussion—Dad was likely to flare up. As production time approached, the flare-ups with which I had been familiar during the *Modern Times* era were again the usual thing.

Along with his work on the screenplay, my father began to study his subject. He got together all the newsreels of Hitler he could lay his hands on and looked at them by the hour, either in his home theater or in a projection room at his studio. There were scenes of Hitler talking to children, cuddling babies, visiting the sick in the hospitals, displaying his forensic art at all possible opportunities. Dad studied the dictator's every pose, picked up his mannerisms and was enthralled by the overall picture.

"That guy's a great actor," he used to say admiringly. "Why, he's the greatest actor of us all."

All this study paid off for my father. His portrayal of Hitler was a perfect imitation, so perfect that Germans watching the picture said you had to listen closely to realize he wasn't speaking their language with a Hitler accent, but just gibberish.

Dad began picking the rest of his cast, too. He was particularly anxious to find just the right man to play Napaloni— Benito Mussolini in real life. Originally Dad had planned to call him Benzino Gassolini, but when his picture was ready for production the war clouds were blacker than ever and Mussolini was still neutral, so Dad decided not to take any chance of offending the gaseous Duce. But fun he meant to have at his expense, and he fastened on Jack Oakie for the part. When Oakie showed up for the interview and learned what Dad wanted of him he clapped his hat back on his head and got to his feet.

"Look," he said, "I'm a Scotch-Irish boy. What you want to look for is an Italian actor."

"What's funny about an Italian playing Mussolini?" Dad shot back.

Oakie saw the point. He took off his hat again and sat down. He was signed for the role.

Dad's selection of extras for a picture was sometimes motivated by more than hard-headed determination to get the best available. There's a sentimental, even tender side to his nature and this comes to the fore when actors are concerned. I found him never so touched as by the spectacle of somebody who had once been an idol and was now reduced to poverty, perhaps because age had impaired his memory. I know Dad has hired such actors and paid them good salaries, too, for doing next to nothing.

Of course Dad couldn't allow sentiment to enter into his choice of the actors and actresses who were to have more important roles. They had to be chosen on merit alone. But even here Dad's sentimental feeling for those in the acting profession was apparent. It was so painful to him to interview people and then have to turn them down that he sometimes spoke of how nice it would be to have a room with a secret window. From that window he could look out at the applicants without anyone's knowing he was there, and select the ones he wanted.

When Dad began his coaching of Paulette, he was even more painstaking than he had been for *Modern Times*, because this was a talking picture and more would be expected of her.

I don't know whether, once Paulette was actually back working with Dad, she ever regretted her urgency to do another picture with him. But she was never much one for tranquillity. She had to give up all thought of the Scarlett O'Hara role, but finding herself with some free time on her hands after finishing *Dramatic School*, she went over to Paramount to do *The Cat and the Canary* with Bob Hope. Even the whirlwind production of Hope's film didn't occupy her whole time. There was still the redecorating of the house to be taken care of.

It had been more than two years since Paulette first brought up the subject of getting the house redecorated. She'd plugged at it intermittently ever since, but without too much enthusiasm, because she had been primarily occupied with getting her career off the ground. But now that everything seemed to be moving forward satisfactorily for her, she attacked the problem of the house with a vengeance. She enlisted the help of a potent ally in the person of the new Mrs. Fairbanks, with whom she had struck up a close friendship.

Sylvia Fairbanks was an ardent decorator herself. She had just redone the Fairbanks' Santa Monica home, and her eyes fairly glittered when she looked round Dad's place. Together she and Paulette worked on Dad. He fought every step of the way, as he had been fighting for two years, but now there were two of them and they were persistent. Gradually the house began to be transformed, though under the most violent protest.

Dad squawked about expenditures and foolish changes like an outraged bird being dispossessed from its nest. But all the same Paulette began throwing out his treasured old pieces and substituting more modern furniture. New wallpaper, new curtains, new carpets; everything began to emerge like a butterfly out of its drab chrysalis. But there was one hatching that didn't take place. I'm sure neither of the two women knew, as they refurbished and modernized the rooms, what lay under the black paint that covered the elegant light fixtures along the wall in the lower hallway. It took the present owners of the house to scrape off that paint and discover that the fixtures were of solid gold.

Though Dad continued to complain bitterly about every change, after it had been made he was usually pleased with the results. He was so proud of the twenty-five-thousand-dollar crystal chandelier which Paulette finally got him to purchase for the front hall that he later had it shipped to him in Vevey. He even began to absorb some of Paulette's enthusiasm. I think the glassed-in sunroom which he added to the living room, and which became his favorite work place, was as much his idea as hers. I know he was the one responsible for the parqueted floors in the hall and the sunroom.

In her redecorating fever, Paulette proceeded upstairs and turned her own room into an exquisitely feminine boudoir. Then Dad found himself making his last stand on a shrunken battle line, his own bedroom. Paulette tried desperately but she was never able to storm that citadel. Dad guarded his room as jealously as a lion its lair, roaring furiously at the very thought of encroachment. It was his, he liked it as it was, even to that faded worn-out rug on the floor, and he meant to keep everything in its place. In the beautifully appointed house, Dad's bedroom now stood out like a sore thumb and attracted the wonder of any guest who saw it.

And what about Syd and me during this tense, exciting period that preceded the big push, the commitment of *The Great Dictator* to film? So rapidly do boys grow that we had left behind the age of irrational escapades. I was approaching my fourteenth birthday, Syd his thirteenth, and our sins now were more those bred of laziness. It was fortunate for us that at this time a new friend came into our lives, or rather an old acquaintanceship was renewed and developed into a lasting friendship.

I'm speaking of Frank Antunez, Jr., son of the former head of transportation at Dad's studio. It was during the filming of *Modern Times* that we had first met Frank, whom we affectionately called Pancho, because he was Mexican. We used to share our bicycles with him at the studio on Saturdays. Now, at the age of seventeen, he came to do odd jobs around the house. He took care of the tennis court and occasionally helped Frank with the inside work. Sometimes he drove Dad to the studio when he was working, and often he brought us home from Black-Foxe. Syd and I looked on him as a big brother. We had riotous pillow fights with him up in our room and shamelessly borrowed ice-cream or theater money from him when we were flat. Often all three of us went to the movies together, sitting in a row, eating popcorn, our eyes glued to the screen.

Recently I saw Frank Antunez, who is now employed in the sound department at MGM, and we began reminiscing about old times.

"You and Sydney were different from the children of so many other celebrities. You never had this air about you of being the sons of someone who was somebody," Frank said, paying Syd and me what I consider a great compliment. "You were always just like ordinary kids. But then your father was that way too. There never was any condescension toward me because I worked for him. Even years later he remembered me, and that's more than a lot of them do when you've quit them."

Then Frank Antunez recalled how, in his job as a delivery and pickup man for Pathé Laboratories after he had left my father, he bounced whistling one evening through the front door of the R.C.A. Recording Studios in Hollywood for their daily quota of film. He found himself confronted by a group of solemn-faced people. "Be quiet," they ordered Frank pontifically. "Mr. Chaplin is coming downstairs!"

Frank was so amazed at all this formality that he choked on his whistling. And while he was trying to recover himself, Dad came running down the stairs in that quick way of his. His eye took in Frank and he hurried over, grabbed his hand and shook it.

"How are you, Frank, and how's business going?" he asked warmly, and he stopped to chat a moment before hurrying on, ignoring the group of gaping people who had been standing at stiff attention waiting for him.

"What does he care for all that solemn fuss?" Frank reminded me. "He was always just people, at least he was with my father and me. He never treated me like a servant. I was more or less one of your family."

As a member of the family it was Pancho's chore to see that Syd and I were ready on time when Dad and Paulette had a dinner engagement in which we were included. This was much more of a task than at first appears, for Syd and I, like most boys that age, hated to get dressed to go to an affair that didn't appeal to us. Pancho often had to tie our ties, and there were many times when he had literally to stuff Syd into his blue suit because Syd couldn't be bothered. Pancho would cajole, pressure and joke until at last, just in the nick of time, there we would both be looking like pieces of sartorial art, with even our hair neatly combed.

If only the affairs to which Dad and Paulette took us had been lively parties glittering with movie stars! But at our awkward age we were seldom included in that kind of gathering and we were beginning to feel left out about it. We were entering a new phase now. We were well on the way to becoming real movie-star fans.

My hero was Jimmy Cagney, and I finally met him one night during a party at the house. Syd was at school doing the "gun beat," and I might as well have been because I was sick with a fever and had to stay in bed. They tried to make it up to me by putting me in Paulette's room, where I could at least hear the clatter below. But that wasn't much comfort and presently I turned my back to the door. All of a sudden there was Paulette.

"I want you to meet someone," she said.

I turned around and a man walked through the door. He looked familiar, but I couldn't place him because he seemed so short. Then I recognized the face: it was James Cagney, Public Enemy Number One. My dream had come true, but all I could feel at the moment was shock at his stature.

I was deeply in love with Hedy Lamarr, whom I knew only by her pictures. And I had a real crush on Paulette. She was no longer just a pretty stepmother who always sided with Syd and me against our father's wrath but also spoke reprovingly to us about keeping up our lessons. She was also a glamorous woman who belonged to us. It was nice to have a stepmother so young and beautiful she could almost be our girl friend too.

Love . . . romance! Syd and I were entering the age of

youthful chivalry. At a private party I stole my first kiss from a girl named Peggy. Someone turned the lights out and all the girls hid. Peggy crouched under the piano. I stuck my head under with dashing enthusiasm. But Peggy wasn't hiding from me after all. Her face was right there and my teeth crashed against hers with a force that almost floored us both.

"You didn't need to knock all my teeth out, Charlie," Peggy said ruefully. "I would have kissed you anyway."

At home the Japanese servants had shrewdly observed the change in Syd and me and discarded their bloodthirsty stories of executions and ghosts.

"You like geisha girls?" Frank would ask instead.

"Well, I guess they're very nice," we would answer, though we'd never met any and didn't know what they were.

This was enough to launch Frank. He would tell us wildly romantic stories with copious interpolations and enthusiastic additions from George, Kay and any of the relatives who happened to be present. It seemed that every one of them was an authority on geisha girls.

Dad wasn't far behind the servants. It was time, he could see, to have a stab at sex education with his sons. I remember the day when he first broached the subject to us. The sun was setting and we were walking around Dad's estate, all three of us, looking at nature in general. Dad always seems to wax most expansive at sunset. It is as though a feeling of tenderness takes possession of him, encouraging him to candor. And so he chose that hour to talk of sex to Syd and me. First he spoke poetically of the flowers and how they grow. From the flowers he passed on to the birds, and then the animal world. And finally he was describing how it was with human beings, how we one and all without exception had come into the world. He told us that in the female body the male cell meets the female and from this mysterious union a new life is conceived.

"There's some Force that causes it," he said. "Who can tell what that Force is? But it's beautiful and mysterious."

Dad never did get around to telling us just how the male cell gets an opportunity to meet the female cell. He seemed relieved when we assured him we had learned all those details from Mr. Mourat. Dad much preferred to stick to his poetic descriptions of the beginning of life. And Syd and I liked to hear him talk that way. Somehow it wrought a veil of beauty, of mystery and poetry, around a subject which Mr. Mourat had dealt with more realistically than esthetically.

It was Paulette, though, who really made me aware that I was leaving childhood behind. One night in the mountains I went to climb into her bed with her as always. But she just threw back the top cover for me.

"What's that for?" I asked her.

"You're an older boy now, Charlie," she said.

"What do you mean?" I insisted.

Paulette laughed. "You! Really, Charlie! You'll be just like your father when you grow up. I can see it now."

So I had to be content with sitting on the bed with the top blanket around me. And the next day Paulette told Dad and they joked about it.

But it took something more than good-natured fun to help me grow in a different way—mentally, so that I found a deeper understanding about things, about myself. It was in March that I had an attack of appendicitis at school. Feeling much like a hero, I was taken away to the hospital in an ambulance.

Once there, it wasn't so much fun. I was on the operating table for two hours, and then there were chest complications because the umbilical cord that had been wrapped around my neck at birth had left me with a weak respiratory tract. I developed pneumonia and was in critical condition for several days.

Mother and Nana and Dad all were notified when I went to the hospital and came down at once. They sat together in the waiting room cheering each other up until the doctors pronounced the operation a success. Then Dad took Mother and Nana to the Brown Derby for breakfast. When I came out of the anesthetic they were all back standing around my bed. I heard them talking before I opened my eyes.

"You know almost everyone has an appendectomy, Lita," Dad was saying. "So you mustn't worry."

"I know, Charlie," it was Mother's voice.

I opened my eyes and saw them looking down at me, smiling, asking how I was doing. Despite his attempt at jocularity, Dad couldn't keep his anxiety from showing. He never could too successfully.

And suddenly it came to me that I wasn't on this earth by sufferance after all. Whatever had happened then, whatever quarrels there had been, it was all over. They cared about me and there was warmth and friendliness between them. In that moment I understood exactly what Dad meant when he had said to me in the living room that day, "It's just one of the things in life." That's all it was, not any more or less important than that. It was life and I was part of it, and I was growing up.

27

It was during that summer of my fourteenth year that I finally met my dream girl, Hedy Lamarr, in a carefully planned romantic comedy engineered by my father.

It took place at Catalina Island. Our small yacht was anchored next to Gene Markey's big one. I knew that Hedy, who was married to Markey at the time, was aboard the yacht, and I hung on the rail of our ship hoping to get a glimpse of her. Dad watched me awhile with amusement.

"Well, son," he said at last, "we're going over there and you're going to meet Hedy Lamarr."

I followed him, speechless, to the little outboard motor, where we were joined by Syd and Paulette. Captain Anderson took us all across. We boarded the Markey yacht, and

213

there was Gene Markey with a captain's cap at a rakish tilt on his head. There were other guests, too; I think the late Robert Benchley was one of them. But the only one I can vividly remember is Hedy, in her white blouse and dark slacks, with her long black hair and scarlet lips. She was smiling at me. But I couldn't look directly at her.

I was at this impasse when Gene Markey suddenly announced there was going to be a chinning contest on the rail of the ship. (Dad had put him up to it, of course, because he knew I prided myself on chinups.) The person who won would get a prize.

"If it's money, Charles and Sydney," Dad warned us, "remember, I told you boys never to accept money from people outside your family."

I knew Dad was serious on this point. He had made it often throughout our childhood—no money gifts from anyone. But I wasn't thinking of money just then. I had a chance to show off to Hedy Lamarr. I went over to the rail with Syd and the other males and we all began doing chinups. I outstripped everyone. It's a wonder I didn't strain myself. I did twenty-five before I had to give up. I sat down on a bench, panting, to rest.

Gene Markey came up to me.

"You won," he said. "Here's the prize."

Of course it was money, a twenty-dollar bill.

I took it and sat looking at it. It was a fabulous amount. But I knew Dad's eyes were on me, waiting, and Dad was inflexible with his rules. I handed it up to him. Suddenly Hedy Lamarr sat down beside me and put her arms around me.

"Oh, please, Char-lie," Hedy said in her charming Austrian accent, putting on the siren act, "don't be so tough on your son. He's such a niiiice boy."

I must have melted down to nothing. I hid my face and smiled and blushed. And everyone around, even Syd, was laughing. But I didn't care.

"Please, Char-lie," Hedy went on, "please let your son

have the mon-ey." And suddenly her lips were on my cheek. Hedy Lamarr was kissing me!

Then Dad handed me back the money as though he had been moved by Hedy's pleas.

"Now don't spend it all in one place," he said.

I don't remember what happened after that. I just remember that I was still unable to look at Hedy when the time came to tell her good-by. But I never forgot that kiss.

That summer my father didn't confine his coaching to Paulette. He also did some work with his second male lead, Jack Oakie.

"Your father taught me so much I couldn't believe I had known so little before," Jack told me. "Why, I felt like a rank amateur before he was through."

The first day of tests Dad wanted to see Jack's bag of tricks. Jack obligingly walked in front of the camera to give him a sample of his take-ums—a special look straight into the camera, to attract the audience's attention. Jack had been doing take-ums so long he'd begun to think he originated them. He finished the take-um but the camera kept on grinding.

"Go on," Dad told him.

"That's it," Jack said.

"Oh, no, there should be more to it," Dad insisted.

He encouraged Jack to milk the take-um dry with every kind of embellishment he could think of. Jack discovered then that it was Dad who was the father of the film take-um, as he was of so much film comedy business. One by one Jack showed off all his tricks and Dad taught him how to improve on each, so that he could wring out five laughs where before he had gotten only one. Dad was going full swing in his favorite role of teacher, and in Jack he had a very apt pupil.

Meanwhile, all through the summer, while Dad was winding up the many details that had to be taken care of before actual production could begin, the Nazi shadow was growing longer and longer. Chamberlain's policy of appeasement had borne its bitter fruit. Despite Hitler's assurance that the Sudeten represented the extent of his territorial ambition, he had moved into Czechoslovakia by the middle of March and had next fixed his hungry eyes on Poland. Thoroughly alarmed now, the British Prime Minister had announced on March 31, 1939, that if Poland was attacked, Great Britain would come to her aid. Ever since that announcement the world had lain in a state of uneasy peace. It was broken September 1 when Hitler's troops goose-stepped into Poland, bringing a war that was to engulf almost every civilized nation and eventually carry Syd and me, along with so many other young men, half across the world.

On September 3, France and England formally announced they were at war with Germany. And a few days later my father began production on *The Great Dictator*.

It was five years almost to the month since he started filming *Modern Times*. All through that period he had been making periodic statements about getting out a picture a year —"quickies" he called them. But by the time he came around to doing *The Great Dictator* he was resigned to the limitation of time imposed on him by his genius and was even shocked when he read about the "quickie" productions of other studios. A *Daily Variety* headline proclaiming that Darryl Zanuck was going to make forty-eight pictures in the current year left him incredulous.

"This is what's wrong with the business," my father exclaimed. "How can you make forty-eight good pictures a year?"

Dad's long absence from actual production, together with the fact that he hadn't yet gone into talkies, put him in the position of a Rip Van Winkle returning to the land of the living after twenty years. By this time unions were firmly intrenched in the motion-picture industry, and if Dad wanted to use his crew for longer than an eight-hour period—and when Dad was on the job it was often customary for his workers to put in a twenty-hour day—he had to pay them overtime. Dad has earned a reputation in certain quarters for being stingy, but none of his former employees will go along with that. All over town producers were hiring replacement crews to cut out overtime expenses, but when one of Dad's budget experts approached him with a suggestion that he do likewise, Dad refused.

"No," he said sternly. "Never cheat on labor. Let them earn the extra money."

Perhaps most perplexing to my father, when he started production on *The Great Dictator*, were the new stand-by employees that, according to union regulations, he now had to add to his staff. What possible use could Dad have for an augmented staff, that one-man dynamo who was used to doing everything for himself? He could never get over all his extra help.

"What are these crowds doing here, anyway?" he would ask, looking about him every morning.

"But what's a script girl?" he would inquire of the script girl when she reported to him. Dad had always been his own script girl, and he kept right on taking care of it even with the girl on hand.

When a makeup man appeared in his dressing room, Dad stared at him. Makeup man for Dad, who had always done his own makeup and would go on doing it because he enjoyed it? He paid the makeup man to stand around and watch him and he got a lot of fun out of putting on a show for him as well. When Syd and I were at the studio with Dad we saw the show ourselves.

Dad took out a thick strand of fake hair about a yard long. He fastidiously dabbed some liquid adhesive on his upper lip and cemented the center of the strand of hair to the adhesive so that the long ends hung down one on either side of his face. Next Dad picked up a tremendous pair of shears and started snipping at the hair—first one side, then the other, in a delicate, precise rhythm. While he snipped he talked to Syd and me.

"What on earth is a makeup man, boys?" he asked with a grimace and a quick snip on one side.

"What do you hire them for, anyway?" Another snip on the other side, another grimace.

"Who needs a makeup man?" Snip, snip—with each snip a grimace and a question. The big scissors flashed in a gay dance closer and closer to Dad's face, until with a last elegant snip he trimmed that tiny mustache expertly right across his upper lip.

Dad didn't have much use for a film cutter, either. He did most of the cutting himself, and the cutter was paid primarily, I guess, to see how a past master did things. One cutter told me that when Dad was impatient he wouldn't bother to reach for the scissors to cut the film. There he would be with it wrapped around his neck in garlands, looking at it against the light. When he came across the offending section he would just rip it out with his fingers, leaving the cutter to trim the edges and fasten the ends together again.

"Whoever heard of tearing film that way?" the cutter said to me. "But your father did."

The new sound-effects technician was someone Dad really needed, but he didn't like to admit it, because he didn't like to admit that anyone could do any phase of picture making better than he. One time he spent two whole days trying to get the sound of an airplane motor. He would sit in front of an electric fan holding a piece of celluloid against the whirring blades and varying the pressure, his head cocked to one side, listening. He would exchange one piece of celluloid for another of a different thickness and one fan for another of a different size while the sound expert stood by humoring him. Finally, when Dad gave up on his experimenting, the sound technician got the effect by simply going down to the airport and recording the sound of a real motor.

But Dad was never too concerned about saving time. Picture making wasn't a business with him. It was creative play and he loved it. I remember the day Uncle Sydney came to him excited over an offer he'd just received from someone who wanted to buy the studio for two million dollars. It looked like a wonderful deal to my uncle, because Dad didn't really need a studio except once about every five years, when he could easily rent one. His own studio was just an expensive luxury. Dad once told me it cost him around a thousand dollars a day to maintain it when it was idle.

At the time Uncle Sydney panted out his proposal Dad was making a test for some kind of sound effect. Uncle Sydney waited eagerly for Dad's reaction, but Dad didn't even lift his head from what he was doing.

"Oh, tell them to leave us alone," he said. "Just where would I play if I didn't have the studio?"

But though Dad's picture making was play, it certainly wasn't a relaxing kind of play. It was more in the nature of a nerve-racking adventure.

Paulette, especially, felt the pressures. She was Dad's wife, but that didn't make any difference on the set. There she was Hannah, the female lead. She had to take more drilling than almost anyone else in the cast—drilling that at times pushed her close to the breaking point. Dad was proud of her finished work. All her best qualities, the independence and courage of her gay pixie spirit, came out in the picture. But the grueling drive that displayed Paulette's personality so brilliantly also helped to shatter the marriage that had so precariously survived the calm between productions.

Syd and I, once again visiting the sets with our father, noticed the change in atmosphere from the old days when *Modern Times* was produced. Things had become much quieter. By quieter I don't mean calmer. The old silent-film camera, with its soft, friendly whine punctuated by faint staccato clickings, was gone. Dad felt awkward at first, acting in front of a camera that made no noise at all. It took him a while to realize that he had used the noise of the silent-film camera to establish his own rhythm. He now had to depend on his own inner timing.

He missed the laughter of the stagehands around the set, too. Now everything had to be acted out in a silence so dead you could hear a pin drop, while a buzzing fly sounded like a miniature dive bomber, especially in my father's ears.

One day when Syd and I were on the set a fly had the temerity to penetrate that sacred precinct in the middle of a particularly difficult scene. They'd been shooting it a number of times without success because one of the players wasn't doing his part to please Dad. Finally Dad got a shot that he thought might pass. But because he's a perfectionist he called for one more take. Just as the camera was ready to roll and everyone was poised in tense expectancy, this fly came flitting across the stage with a gay little buzz. Dad blew his top just as though that tiny fly were a P-38.

"Goddam it!" he yelled. "Get that bloody vulture out of here!"

Five men each reached for a fly swatter. Dad must have kept dozens of the things hanging around the place. They all started chasing the fly, leaping, pirouetting, racing around and flailing their fly swatters energetically.

In the midst of the bedlam Dad paced back and forth, back and forth, hands behind his back, head bent, ignoring the pandemonium around him.

"The scene'll have to go better. It'll just *have* to go better," he kept muttering to himself.

After what seemed about twenty minutes of pursuit, the men got the fly. Shooting was resumed and the scene went over beautifully. Then all at once someone began to laugh. There was another and another laugh. Soon the whole set was in an uproar, Dad laughing along with the rest of us. No matter how angry he gets or what an embarrassing situation he may find himself in, when things die down he's quick to see the humor in it.

Another time it was Syd, not a fly, who was the culprit.

This time they were shooting the scene of the firing of the Big Bertha. They'd been through rehearsals several times and it was a lot of fun. Dad would get ready to pull the lanyard on the gun. But first he would go through some kind of quick jig that was hilarious. Then would come the *boom* of the gun and Dad would do a few startled somersaults and other business, all of which was side-splitting. Everyone was holding his mouth to keep from laughing, and doing a good job of it.

Then they were ready for the take. The camera rolled. Dad did his funny business and in the midst of the silence a sudden peal of laughter rang out. It was Syd. In a twinkling, from being the funniest man alive Dad became the most furious.

"Who laughed?" he shouted.

No one answered. I guess Syd was hoping Dad's anger would cool down, as we had discovered it did. But Dad kept insisting, "Now who laughed? Who laughed?"

"I did," Syd said at last, getting his courage up.

Dad rushed up to him in that characteristic running way he has.

"Do you know your laugh just cost me fifteen thousand dollars?" he exclaimed.

He had his hand raised. I thought he was going to strike Syd and I was terrified, because I could see he had been so completely concentrated on the scene he had forgotten for a moment who he was or where he was.

"You . . ." he said. Then he let his hand fall. "You laughed at me!"

Suddenly he was laughing himself. He turned to the crew.

"Even my own son thinks I'm funny," he said, as though he had just received an extraordinary accolade.

He turned back to Syd. "Well, it was fifteen thousand dollars' worth of laugh," he said, "but if you appreciated it that much, it's all right." He paused, looked at Syd meaningly and added, "Just don't let it happen again, son."

Believe me, Syd didn't.

Dad was more tense at the beginning of production on *The Great Dictator* than he had been with *Modern Times.* His worry with *Modern Times* had been over doing a silent in a world of sound. With *The Great Dictator* his anxiety came from a more positive source. He had to master new techniques as a beginner in a field where other producers were by this time old hands. It wasn't long, however, before Dad began to realize that talkies weren't the bugaboo he'd been picturing them. And presently he was enjoying the new medium so much that he even started speaking regretfully of not having made *Modern Times* with sound.

"I don't think some of my funniest scenes were understood by the children," he would say. "Talking would have made them plain."

"Of course," he would add, "even then the picture wasn't too much of a failure." That particular film has been making money in the millions for Dad ever since its first release.

One of the pleasantest things about the new film was the affable relationship between Dad and Jack Oakie. Jack has a tough hide and was able to take Dad's drive in stride. Dad, on his part, has always had a great admiration for Jack. As one of the most exuberant comics in the business, he was a perfect counterpart of the effusive Mussolini. Even his shape resembled that of the pudgy Italian dictator. But Jack was on a diet at the time the picture was being shot, and this worried Dad. What would be funny about a slender Mussolini? My father tackled the problem with his characteristic thoroughness. He used to bring George down to the studio to prepare lunch, and he instructed him to fix his choicest and most fattening dishes. Then he began to invite Jack to his dressing room as a luncheon guest.

I remember being in on those sessions, which always ended so hilariously that Syd and I couldn't keep straight faces. Dad never ate much lunch as a rule, but he would ply Jack with generous portions of food so tantalizing a gourmet would have been in rapture.

"Charlie, I can't eat it," Jack would exclaim desperately. "I tell you I'm on a diet. A little fruit and some cottage cheese, maybe."

For answer Dad would put a forkful of the food in his own mouth and sample it with an expression of ecstatic pleasure. Jack would stare at him with longing sheep eyes.

"I know what you're trying to do, Charlie," he would moan. "But I'm not going to fall for it. I'm on a diet and I'm sticking to it."

"Oh, come on, Jack. Just this once," Dad would beg, and he would take another mouthful and savor it.

In the end Jack always broke down and ate everything in sight. He didn't just retain weight, he put on more. Dad took to calling him Muscles, and Muscles he remained throughout most of the picture.

During the shooting of *The Great Dictator*, Jack was mostly the pupil, my father the master. But I know there was one time at least that Jack was able to teach Dad something. I know of it because Jack is so proud he still likes to tell about it.

My father's directorial methods are mainly intuitive, like so much else about him. He knows when a scene is right. But Jack noticed that sometimes he had trouble defining for others just what he wanted. One day he used up film by the yard on a dining scene with a blond waitress who was bringing a tray of spaghetti to a table where Jack sat. The girl kept doing everything persistently wrong, and under Dad's merciless drilling she was becoming so nervous she was almost in tears. It was Jack, from his vantage point at the table, who suddenly realized what the trouble was. Dad, not the girl, was at fault.

"Charlie," Jack said, "you're directing the scene left-handed and the girl is right-handed."

Dad's face brightened. He crossed to the other side of the set, and when the girl came in this time he saw at once what was wrong, and they got a perfect take.

Though I don't believe Jack played the instructor more than once—at least he hasn't told me about it—he did prove not only an apt but an ambitious pupil. Now that he had Dad's secrets, he went all out to steal at least one scene from the King of Comedy. He tried everything he'd learned, but it wasn't quite good enough. My father still kept taking the scenes away from him.

One day in the middle of one of Jack's desperate efforts, Dad turned to his sweating pupil with a grin and divulged his final secret. "If you really want to steal a scene from me, you son of a bitch," he said affably, "just look straight into the camera. That'll do it every time."

Dad could afford to be free with his secrets. He, as well as everyone else, knew he was the master of living comics. I say *living* because Dad did admit serious competition from another quarter .He spoke about it often after he saw Walt Disney's *Snow White* at the Carthay Circle Theater that year. All through the showing he analyzed Disney's techniques, looking for things he could adapt to his own work. Dad was able to learn even from animated cartoons, and he had the greatest admiration for Walt Disney both as an artist and as a master technician.

"Disney's making it tough on us comics," he used to say with a shake of his head. "The timing of his characters is always superb because they don't even have to stop to take a breath."

28

On December 12 of that year a tragic event occurred which threw a shadow over the Christmas season. Douglas Fairbanks, Sr., who was only fifty-six at the time, died unexpectedly of a heart attack at his beach home. He had been my father's oldest and dearest friend in the acting profession. My father was a pallbearer at the funeral, and this must have cost him dearly in emotional strain, for he has always made a point of avoiding funerals if possible.

"They ought to be outlawed," he once told me vehemently. "The grief they cause the family. I just don't dare go."

My father's floral contribution to the funeral was an urn of white sweet peas, red roses and orchids. The message read, "In loving remembrance of my good friend Douglas. I shall always treasure his memory."

What memories! Dad and Doug Fairbanks were like a couple of schoolboys together, always ready for a harmless practical joke and a few laughs, and they could find their amusement in the simplest antics. In the days of silent movies, before people knew what their voices were like, they used to drive slowly around Beverly Hills until they came upon a group of tourists. They would stop and Dad would lean out.

"I say," he would exclaim in a high-pitched voice, "would you tell me where Sunset Boulevard and Benedict Canyon meet?"

The people, nonplused at being accosted by the two famous stars, and never once stopping to wonder why they weren't conversant with the streets of their own town, would stammer out directions.

"Thank you very much," Dad would reply in his quavering voice.

"Charlie, shall we go now?" Doug would put in, in a falsetto almost as high. "We have to get to that party tonight."

Then they would drive off slowly, their ears cocked.

"I didn't know Charlie Chaplin and Doug Fairbanks spoke with such high-pitched voices," the disillusioned exclamations would rise behind them.

Convulsed with laughter, Dad and Doug would feel their day had been crowned with success.

Sometimes they'd plan a gag beforehand. Doug Fairbanks would come to a party wearing a trick shirt under his dinner jacket. My father would pretend to get into an argument with him and at its height would shout, "If you don't shut up I'll rip your shirt off."

"Go ahead, try it!" Fairbanks would reply, eying Dad contemptuously.

Dad would dart up and grab the front of Fairbanks' shirt. *Whhup*, the whole front would come off, sleeves and all, leaving only the cuffs behind. Fairbanks would just sit staring at him while Dad would stare at the shirt.

"Oh, I'm so sorry," he'd finally say as politely as though what he'd done was just a little *faux pas*. "I had no idea!"

Then, turning to the shocked guests he'd explain mildly, "It's nothing—just a small argument."

There were the poker games, too, down at Fairbanks' beach home. You have heard of the traditional poker face, but there was never one for long at those games. Dad couldn't resist pantomiming a typical poker player over his cards. Then Doug would throw in his two bits' worth of hamming, until what had started out as a sober game of cards would be turned into a hilarious evening. Now those games were over forever, along with so much else Dad had enjoyed with Fairbanks.

It must have seemed to my father that with his friend's passing the whole world of Hollywood as he had known it was breaking up. As indeed it was, for Fairbanks had been a symbol of the movie colony's exuberant childhood.

That Christmas Syd and I received two more dogs from Paulette. They were St. Bernard pups, which we called Samson and Delilah. Now, much to our father's consternation, there were four dogs around the house. (Puddles had either wandered off or been kidnaped.) The St. Bernards were the worst of them all, despite their being such gentle creatures. They grew into monsters, prowling everywhere, tearing up the yard, bounding into the house whenever they could find a crack in a door that they could paw open.

"You'd better take them out to your mother, she probably needs some watchdogs," Dad suggested solicitously.

So we took them to the ranch, though no one there seemed particularly grateful for Paulette's gifts, either.

Christmas was only a short respite in the Chaplin home that year. Dad was pounding down the home stretch now on *The Great Dictator*, driving all before him like Shelley's west wind. I remember seeing Paulette unhappy, even in tears, much of that time. It wasn't just the strain of work that was affecting her. There was an element of hurt pride, too.

Paulette was no longer the green newcomer she had been

when she so gratefully accepted my father's coaching in *Modern Times*. Now she was regarded in Hollywood as a promising young actress. And Dad's grueling, sometimes impatient coaching of her on the set in front of the other players was on occasion very humiliating to her. Sometimes she came home from work looking so woebegone that Syd and I would ask Dad anxiously about her.

"Your stepmother worked very hard today," Dad would explain, "and I had to tell her a few things about acting, which isn't easy." Then Dad would try again to explain to Paulette what had been wrong with the scene that had caused the trouble in the first place.

"Oh, don't talk any more about it, Charlie," Paulette would burst out. "You're just a slave driver." And she would lie down on the couch and start to cry.

Dad would turn to us and ask us to leave and let Paulette rest. When we had gone he would make it up with her. She was always too bright a person to stay downcast for long, anyway, and afterwards she and Dad would be as affectionate as ever with each other. It still never occurred to Syd and me that these quarrels were anything more than temporary explosions due to the tensions of the production, quarrels which would stop as soon as the picture was finished.

Things did relax for Paulette and the rest of the cast when the shooting came to an end in the spring of 1940, but not for Dad. Still the human dynamo, he turned his attention to composing the music for *The Great Dictator*. And because many of his sessions with the musicians were held at the house, I had the opportunity of watching first-hand a man who couldn't read a note and knew nothing of the mechanics of the art, work at being a composer—and drive men mad as he had Al Newman in earlier years.

The musicians were actually musical secretaries taking Dad's dictation. The music was always his. He would hum or play his tune and the musicians would take it down and then play it back for him. Dad would listen carefully. He has a wonderful ear.

"That part's good," he'd say. "But there's something wrong here. Wait a minute."

He would concentrate and hum the phrase again, and the musicians would get back to their dictation. It might take a number of tries before Dad had the tune to his satisfaction.

He and the musicians not only worked long hours at home, but more long hours at the studio, where they used a Movieola so that a scene could be played, reversed and played again until the music to match it popped into Dad's head. Once he had it in its entirety he would give the musicians a description of how he wanted it scored for each scene—the tempo, the rhythm, the style. Though he knew some of the various musical forms and could correctly use a great deal of terminology such as pizzicato, rubato, allegro and the like, he preferred to describe what he wanted by referring to a composer's name or an instrumental label by way of illustration.

"We should make this Wagnerian," he would say, or, "This part should be more Chopin. Let's make this light and airy, a lot of violins. I think we could use an oboe effect in this passage."

Sometimes when Dad described what he wanted the musicians would shake their heads, because Dad's timing of a musical phrase to suit a bit of action was sometimes so unorthodox it threw them off. They would try to explain the technical reasons for not being able to give him what he asked for.

"Well, I'm not concerned about that," Dad would say. "Just put it down here the way I want it."

It was only after they'd done so that they could see that, though unorthodox, Dad's dramatic instinct as it related to music was brilliant. So phrase after phrase, literally note by note, Dad and his valiant musicians worked their way through *The Great Dictator*. The musicians turned gray and were on the verge of nervous breakdowns by the time it was over, but whatever they suffered they couldn't say that working with Dad was ever dull. He gave them a free performance at every session, because he didn't just hum or sing, or knock out a tune on the piano. He couldn't stay quiet that long. He would start gesturing with the music, acting out the parts of the various people in the scene he was working on, but caricaturing their movements to evoke a tonal response in himself. At those times his acting was closer than ever to ballet.

My father's comedy in general more nearly resembles ballet than any other art. He has a dancer's movements and mannerisms—almost feminine mannerisms, though not effeminate. He's light on his feet, with an acrobat's sure sense of timing. His small, delicate hands are so articulate that if you follow them you can usually tell exactly the impression he wants to convey. Ballet dancers are the first to recognize my father's proficiency in their field. Most of those who have seen him perform will tell you frankly that he is as good a dancer as they. And Robert Helpmann, one of the stars of the famed Sadler's Wells troupe, once told screen writer Dudley Nichols that Dad was far better than he could ever be.

Dad loves ballet. He is familiar with all the dancers, even the minor ones. Among the ballerinas Dad used to admire Alicia Markova and Alexandra Danilova, especially Danilova. Of the male ballet dancers I remember his mentioning Fedor Lensky, Igor Youskevitch and Frederic Franklin.

Years before, he had met Nijinsky, and he still spoke with awe of his performance in *The Specter of the Rose*. Dad would tell me the plot, and when he came to the part in which Nijinsky dives through the window with the rose in his mouth, Dad would imitate him and with an imaginary rose between his teeth go diving off somewhere himself.

"He'd go backstage spitting blood," Dad would say. And I could tell by the tone of his voice how deeply he admired this man who gave himself so wholeheartedly to his art that it wrecked his health.

When speaking of Nijinsky, Dad would invariably add

the melancholy fact that Nijinsky had gone insane. "Oh, he was mad, mad," he would exclaim. It seemed to amaze and trouble him, and as always whenever he speaks of insanity he would add, "Of course you know there's some insanity in our family, too."

With regard to himself I don't think my father gave much thought to the slender borderline that so many people believe lies between insanity and genius. So far as I know he never admitted to genius himself, though he liked to brag about being an egocentric. "They call me a genius," he would say, laughing. "I've never aspired to be one. I just make things as I see them and feel them."

Every time a ballet troupe came to town Dad would take in the performance, not once but several times. He knew the stories, the music and all the parts by heart. He usually visited the troupe backstage afterwards and always extended a cordial invitation to them to come to the house on the hill. The famous Ballet Russe de Monte Carlo and the equally famous Sadler's Wells troupe were guests at his home. Dad and the ballet dancers had a lot of fun together. Dad has never studied ballet, but he could mimic the dancers superbly.

"Oh, you did a wonderful arabesque there in the second act of *Swan Lake*," he would say to a ballerina, and he would immediately strike the pose. "You did this," he would go on. "Oh, it was lovely!" and he would pirouette gracefully. "Oh, that leap!" Dad himself would imitate the leap, but in exaggerated form. From then on it was burlesque every step of the way in a wilder and wilder tempo, until the ballet dancers would be in hysterics.

I wasn't there the afternoon that a visit from a ballet troupe almost ended in tragedy, but Dad told me about it, acting it out for me, of course. Around the circular driveway of his home, to the right as you approach the house, there is a parapet. The side that faces the driveway is about a foot high. But on the other side there is a ten-foot sheer drop down into the steep wooded slopes below.

231

It had been a pleasant afternoon, with drinks and dance demonstrations and joking all round. And now in a jocular mood everyone was on the driveway, where the dancers were telling Dad good-by and getting ready to go home. Suddenly Casimir Kokitch jumped up on the parapet without looking on the other side.

"This is how we do it," he announced, and stood there poised as gracefully as a bird. "Then the leap in the grand manner."

Before Dad could stop him he sprang lightly into the air and immediately disappeared from view.

Everyone crowded to the wall and looked over. There lay poor Casimir Kokitch limp and motionless, sprawled among the pine trees. He'd been conditioned for doing leaps, but obviously not for this ten-foot flight straight down to a steep slope.

Some of the women started screaming.

"Oh, my God," Dad cried, in his mind's eye seeing Casimir Kokitch with every bone in his body broken. He called for Frank to phone the doctor. Then they all made their way to the foot of the wall and gathered round the unconscious man, afraid to move him. The women were crying. The whole company was conjecturing about broken bones, broken back, broken neck, internal injuries, fractured skull—everything including the melancholy fact that Kokitch might at that very moment be dying.

"Damn it," Dad kept muttering. "Where's that doctor? Where is the blockhead? Why doesn't he come?"

In the middle of everything Casimir Kokitch suddenly opened his eyes, shook himself and got to his feet, looking around inquiringly. So far as anyone could see there wasn't much wrong with him. The liquor had so relaxed him that he had easily performed a feat he would never have dreamed of attempting intentionally.

The women who had been crying began to laugh, and then everyone joined in; Kokitch laughed too, though a little shamefacedly. They all trooped back to the driveway, and of course they had to have another round of drinks to celebrate. The doctor arrived in time to join in the toast.

Dad liked to tell that story as a good illustration of the difference between tragedy and comedy.

"If you kick a man in the rear, but not too hard, and he goes sprawling in a funny fashion but doesn't get hurt, it's funny," he used to tell me. "If you kick him too hard, it's tragic. It's only a matter of degree."

Dad himself has always managed carefully to keep his comedies balanced on the very borderline of tragedy. Jack Oakie likes to call the result "dramady."

"Your father," he told me, "has the talent for putting a tear in your throat and making you cough it up with a laugh."

29

In the spring and summer of 1940, Syd and I were entering a new phase of our teenage life. We were fourteen and fifteen years old and the first bashful feelings of love were giving way to a slightly more knowledgeable attitude. Movie romances with those long, passionate kisses between hero and heroine made us feel sadly deficient in the art. Eager to be as capable as the screen Romeos, we would sometimes grab Paulette and kiss her just for practice.

"Oh, that's a terrible kiss," Paulette would laugh, wiping off our clumsy attempts. And then addressing herself to Dad she would say, as always, "Charlie, your sons are getting more like you every day."

Perhaps we were getting more like Dad. In size we were actually outstripping him; we had both grown taller than he. Paulette, who long before had started calling Dad "Big Charlie" and me "Little Charlie," so that we wouldn't both come running at her summons, had to cast about for something more appropriate, and I became Charlie, Jr.

Syd and I weren't just growing in height. We were also becoming more astute—in money matters, for instance. Our allowance had been raised to a dollar a week, but it still wasn't enough. We had discovered, however, that Dad was an easy touch when he was in a jubilant, creative mood. By timing things right, Syd, who was bolder than I, was able to borrow the yacht from him several week ends. But usually what we needed was cash. We learned to ask for about twice as much as we expected to get.

We became aware, too, of how sensitive Dad was about one of his idiosyncrasies, his poor memory where names were concerned. He could never remember names, not even those of people whom he most admires. He labels people exclusively by their occupations. I recall the day he went to introduce me to Vladimir Horowitz and found himself stuck.

"Oh, ah, uh, this is my son, Charlie, Jr.," he said in a low, running monotone, so that you could not be sure what he was saying, "and this is uh-ah-yes, you remember him, Charles, the great pianist. My son here is very interested in classical music."

I was amused at how successfully he passed it off with pantomime. But he wasn't always able to cover up his failing so easily. I remember how one day he stayed in the Hollywood Brown Derby several hours because he was too embarrassed to pass Joe E. Brown, the comedian, whom he had greeted upon entering with "Hello, Harry." In his inimitable way he had confused Joe E.'s name with that of the producer Harry Joe Brown.

Dad was the same with telephone numbers, including his own, which he'd had for years. "Oh, let me give you my phone number . . . I . . ." he would say, and then turn to Paulette or Syd or me with "Now what is that number again?" He couldn't even remember his address, though he knew well enough how to get there.

Dad once explained his poor showing on numbers and names to me. He was a slow reader, he said, and had to work at memorizing anything. So he spent his time only on what he liked. He knew reams of Shakespeare.

By this time Syd and I were old enough to be included in the dinner parties Dad gave. There were very few big affairs at his house. Small, select gatherings were the usual order of things. When Dad was in the mood he would jump to his feet right in the middle of the meal and start pantomiming something. If other comedians were present you could count on a real ball, because all those hams would be trying to outdo one another.

After dinner the fun went on late into the night. Sometimes Dad would put on his Balinese records and dance for his guests. Sometimes he would do his side-splitting one-man imitation of a bull fight. At other times he would spend a whole evening acting out a story he had written, or dish up a real-life drama. One of his favorite subjects was still Dr. Reynolds. He liked to pantomime the time Dr. Reynolds put on a production of *Hamlet* in a local theater. Dr. Reynolds, playing the part of Hamlet, portrayed him as a dangerous paranoiac. Dad squirmed through the performance and afterwards had to go backstage and congratulate the doctor.

Dr. Reynolds, in his black tights, was standing in an affected pose, his legs crossed, his back to the door, a lighted cigarette in a long holder in one hand, waiting for Dad's accolades with a great show of indifference. Dad is an honest man when it comes to appraising an actor's work, even to his face. But Dr. Reynolds wasn't an actor. He was a friend who thought he could act. Dad says that getting any words out of his mouth at all was one of the most painful experiences of his life.

"Wellll. . ." he began, ". . . it was . . . you know . . . nice." Dr. Reynolds whirled around. "Was I that good?" he shot back. "Did you really like it that much?"

My father always got a howl when he did this scene.

Sometimes with the late Lenore Cotten, wife of the actor Joseph Cotten, at the piano, Dad would mimic various opera singers in their native tongues. Once after giving a beautiful rendition of a Russian opera, he shrugged off the astonished admiration of his friends with the explanation, "I can't sing. I'm only imitating Chaliapin singing well."

The songs Dad loved best were Irish ballads. (He has always been partial to the Irish and likes to brag that his father was part Irish.) Sitting cross-legged on the floor among his guests, he would sing those ballads in the manner of John McCormack, whom he admired and who was his friend.

My father's best audience at these song fests wasn't Irish, though, but Swedish. She was Greta Garbo. She would be sitting there with that grave, almost austere, look of loneliness which has become her trademark, holding a drink in her hand and twisting it around and around, but never drinking much. As she listened to Dad you could see her relax. Her withdrawn face would begin to sparkle, and before the evening was over she would be as giggling and gay as any schoolgirl. Presently she and the whole group would join Dad in singing.

So far as I know Dad never dated Garbo, either before or after his marriage to Paulette, but they were friends. My father admired her for her intellect as well as her beauty, and when he spoke of her there was always a note of deference in his voice. His conversations with her were usually about some creative aspect of motion picture making, the arts or ballet. Every now and then when they were talking, Dad would get expansive and come out with an idea for a picture he wanted to do with her. Unlike the people who took Dad's sudden enthusiasms seriously and then were angry or hurt when nothing came of them, Garbo accepted it all with a grain of salt. "I'd love to do a picture for you, Charlie," she would say. And then she would discuss the idea with him without expecting to hear anything more about it after that. It was like a little game between them.

30

Toward the end of the summer my father again entered that
final painful phase of picture making, the time of anxiety
when a producer tensely awaits the public's verdict on his efforts. Dad felt a special concern about *The Great Dictator*,
for it was different in kind from any of his other pictures.
Always with them he had hoped for two things, to make
people laugh and to make money. But with *The Great Dictator* there was something else involved: it had become imperative to him to get across his outcry against the hell of war
and the evils of oppression. For the first time I heard my
father speak seriously of prayer in connection with a picture.

"I'm praying, son, that this picture will have a good message and maybe help mankind a bit," he said to me suddenly

one day. But he wouldn't have been my father if he hadn't added in a humorous aside, "I'm also praying it will be a big hit, because I've spent a lot of money on it."

Dad was vague about who it was to whom he addressed his prayer. I never heard him speak of God as a personal power or conjecture about what comes after death. He never even mentioned death as far as I can recall. He wasn't one to adopt an organized religion, and he didn't care for ritualistic services, though he openly and ardently admired the architecture of churches and synagogues. He never forced his own beliefs on Syd and me, though occasionally he would speak of them to us.

"I'm not an atheist," I can remember his saying on more than one occasion. "I'm definitely an agnostic. Some scientists say that if the world were to stop revolving we'd all disintegrate. But the world keeps on going. Something must be holding us all in place—some Supreme Force. But what it is I couldn't tell you."

Dad's opinion of this Supreme Force varied with his moods. Sometimes, reading the headlines of the bloody battles raging in Europe, he would shake his head and say, "It must be Something very vicious that permits people to kill one another in this way."

Sometimes in the solitude of seashore or mountain he would speak of the Supreme Force almost tenderly, as of Something sublimely beautiful, mirroring itself so eloquently in rushing waves or snowdrifts, solemn rocks and ancient trees.

It was to this Something that he addressed his prayers for the success of *The Great Dictator*.

Dad and Paulette didn't go to New York together for the première. That should have looked strange to Syd and me if we had stopped to think about it. Paulette was in Mexico City, on her second trip there in recent months. On a similar visit in May with her mother she had struck up a friendship with Diego Rivera, the well-known Mexican painter. Paulette has

240

a penchant for meeting talented people. She was always bringing them up to the house for dinner.

Though she wasn't going with Dad, Paulette did plan to
fly to New York from Mexico City in time for the première.
Dad left Hollywood by train with Tim Durant. Whenever
possible Dad traveled by train rather than plane. He wasn't
completely relaxed in planes, especially after one rather hair-
raising experience when his plane came down out of the
clouds over New York City. "All of a sudden," he recalled
with a shudder, "I looked out of the window and I could see
the secretaries typing inside the Empire State Building. After
that I hated flying."

But whether Dad goes by plane or train or boat, there has
always been something melodramatic about his leave-takings.
He's one of those split-second travelers who arrive just in the
nick of time. He never had to bother about packing, because
Frank took care of this well ahead of time and then went
down to the station to check in the baggage. After that he
had to wait for Dad, whom Kay would drive down. I don't
know how many times good, faithful Frank was left pacing
back and forth in the station, looking at his watch, comparing
it with the station clock, checking his watch again, eying the
door through which he expected Dad. I know that each time
he wondered if the luggage would in the end go off without
him.

I don't know what always delayed Dad, except that it was
usually little things. He would run out of doors and look at
the weather. "Oh, I need my coat," he would cry, and rush
back for it and put it on. He would come out wearing it.
"No, I don't think I need it after all." And he would take it
back again.

He would rush around the house looking for various little
items, finding them, deciding he didn't need them and replac-
ing them. Toward the end of all this maneuvering Kay, who
had been striding along behind him wherever he went, would
start urging him to hurry. "Mr. Chapilaine, Mr. Chapilaine,

241

your train," he would say in anguished tones. And then he
would whip up his arm and look at his watch. "Mr. Chapilaine, you'll be late. Must hurry now."

At last Dad would pull out his own watch, fumble for his
glasses, put them on and look at the time for himself. An expression of consternation would cross his face. "Kay, why
didn't you warn me? It's getting late," he would moan.

Then everyone would dash for the car, and Kay, weaving
in and out of traffic, would make for the station with Dad sitting on the edge of the back seat, anxiously urging him on.

At the station everyone would jump out and run, with
Dad far in advance, scurrying along. Frank, perspiring by this
time, would rush forward to greet him, calling, "Hurry!
Hurry, Mr. Chaplin! Can't you see the train's leaving?"

So he would take Dad's arm and, urging and shoving him
along, would literally boost him onto the moving train. It
was exactly in that way that Dad and Tim finally got aboard
that October day for the New York opening of *The Great
Dictator*.

The première was a memorable affair, as were all the
premières of my father's pictures. There were crowds of fans
around the Astor and Capitol theaters, where it was being
shown simultaneously, and both houses were packed with
scintillating personalities both in and out of show business.
And of course there were the ever ready critics. As usual they
received Dad's picture with mixed reactions. They thought
the Little Tramp had exceeded himself, and had tackled something beyond his powers. They objected to the closing speech,
Dad's impassioned outcry for the oppressed of the world, as
being too long and rhetorical. Many people in show business
agreed with the critics. Perhaps Mary Pickford, who calls the
Little Tramp the Little Philosopher, best voices the sentiments
of this school of thought: "It is deplorable that he who gave
so much to the world turned his back on the tramp and entered politics by introducing such themes into his pictures.
When he did he lost me."

But the opinions of the critics and such professionals as Mary Pickford were not supported by those whom Dad has always regarded as his final judge and jury—the people. *The Great Dictator* was accepted with enthusiasm, first by United States audiences and later by those around the world.

"I've made more than a hundred pictures," Jack Oakie says, "but the only one they remember me by is *The Great Dictator*. Why, even on my last trip to Mexico the people greeted me at the plane with the Fascist salute."

My father had crossed the first hurdle with *The Great Dictator* in getting it to the screen. Nonetheless, he was eventually to feel that he paid dearly for making it. He was convinced that it was the cause of most of his subsequent troubles, claiming it antagonized certain powerful pro-Nazi propaganda groups in this country which then began working against him. I know that because of its controversial theme *The Great Dictator* was banned from many foreign markets at the time. German and Italian diplomats worked feverishly to have it barred in Latin America.

But during its revival in Europe in 1958 it played to crowded houses in England, France and Germany. When it was shown in Germany the critics hailed it as a "macabre masterpiece." Only the young could laugh at that picture, said the critics. The old wept as at remembered sins.

At the Capitol Theater opening Dad galvanized his audience with a piece of information which reporters had been trying for years to worm out of him and Paulette. At the close of the picture he appeared on the stage and made a short speech in which he introduced Paulette as "my wife." It was the first time Dad had ever publicly bestowed that title on her, and it sent the newsmen scurrying from the theater to phone in the story.

There was a lot of speculation then and later about why Dad chose this particular time, with his separation from Paulette so imminent, to make the announcement. There was, of course, the angle of the clubwomen who had been getting more and more vociferous about Paulette's status, until Dad was afraid it might hurt his box office. But Dad, though naturally strongly motivated by concern for the box office, usually has more than one reason for what he does, and I think he may have felt that this belated announcement might help to patch up his marriage.

After the première Dad remained in the East, ostensibly to open *The Great Dictator* in key cities, while Paulette returned to Hollywood to play hostess to H. G. Wells, who was on a lecture tour and would stay at Dad's house for two weeks. But Paulette didn't remain long at the house on the hill. Sometime in the early part of December she moved into the empty beach house of her agent, Myron Selznick.

It was Pancho who helped Paulette move. I guess we might consider him the first casualty of our close-knit family, because one day shortly before *The Great Dictator* opened he showed up at the house to announce with a proud grin that he was married. Dad and Paulette each gave him a gift of a check. As for Syd and me, now that Pancho was married, he was no longer in our class. He became Frank to us, and in five months the break was made complete when he left my father's employ and went into defense work. When in '46 he returned as a driver for Dad's studio, the old relationship was gone because Syd and I, too, were no longer children. All three of us had been through a war and had lived to talk about it—it was this kind of relationship between us from then on.

I think Paulette took the Bedlington terriers away with her at the time she moved to Selznick's beach house. She was attached to them and Dad was not. And she knew Syd and I would not be able to care for them much longer because it had been arranged for us to go to Lawrenceville, New Jersey, the following year to prep for Princeton. The departure of the Bedlington terriers, with which Syd and I had had so many years of fun, was another breach in our family circle.

Dad wasn't home when Paulette moved away, though he knew about it, because Alf Reeves kept him informed. But Syd and I remained in the dark. When Dad returned home from the East and we went up to see him on week ends again, we just didn't find Paulette around. Dad would explain to us that she was away on business, but that seemed strange, because she had never been absent so long before.

We wondered too why Paulette didn't go along with Dad when he went to President Roosevelt's inauguration in January of '41. My father, as an influential citizen of Hollywood, headed a delegation of actors who were to provide entertainment for the festivities.

It was the climax of a long association with President Roosevelt which had begun for Dad during the First World War. Dad has always maintained that President Roosevelt was the greatest president the United States has ever had. He even holds him above Lincoln, though in this particular he finds himself almost alone in Europe.

Dad has the same admiration for Mrs. Eleanor Roosevelt. "That woman is so homely she's beautiful," he used to remark. "It's the aura that surrounds her."

At a preinaugural concert on January 19, which Mrs. Roosevelt and other members of the President's family attended, my father highlighted the evening by delivering the final speech from *The Great Dictator*. The critics had called it rhetorical, but my father had meant every word of it. In the midst of his appeal for world freedom his voice broke and he had to ask for water. While he waited for Doug Fairbanks, Jr., to hand him the glass, the audience burst into applause that lasted for more than a minute. My father's appearance at that gathering, the heartfelt applause at his earnest words, might be called the pinnacle of his public success in this country. From then on the path led downward by subtle degrees until it ended in his self-imposed exile.

When Dad returned from the inaugural his mind was full of ideas for another picture. It was to be a story about immigrants in New York, he said, and he was going to give Paulette the leading role in it. This must be the picture that Dad developed years later in Europe as *The King in New York*. Like Charles Dickens' *Martin Chuzzlewit*, it became a bitter satire of the way he had been treated by his American cousins. But a lot of water was to flow under the bridge before that picture came to fruition.

While Dad was toying with the thought of doing the immigrant story he was also working on another idea. It seems that, as in the case of *The Great Dictator*, several ideas at a time war with one another in the arena of my father's mind, and it is only after a knockdown struggle that the strongest wins. This idea, which my father told Louella Parsons about that spring, was the story of a perennial drunk who comes across a little chorus girl who doesn't know he exists, but with whom, in his loneliness, he falls in love. Eventually the nucleus of this story was to be enlarged to *Limelight*, the last picture Dad made in America. The difference in the plot is that the chorus girl in *Limelight* does know the man exists and loves him for what he is, despite his being so much older than she. Perhaps it was Dad's happy marriage to Oona that twisted the plot around in this way.

There was a third idea which Dad had in mind at this time. It was the story of Monsieur Landru, the French Bluebeard. This picture was eventually to win over the other two, but it was not to see the screen for six years.

At the end of March, Dad went back East again, this time to testify as a character witness for Joseph M. Schenck in the suit the federal government was bringing against him on a charge of income-tax evasion.

My father stayed in the East a long while. At that time I believe he was more partial to the immigrant story than to either of the others and was thinking seriously of remaining in New York to do it. It is ironic to think that if he had he might have escaped the whole sequence of unhappy events that began that June when he met a girl by the name of Joan Barry.

By the time Dad returned to Hollywood the separation between him and Paulette was so complete that there was nothing to do but explain it to Syd and me.

"Well, your stepmother and I don't see eye to eye any more," Dad told us, "so we've separated."

Our father's announcement was a shock. Though we might have expected this kind of solution to domestic problems from our mother, whose last two marriages were well within our ken, we had never dreamed that it would happen to Paulette and Dad.

I tried to think back to see when the incompatibility had started, how it had manifested itself. There had been tears during the filming of *The Great Dictator*, but never any real quarrels that I could remember. I supposed there were arguments now and then in private because sometimes Paulette would come downstairs looking irritated.

"Your father's so stubborn," she might say, but no more. In the next minute she would be all gaiety again.

But that kind of thing was just the normal give and take of domesticity. I couldn't even recall seeing anything that might have passed for serious jealousy.

"You know, a lot of men were looking at you last night," Dad might say to Paulette the morning after a party.

"Well, the women weren't exactly overlooking you, Charlie," Paulette would respond.

Then they would kid back and forth about it. There had always been so much kidding between them, so much joking and laughter and fun around the place—in the main everyone had seemed happy and contented. Yet it had all suddenly blown up. How could you rely on stability in anything after this? Life began to take on an ephemeral look to my youthful eyes. Everything appeared to be fleeting; nothing endured for long, married happiness least of all. The house on the hill seemed sad, now that Paulette was not around with her gay spirits and her laughter.

"It's too bad Paulette isn't here," I'd say to Dad sometimes when we were enjoying something that once all four of us had had fun doing together.

"It's just one of those sad things, son," Dad would answer. "That's life for you."

It was almost the same answer he had given when explaining my changed birth dates to me. It was Dad's philosophy for all the vagaries of existence.

31

I'm sure it wasn't easy for my father, after a marriage of five years or so, suddenly to find himself alone again. When Paulette left, his moods of depression seemed to become more frequent, and sometimes when he got to philosophizing about human nature and the world, his disappointments and disillusionments, he would talk unhappily of the failures in his life. He didn't speak of his marriage, but I could guess this was one of the things that troubled him. He told me instead about how he had dreamed of being a concert violinist and had never carried the dream through. He even spoke of how his pictures had failed in one way or another. It was strange to hear him discussing his failures at the height of his success, but my heart went out to him, because I could see he was genuinely troubled and unhappy.

Syd's and my position with our father had changed once more. We were no longer just children to him. We had become companions. He depended on us a great deal during that period of his loneliness. I didn't realize then how much store my father set on the bond of our common blood. Kindred blood gives him a feeling of unity and solidarity. Because of it he had amply provided for his mother as soon as he began to earn his own way, had made places in Hollywood for his half brothers, Uncle Sydney and Uncle Wheeler, and had cared for Syd and me. It was on the alchemy of blood that he depended for our loyalty and love in return. I remember the day he revealed his feeling to us. That day has always meant a great deal to me.

He had been wrapped in the silence of his own thoughts and then suddenly there was a quick urge to speak. He turned to us. "Sometimes," he said, "I think you two, you, Charles and Sydney, are the only ones in the whole world who have ever really loved me."

Just that one sentence, but it revealed to us both the depth of his inward loneliness and his dependence on us.

Now that Dad was in effect a bachelor, he was free to take out other girls. Yet he went about it discreetly, for the last thing he wished was to attract unfavorable publicity. Syd and I often acted as his chaperones whenever he appeared in public with a date.

I remember I was the chaperone on his first date with Carole Landis. I had a crush on Carole at the time, though she was about twenty-two and I was just sixteen, so I jumped at Dad's invitation to have dinner with them. But there was a string attached.

"I'm going to take Carole to a little party afterwards where we'll be with intimate friends," Dad said. "So after dinner you just tell her you're very tired and have to go to bed early."

"Fine," I said. "Oh, just fine, Dad."

So I dressed myself up in my best dark suit, put a tie on and brushed and curried my hair as though for a grand reception. With Kay at the wheel we drove over to Carole's place. I'll never forget how she appeared that night, limned in the light as Dad escorted her to the limousine. She wore a black dress that followed the lines of her fabulous figure, and her blond hair was swinging at her shoulders. Seeing her I could understand why that year they had given her the title of Miss Ping. They were always hanging a title of some kind on Carole. My own heart began to *ping* as she climbed in beside me.

"Oh, this is your son," Carole said, turning to me as she sat down. "Nice-looking, Charlie."

There she was right beside me, blond and laughing, and I was so bashful I couldn't get a word out. I just sat there like a goofy kid trying to keep my big crush from showing. But warm-hearted Carole saw it and her eyes were dancing, while Dad on the other side wore a broad smile.

All through the meal I couldn't take my eyes off Carole. I hung on every word she said and I hardly heard Dad when, over coffee, he threw me the clue.

"Well, son, we're going to . . ." He had to say it twice before I woke up.

"Oh, Dad, that's right," I said, almost choking on my words. "I have to get up early in the morning for the beach. Do you mind if I go home now?"

Dad went out with Carole occasionally for a couple of months, but I saw her only once more. After a party he brought her by the house with another couple for a nightcap before taking her home. They put on some tango records and danced awhile and finally I found the courage to cut in.

"May I have a dance with you?" I asked her.

Carole laughed and danced with me good-naturedly while my head spun like a top. I kept thinking of how nice it would be to have a date with her, to take her to the movies and then out for a soda or something, but I never dreamed of asking her. After all, she was Dad's girl. I told my father how I felt only after I noticed he had stopped dating her. Dad was amused.

"Had I known it, Carole would have loved a date with you," he said.

But it was too late then. It was almost time for me to go East to school. That was a cruel wrench. "To heck with it, with people like Carole around," I told myself. But Dad wanted me to finish my education, and I wanted to please him. So I tore myself away from my daydreams and I never saw Carole again.

It was a shock to all of us when she committed suicide in 1948, seven years after my father had dated her and I had been so struck with her warm heart and her charms.

Another girl my father dated at the time of his separation from Paulette was Hedy Lamarr. I still thought she was beautiful, though this was after I'd lost my heart to Carole Landis. Dad has always been a connoisseur of women's charms, and not just those of the women he went out with. He liked to pick out the best features of each for comment. He preferred long hair to short and I think brunettes to blondes. He commented on my mother's vivacious brunette beauty, the vibrant way she carried herself. He spoke of Carole Landis' wonderful figure and of Hedy Lamarr's face—a Madonna-like face, he said, that in repose could capture the heart of any man in the world. But he thought the serene quality was marred when Hedy smiled, and was of the opinion that she should never do so. He admired the ethereal, exotic beauty of Merle Oberon, who, with her husband, the late Alexander Korda, used to visit us often. But it was Garbo's spirit, shining through the envelope of flesh, that most attracted him to that lovely actress.

Yet it wasn't girls that occupied the most important place in my father's life after Paulette left. It was tennis. It was the only sport into which he flung himself with wholehearted abandon, though he was also a fine swimmer and he liked to tell us of how he had placed in the marathon foot races in England when he was young. Football he abhorred and he cautioned us against playing it; he was sure we'd get our collarbones or our skulls fractured. He didn't like boxing, either.

I ignored Dad's opinion about boxing when I entered the army and found that because my father was Charlie Chaplin I had to prove myself doubly. It was in an army boxing ring in France, fighting a losing battle with a near-professional much heavier than I, that I suffered a cracked nose and won the right to be respected as an individual.

When I came back Dad noticed my nose at once and was distressed. He had always insisted that tennis was the proper game for Syd and me to play. But I never took him up on it, no matter how much he urged. I'm the type who's embarrassed to miss the ball, which you do more often than not when you're a beginner. Perhaps, too, I really didn't want to be in competition with Dad—not with his girls or his tennis. Syd was of braver stuff. Though he felt the same way I did about Dad's girls, he accepted his challenge on tennis and started learning to play it.

I remember those pitiful beginnings when Syd practiced with Dad and Dad shut him out so easily each time—six-love, six-love. Syd never got a game, though Dad could have thrown him one now and then to keep him from losing morale. But Dad said catering to a person's sensitivity like that wouldn't make him a good tennis player.

Take a boy like Sydney. He really didn't need any buildup of morale to keep him going on anything. He never gave in, once he made up his mind to something. I remember how, when bowling took hold of him, Mother couldn't get him away from the bowling alleys no matter how hard she tried. He spent day and night there—and all his allowance—and went around with circles under his eyes while the obsession lasted.

So it was with Sydney and tennis. He kept practicing and practicing. I think Dad helped him along by buying tennis lessons for him from Bill Tilden. In addition, Syd spent his own money on instruction away from the house, where it wasn't so embarrassing to miss a ball now and then. Finally he began to take a game or two away from Dad. But that still wasn't enough for Syd. He spent several years practicing and then one day he gave Dad such a beating that Dad treated him with real respect from then on.

Beating Dad was a formidable accomplishment. Out here on the Coast, where most of the best tennis players live, Dad was always in the top bracket. Back East the social set considered him practically a champion. He should have been. He went to every tennis match at the club in Beverly Hills and knew the good players. He had all the professionals up at his house. Helen Wills, Pauline Betz, Bill Tilden, Fred Perry and Don Budge were frequent and welcome visitors there. Dad played them all and picked up pointers from them. Of course he couldn't take a game from a pro like Bill Tilden unless Tilden wasn't in form or, as he sometimes did, let Dad have a game. Dad used to brag about that but in a joking way, because he knew what Tilden was doing.

Like many tennis players, Dad seemed to attach an almost mystic power to the racket he used. I remember the week end he bought a new one. It was an expensive but not an extraordinary racket, but when he won the first game he was sure there was something special about it. When he won the second game the racket became almost sacred to him. From then on he played all his games with that one racket, and for the longest stretch he was invincible. Then one day he picked up the racket and started to play. The game hadn't gone far before a puzzled frown came over his face.

"I don't think this is my racket," he said suddenly.

Both Tim and Frank assured him it was and he went on playing the game, and lost. He played two more games and lost them too. So far as he was concerned that was genuine proof.

"This just isn't my racket," he insisted. "Somebody must have gone off with mine and left this one."

On this theory he sent Frank all over town to ask the various guests who had been at his place the Sunday before if they had taken the racket by mistake. Frank, of course, returned from that fanciful quest empty-handed, but Dad still refused to be convinced.

"Somebody must have stolen my good racket," he mourned. "I'll never find another like it." You would have thought he had lost a dear friend.

As time went by, the circle of tennis players who came up to the house widened. Presently the quiet Sunday afternoon tea and crumpets routine which Syd and I had known as children became a gala weekly open house, where you could meet such Hollywood luminaries as Katharine Hepburn, Greta Garbo, Ronald Colman, Gary Cooper, John Garfield, Errol Flynn, David Niven and John McCormack. The list was endless.

Presently those who couldn't play tennis began to come just to be seen at Dad's house. People fought for invitations, knowns and unknowns came as guests of guests. They were all welcome, especially if they could play tennis. Syd and I brought our young friends, and there was always a bevy of beautiful girls around, most of whom had come with the hope that Charlie Chaplin would notice them and put them in one of his pictures. Wasn't he the man who preferred to create his female leads out of youthful unknowns?

The guests gathered on the courts at the foot of the terraced lawn. They engaged in cut-in matches or sat around talking in the adjacent tennis house or watched the games from its balcony. For those who didn't play tennis there was the nearby swimming pool, but tennis was always the center of attraction on these days.

Tea was served in a magnificent silver teapot. There was coffee, too, and sandwiches—white chicken and turkey meat between slices of trimmed white bread. The sandwiches were stacked in tiers on a huge platter three feet in diameter. Most of the people ate as though they hadn't seen food in weeks— Dad ate right along with them—and the platter had to be replenished from time to time. But no matter how many guests were present or how much they ate, the supply never seemed to run out. There were also crumpets, always George's delicious crumpets.

While the matches were going on, Dad would concentrate everything on tennis, but afterwards he would hold court in the little tennis house. Then there would be lively discussions on all sorts of subjects, joking, storytelling—as was always the case with Dad around. When finally the gathering broke up, people went away feeling that it had been a great experience, a privilege, to have spent an afternoon with Charlie Chaplin.

It was at a Sunday open house that summer that Dad met Joan Berry, who had taken the stage name of Joan Barry. She had come up from Mexico City with a letter of introduction to Tim Durant from the late A. C. Blumenthal, who had become acquainted with her down there. She went with the letter to Tim Durant's house, where she met Tim and his mother, who were both favorably impressed with her. She was pretty, with a demure freckled Irish face and beautiful red hair. To Tim she resembled a respectable Brooklyn stenographer—she came from that section of the country. She was attractive and quiet and apparently cultured. He invited her to Dad's open house any Sunday she chose to come. It was an easy way to pay off a Hollywood friend, Mr. Blumenthal.

So Joan Barry and her mother, Mrs. Gertrude Berry, came up one Sunday afternoon and my father welcomed them with the same graciousness he showed to all his visitors.

32

That fall of 1941, Syd and I set off for Lawrenceville, fully determined to make a go of our new school and to acquire such learning as would make our father proud of us. It was the first time we had been so far away from our family and we were very homesick. We might have become used to the separation in time, but December 7 Pearl Harbor was bombed and our country entered the war. Draft boards began signing recruits up by the thousands. Syd and I and millions of other boys in our age bracket knew it wouldn't be long before we, too, would be in the army. That realization made any planning for the future, any concern to get an education, look like a foolish waste of time.

Because of the war we lost three more members of our

household, Frank, Kay and George, Dad's faithful Japanese servants and the fond companions of our childhood. All three were ordered by the government to leave for the internment camp at Manzanar. Dad was deeply depressed, but of course there was nothing he could do about it. Frank, who had come from Hawaii, and George and Kay, together with a lot of other Japanese, had to sell as many of their belongings as they could and throw away the rest. Taking only a couple of suit-cases with them, they and their families boarded the bus for Manzanar, leaving behind a great emptiness in the house on the hill.

Dad never wrote to Frank, but he didn't forget him either. Every month during his stay at Manzanar, Frank received a pension check. And even now that Dad is in Vevey he still remembers Frank with a check at Christmas.

When Syd and I came back from school that summer of '42, we found English servants in our old home. They were capable but aloof, and Syd and I could never get used to them after the friendly folksy Japanese, with whom we had grown up and who had seemed like part of our family. Dad missed the Japanese, too—their lightning-quick efficiency and the in-tuitive care with which Frank had spoiled him. "They're pretty good," he would say sometimes of the English. "Only they're so *slow*. It takes hours now just to serve me a little cake."

That summer Paulette sealed her separation from our father with a divorce in Mexico. She received the decree *in absentia* from Judge Javier Rosas Seballos of the Mexican Civil Court at Juárez. It was he who disclosed not only the divorce but the year and place of the wedding, which Dad and Paulette had so assiduously kept from the press. It was in 1936 in Canton, China, just as Dad had told us. Paulette's charges were incompatibility and separation for more than a year.

That divorce marked *finis* to a relationship that had meant much to Syd and me throughout our childhood. But Paulette's departure wasn't really the end between us. Everything remained on the friendliest terms. Syd and I always considered her part of the family. We still do.

Dad continued to see her now and then. And when she was in town and he was too busy for us, she would invite Syd and me over for a dinner or a movie or a little party at her place. Even after I was out of the army and in New York doing the play, *Now I Lay Me Down to Sleep*, with Fredric March and Florence Eldridge, I got a call from Paulette one day. She had married Burgess Meredith in May of 1944 and divorced him in Mexico in June of 1949. Now she was an unattached bachelor girl again.

"I've been dating a rear admiral and he's very dull," she said. "Why don't you take me out, Charlie?"

"I'd love to, Paulette," I told her, "but you know how actors are—broke."

"Oh, don't worry about that," she laughed. "You know your ex has a little money stashed away, especially having been married to your father."

Paulette enjoyed joking about the settlement Dad made on her. "I think your father lost a lot when he married me," she used to say. "I even got the yacht."

I was never told how much Dad gave Paulette, but gossip said it was around a million. When Paulette joked about the settlement she never failed to add, "Your father is a wonderful man, and you must treat him as such."

Dad always praised Paulette, too, and he also liked to joke about the settlement. "Your ex is a very lovely gal—and a shrewd one," he would say. "She took me for a little bit."

I had the feeling that though Dad was joking, it was joking on the level. He often warned Syd and me to be cautious of the female sex. No matter how nice they are, he used to tell us, they will still sometimes try to get what they can. Syd and I had reached the age where Dad was beginning to worry about us and our dating. We had become old hands at it now and were bringing our girl friends up to the house to go swimming or strolling through his wooded estate.

That summer of '42 I met Joan Barry. It was up at the house in the glassed-in study which was always so bright and cheerful. She was wearing a dark dress and her hair, very red, hung like a cloud about her shoulders. She had a nice figure, a cute, sweet face. She looked between twenty-one and twenty-five.

"Oh, this is Joan Barry, son," Dad said as I came in. "She'll be the lead in my next picture, *Shadow and Substance*."

He was really enthusiastic over Miss Barry. He sometimes talked to Syd and me about her potentialities.

"She has a quality, an ethereal something that's truly marvelous," he said. "A talent as great as any I've seen in my whole life. If it could be channeled I could make the most wonderful picture with her."

Dad was sincere in his desire to make a great actress of Miss Barry. This fact was often lost sight of in all the ballyhoo of the subsequent trials, in which the prosecuting attorneys tried to picture him as a ruthless philanderer. My father's artistic integrity has always been the foremost thing in his life, as those who have worked with him will testify. No girl ever got into any of his pictures by way of a boudoir promise. She had to have real potentialities before he would invest time and money in her.

When he met Joan Barry he was convinced she was right for the lead in the play, *Shadow and Substance*, which is the story of a young Irish girl of simple faith and a cynical canon. Dad had already paid twenty thousand dollars for the movie rights to the play. Now he put Miss Barry under contract, first at seventy-five and then at a hundred dollars a week. He sent her for three months to Max Reinhardt's drama school, had her wardrobe designed and prepared for the picture, and paid for extensive dental work. He had thrown himself into writing the screenplay and was working on it that summer with all the intensity of his nature.

At the same time he was coaching Miss Barry. He would do bits out of Shakespeare with her for guests, and everyone commented on her exceptional ability. But this was only drawing-room acting. Real acting isn't glamorous, as so many people assume. It takes long hours of grueling work to bring what looks like a spontaneous performance to the stage. Though Miss Barry had many fine qualities, she lacked other qualities just as vital. She didn't have the discipline or the wholehearted devotion to the theater which is a prerequisite for a good actor. Much less did she have the hardihood to stand up under my father's persistent demand for perfection. She was undependable, sometimes coming late to rehearsals, sometimes not even showing up. Sometimes she would be brilliant. This would be followed by periods when she refused or was unable to concentrate on her work.

Almost from the first Tim Durant and other close friends urged my father to drop Miss Barry, whom they recognized as a very emotionally disturbed person. But Dad felt he could help her by forwarding her career. Finally, however, even he began to realize that despite the appealing, really lovely qualities he saw in her, she couldn't become an actress. Actually she was a tragic figure from the start.

But none of the unfortunate events that were to take place as a result of my father's association with Joan Barry had yet occurred that summer. I spent an evening with her once at Dad's request. He was busy working on *Shadow and Substance* and as usual when the mood was with him, didn't want to be interrupted. So he asked Nana and me to escort Miss Barry to the Hollywood Bowl concert that night. My grandmother found her as charming as Tim Durant's mother had— a very friendly person who could talk about nothing but the opportunity Dad was giving her, an unknown, to be the lead in one of his pictures.

It didn't seem to me at the time that there was any profound attachment between Dad and Miss Barry. She was just his protégée. I supposed, of course, that he dated her now and then. But she was dating others, too. Even at the time Nana and I went up to her apartment to call for her there was a gentleman visiting her.

That was how things stood when I went back to Lawrenceville in the fall. Syd didn't go with me. He had had enough of regimentation and boys' schools, and had decided to go to North Hollywood High that year. I was sticking it out to please Dad, though almost as soon as I got back there I began to wish I had followed Syd's example. I felt more lonely than ever, more isolated. And I was plagued by the thought that life was passing me up and that soon the army and a European battlefront would claim me.

I was delighted when, that October, my father came East to make a speech. He obtained permission from the school for me to come in to see him, and I went at once.

This speech was one of several my father made for a second front at the beginning of the war. I believe his first was in San Francisco's Cow Palace, where he spoke for the benefit of Russian war relief. He was substituting for Ambassador Joseph E. Davies, whom President Roosevelt had asked to speak but who had become too ill to do so. As usual, my father prepared his speech with a great deal of care and anxiety. But just before he was supposed to go on, he was attacked by his usual state of nerves and had to hurry backstage and throw up. In the confusion he lost his notes, and he had to face about eight thousand people with an impromptu speech. He talked for an hour and a half, holding his audience so spellbound you could have heard a pin drop. It was then that he came out for a second front.

The second front speech in New York was made under the auspices of the Artists Front to Win the War, which, I understand, was considered a pink organization. Whether it was or not, Dad himself was never a Communist. He did sincerely admire Russia for her stand against Germany and felt not only that she should have help, but that a second front would win the war more quickly for us all. As usual, his enthusiasm ran away with him, so that some of the English began to complain he might have been a little more appreciative of the war efforts of his own homeland, while Americans thought his gratuitous advice a breach of etiquette, since he wasn't a United States citizen. Still others felt he was being presumptuous in trying to tell the military how to run things. On the other hand, there were a lot of people who agreed with him. It was only much later that the second front speeches were resurrected and, taken out of context of their times, when Russia was our ally, held as proof positive that my father was a Communist or fellow traveler.

When I arrived at the Waldorf Towers I found my father in his suite pacing back and forth with his glasses on, muttering phrases to himself as he worked on his speech. He was nervous and sick again, as usual before a public appearance. Every now and then he would have to hurry to the bathroom. I felt sorry for him.

I couldn't stay for the speech, since I had to get back to the school by curfew time. I was disappointed about that. I think I was more unhappy about not being able to stick around and enjoy New York with Dad and Tim and Paulette, who was also in town. I thought enviously of all the fun they would be having while I was tucked away in school.

Actually, Dad didn't have as much fun as I was imagining. That visit to New York became another link in the long chain of events that seemed to bind him to a peculiar nemesis at this period of his life. Miss Barry was the motivating force.

I remember how my father used to speculate on the tragedy of happenstance in life. A person takes a wrong turn or makes some minor move, innocuous in itself, and because of it he has to live the rest of his life with the unfortunate results of that irrevocable moment. After the Joan Barry case started unraveling, I thought sometimes that something of the sort had happened to my father. Only the move he made was one of kindness.

Shortly after I had gone away to school, Dad decided to shelve *Shadow and Substance*. He had already spent more than five hundred thousand dollars on the picture, but he felt that, because of Miss Barry's unpredictability, he could not afford to launch a two- or three-million-dollar project with her as the star. At the same time Miss Barry, too, came to the conclusion that she was not suited for the life of an actress and told my father that she would like to terminate her contract and go back East if he would pay her fare. After some importuning on Miss Barry's part Dad had agreed. Through the studio he arranged to buy two one-way train fares for Miss Barry and her mother and also settled some five hundred dollars' worth of debts for her so that she could leave town unencumbered.

Miss Barry, with her mother, had gone East two weeks before Dad left to make his second front speech. My father supposed she was now out of his life forever. She was certainly the last person he wished to have contact with in New York, and he was upset when she got in touch with him at the Waldorf Towers. She kept calling him up, but my father steadfastly refused to talk to her until she told him she was on the twentieth floor and would throw herself out the window if he wouldn't see her. This suicide threat was the first of several which Miss Barry made in the following months.

When my father saw Miss Barry she told him she was destitute and he gave her three hundred dollars to tide her over. Miss Barry used the three hundred dollars to return to Hollywood instead. This was the basis for the Mann Act charge which was brought against my father, forcing him and the government to go through a trial that had all the attributes of a three-ring circus—though it didn't look like a circus to Dad at the time, because he was faced with a prison term if the judgment went against him.

Of course I didn't know anything about it at the time. The first inkling my brother and I had that anything was wrong was during the Christmas season, when I was at home for the holidays. It was December 23. Syd and I, who were staying at Dad's house, had been out with a bunch of the fellows. We returned home about two in the morning, coming around by the terraced lawn as we usually did to let ourselves in the back way. When we reached the study we stopped short, seeing that something was seriously amiss.

A ladder was propped against the wall with its upper rungs leaning on the window sill of Dad's room. A purse, a pair of women's shoes and a pair of silk stockings lay on the grass at the foot of the ladder. Then we saw that the glass of the study door had been shattered around the handle and the door stood ajar. The curtains were flapping to and fro in the breeze.

Syd and I stood there a minute looking wordlessly at each other. I was remembering the pistol in the drawer of my father's night stand, Dad's quiet feet moving through the house in search of prowlers. He had often explained to Syd and me that if you were famous you became the target for all kinds of crackpots.

"Dad's in trouble, real trouble," we thought.

We went in through the door and started quietly investigating, passing from the study into the living room with its Oriental cabinet that held the samurai swords which had provided me with such comfort in my childhood. We went on into the hall, past the dining room, where Dr. Reynolds' cadaver had once held a reign of terror in my childish imagination. There was something else about now, something ominous. You could breathe it in the quiet of the house. Why was everything so still?

We reached the stairway. There were lights above, but the same silence. Now we were filled with genuine alarm, not knowing what we would find up there. We were just going to investigate when suddenly Dad, whose quick ear had caught the sound of our footsteps, appeared in the upper hall. Leaning over the balustrade, he looked down at us. He had a bow tie on, a shirt, trousers and a smoking jacket. It was his favorite attire for a comfortable cocktail party at the house.

"What are you doing here?" he asked us sharply, as though his mind were not focused on us and he had not recognized us. Then he caught himself.

"Oh, that's right, you live here. I didn't mean to . . ." He never wanted us to feel unwelcome at the house on the hill. "I'm very nervous, boys. I've got an important . . . Go to bed. Lock your door. I'll tell you about it in the morning."

Dad's manner told us he was in danger. We were worried about him and wanted to help, but we didn't know exactly what to do. Everything was so mysterious.

"What's the matter, Dad?" I ventured to inquire.

He shook his head brusquely. "Don't ask questions," he said. "Go to bed. I'll tell you in the morning."

Syd and I hardly slept that night. We lay there whispering to each other, listening for sounds in the hall, wondering, anxious. Early the next morning Dad knocked on our door.

"Come on downstairs, boys," he told us.

Syd and I came out and followed him silently down. Dad didn't speak again till we reached the living room.

"Well, I got the gun away from her," he said abruptly then, starting in the middle of his narrative.

"Gun?" we asked, shocked. "What do you mean, gun, Dad?"

"From Joan," he told us.

"Oh, Miss Barry," I said, remembering. "But what's wrong, Dad?"

"Well, she said she would kill herself," Dad went on in his strange, preoccupied way that made him tell the story in disjointed sentences. He was still very nervous. "Kill herself here and I'd be blamed for it. I have the gun."

He showed the gun to us. It was a small lady's gun which, we learned from later newspaper accounts, she had purchased at the Hollywood Gun Shop before going up to Dad's place. "It took me hours and hours to talk her out of doing it," Dad went on.

He looked sad. "She's in love with me," he said, "and I'm not in love with her. And I can't help it. Would you boys go across the street and visit with your friends today?"

Dad didn't tell us that Miss Barry was still in the house, but we could guess she was and that he wanted to get us out for fear we might be witnesses to another hysterical scene. We obeyed him without a word and went across the street to visit the Krisel brothers. We didn't come home until evening. The house was very quiet then. Dad was there. He looked unhappy, still shaken and nervous. But Miss Barry was gone and Syd and I never saw her again.

My father didn't say anything more about the incident, and of course Syd and I didn't bring it up. But during the next months we noticed that a change had come over him. He was often sad, often preoccupied. Syd and I thought he was disturbed because he was unable to reciprocate Miss Barry's love. We did not know until later testimony brought it out that the gun episode was only one of a series of harassments to which Miss Barry subjected him after she returned to Hollywood from New York. (He was to testify in court that she smashed in the windows of his home on four different occasions and that he had to have the locks on his house changed four times because she was always breaking in.) It was a problem for which he could find no solution, especially as he also felt sorry for Miss Barry, who, he fully recognized by this time, was a truly disturbed person. She kept doing erratic things such as bathing in his sprinklers fully clothed and driving so fast around his circular driveway that the car almost careened over. And there were spells when her speech was so incoherent she could not be understood. As I've said before, suffering, when it manifests itself in outward symptoms, affects my father, and he was affected in this way by Miss Barry.

33

It was only six months until I would be eighteen and I knew it wouldn't be long after that before I would be called for the draft. I had so short a while as a civilian that I didn't want to waste any more of it away from home in a boys' school, no matter how proud it made my father. Syd gave such glowing accounts of his experiences at North Hollwood High that I decided to stay home and go there too.

I wasn't in the new school long before I realized the change of atmosphere from the old days. It was the war and our country's being in it that was responsible, especially where Dad was concerned. Never before had his British citizenship been a matter for discussion among our school friends. Now some of them began to ask us about it rather pointedly.

What could we answer? We were young boys expecting to be called in to do our bit before it was over, and the way the question was put made us feel that because our father wasn't a citizen we, his sons, weren't one hundred percent Americans. We found the temerity to take the matter up with him during our visits at his home. It was the only subject we ever argued over.

Dad gave us his customary rebuttal, which didn't seem to carry much weight when we repeated it to our insistent friends.

"I consider myself a citizen of the world, an internationalist," he told us. "I just happen to have been born in London, England. It could have been Burma or China or Timbuktu, I'd still be the way I am. I'd keep my first citizenship because, being an accident of birth, it wouldn't have any real significance. But wherever I live I'll conform to the rules, laws and regulations of that country."

This was a basic conviction with my father. But later I came to realize that his refusal to take out citizenship papers was motivated by something more than mere conviction. To close friends who also were importuning him to become an American he had a different answer.

"If you, as an American, were living in England earning your living there, even if you had lived there for years, would you care to renounce your United States citizenship?" he would ask. And when they remained silent he would add, "Well, that's how I feel about England."

My father had still another reason for not becoming a United States citizen. He confessed to friends that he had a horror of taking the examination and, because of his faulty memory for dates, flunking it. He knew that the event would be splashed across the pages of all the papers. The very thought of it made him cringe.

Now that we were older, Syd and I popped in on him whenever we chose. Or rather Syd did so. I was still as awed by my father as ever, and as reticent about disturbing him at his work. So I always phoned first to ask him if I might come up. The English servants, unused to my idiosyncrasy in this matter, seemed each time to be taken by surprise.

It was a strange thing about my father and me. I loved him and wanted to be close to him, yet whenever I was with him alone I had the feeling, which had been carried over from my childhood, that I should be on my guard. I began to have another feeling, too, that Dad was studying me carefully, as though trying to figure me out. Why all this awe, this lingering formality? his eyes seemed to be asking. But one day I learned there was another reason for his quizzical appraisal.

"You know," he suddenly exclaimed in astonishment, "I can see a lot of me in you. My God, you *are* like me, your gestures . . . everything."

Much I must have inherited from him. Perhaps as much I had picked up from him, from the long, close association of my childhood when, following him around, I had wanted more than anything else to be like him. And now his words marked the fruition of that dream. I felt it was the greatest compliment I had ever received.

However, that winter and spring of '43 my father had more to occupy his mind than a study of his sons. Two skeins, one bright, one dark, were being woven into his life. The dark one was Miss Barry, whom I had met the summer before and who had been an unseen but disturbing visitor at our home the December just past. The bright one I was now about to meet.

Oona O'Neill! Her name sounds like a spring breeze—as ethereal, as lovely as the girl herself. She is the daughter of the famous playwright Eugene O'Neill, and she is exactly my age, even to the month—the month of May. The previous spring she had been café society's Debutante Number One in the Stork Club. She had taken her Vassar entrance examinations but had decided against college because she was interested in a screen career. So she had come out to Hollywood instead, where her mother and stepfather were living, and had met Dad some time that November.

Minna Wallis, a good friend of Tim Durant's, was giving a dinner party, a foursome to which she was inviting my father and Tim. She thought it would be nice to include Oona, because Tim Durant's father had been a good friend of Eugene O'Neill's. Tim himself had been somewhat acquainted with the playwright and was interested in meeting his daughter. It looked as though it would be an interesting evening all around, because in his earlier days Eugene O'Neill had expressed great admiration for my father and his comedies, and my father was as great an admirer of Eugene O'Neill and his tragedies. So Oona and Dad met and that was the beginning of everything.

I first saw Oona at one of Dad's open-house teas. She had come up with Tim Durant and Tim's young daughter, Marjorie, to play tennis. Neither Syd nor I linked Oona's name with that of the great playwright. We just saw her as a pretty girl who was completely different from the ordinary run of Hollywood glamor. She was always herself—quiet, quick to be amused but never ostentatious, with an almost elfin quality about her that appealed to us immensely. She was very attractive in an offbeat way—her slender, long-stemmed figure, the way she wore her straight black hair, the brooding look in her dark eyes that could so quickly sparkle with an inward humor. She was shy and yet there was a calm about her, a native sweetness that drew Syd and me to her. We thought it would be nice to know her better.

Oona didn't play tennis, at least not well. I didn't play at all, and though Sydney could play a good game, he was more interested in Oona than tennis. She was friendly but shy. When we joked with her she would reply with the bashful good humor of a child. But just when she seemed most naïve, she would catch us off guard with a quick pertinent remark that would make us realize, almost ruefully, how intelligent, even deep she was, how much more mature in many ways than we were.

During those first weeks Syd and I engaged in a friendly unspoken rivalry to see which one of us would be the first to get a date with Oona. After several weeks we compared notes.

"You have eyes for Oona, I see it," Syd said to me jokingly.

"You do too, Syd," I countered.

"It won't do us any good, Chuck," Syd said, "because Oona has eyes for Dad. We might as well lay off."

That was true, and it was so obvious that there was no use hiding from the fact any longer. Whenever Oona was with our father a rapt expression would come into her eyes. She would sit quietly, hanging on his every word. Most women are charmed by Dad, but in Oona's case it was different. She worshiped him, drinking in every word he spoke, whether it was about his latest script, the weather or some bit of philosophy. She seldom spoke, but every now and then she would come up with one of those penetrating remarks that impressed even our father with her insight.

"Oh, a lovely girl," he would say. He would commit himself no further in words, but that was unnecessary. The expression on his face told us plainly that he was as fascinated by Oona as she was by him.

During the next months Oona and her mother were frequent visitors at my father's home, where he had begun giving Oona dramatic lessons to help her fulfill her dream of being an actress. Oona wasn't getting any encouragement along this line from her father, who was at the time living near San Francisco. According to all accounts, he had almost completely alienated himself from her because of her interest in the stage. But even before that he couldn't have been very close to her or seen much of her, for he had separated from her mother when Oona was only two.

It was far more, however, than a teacher-pupil relationship

between Dad and Oona. Presently he began going out with her openly and the gossip columns started speculating on whether it would end in a fourth marriage for him.

Then things began to break. In the early part of June, Joan Barry gave a statement to the press saying that she was expecting a child and that it was my father's. My father responded with a counterstatement that he was not responsible for Miss Barry's condition, that she had first approached him in May with her accusation, together with a demand for a settlement, and that he had promptly rejected it.

Tim Durant, who acted as middleman in the case, told me that her offer to settle was bona fide, that the lawyer who came to him with the terms was a prominent and honest attorney. Tim, who could see from the start all the consequences of a public airing, had entreated my father to make a settlement.

"Even if you win you're going to lose," he said. "You're a famous man, so it will be spread all over. And you've got a duty to more than yourself—your two boys, if nothing else. Don't get mixed up in it."

But my father wouldn't hear of compromise.

"No, I'm in the right," he said. "If I settle now they'll come back for more. I'll be hounded the rest of my life. I am not the father of the child. If it had my blood in its veins you know I would take care of it."

I'm sure my father was sincere about this, simply because blood ties have always been so important to him. I don't believe, either, that money was the prime reason for his rejection of the settlement offer. I know he has a reputation for being close with a dollar, but even then he must have realized that the costs of a legal battle, if it came to that, would amount to far more than an out-of-court settlement. He was only indignant because he was innocent. It was all part of the strain of stubborn integrity which runs through him and which is such an admirable and exasperating characteristic.

273

After Joan Barry's accusation it was just as Tim Durant had warned. The papers had a Roman holiday with the story. Joan Barry's visit to my father with her gun on the twenty-third of December was thoroughly aired, and I learned from the papers of his second ill-advised charitable act to her. The previous January Miss Barry had been discovered by the police wandering along Olympic Boulevard in a man's bathrobe and a pair of slippers and was arrested on a charge of vagrancy and jailed.

(Ten years later, in 1953, Miss Barry was again picked up wandering around barefoot and in a dazed condition in Torrance, California. At that time she was taken to the psychopathic ward of Harbor General Hospital for observation and then released. A few hours later she was found wandering about the same place and was returned to the hospital, where she was examined by Dr. V. J. Miller, a staff psychiatrist. He described her as a schizophrenic with a very well-organized delusional pattern. The prominent characteristic of this serious mental ailment is that the sufferer lives in a world of fantasy, believing it to be absolutely real. Miss Barry herself realized her need for treatment and her mother signed commitment papers. She was then committed by Superior Court Judge William P. Haughton to the state mental hospital at Patton.)

But the fact that Miss Barry might have been suffering from incipient schizophrenia at the time of her first arrest in 1943 didn't occur to the Beverly Hills police. It was just a routine case to them. Judge Charles J. Griffin of the Beverly Hills Police Court, who heard her case, suspended sentence on condition she leave town permanently.

While in jail Miss Barry had been allowed one phone call and had made it to Robert Arden, a radio commentator who was a friend of my father, with whom Arden got in touch at once. Through Mr. Arden my father offered to pay all Miss Barry's debts and to provide her with a train ticket to her former home in the East. Miss Barry accepted the offer and was escorted to the train by Police Captain W. W. White.

This gratuitous deed of charity on my father's part was to cost him dear. He was to be indicted with six others—Tim Durant; Robert Arden; Police Lieutenant Claude Marple, who locked up Miss Barry; Judge Griffin; Captain White; and Mrs. Jessie Billie Reno, part-time police matron. They were all to be arraigned for violating Miss Barry's civil rights by conniving to give her a "floater" sentence. The penalty for such a violation is two years' imprisonment, a ten-thousand-dollar fine or both.

Miss Barry went only halfway across the country; she turned back at Omaha and reappeared in Beverly Hills. She broke into my father's home again. In desperation he had the police called and again Miss Barry was jailed. This time she was given a ninety-day sentence. My father, who could never bear the thought of jails, interfered once more by sending an attorney, Cecil D. Holland, who has since become a judge, to intercede for her. She had been five days in jail then and had made her pregnant condition known, but she had not yet publicly blamed my father for it.

As soon as Mr. Holland learned that Miss Barry was accusing my father, he withdrew from representing her, though he obtained her release from jail so that she could go to a sanitarium. It was at this time that John J. Irwin took over the chore of representing Miss Barry in her paternity suit against my father.

These were the events that formed the turbulent background of the Chaplin fortunes that late May and early summer. Everything was in a state of confusion, with investigations right and left. Even Oona was questioned, but she was able to say she knew nothing about Miss Barry. As for herself, she and her mother were just good friends of my father's. But Syd and I were his sons and so it was natural that, as Tim Durant had predicted, we should be sucked into the middle of everything. We were ordered one day to report to the district attorney's office for questioning.

That session came as a shock to us both. We loved our father. It wasn't just that he had been good to us. It was also that he was our father, whatever he did. It's hard to explain it, but we feel a definite and very strong loyalty toward him. We would have done anything, even lied, to protect him, though it might have meant jail for us. But it wasn't necessary. He had never done anything out of the way. We had been at his home any number of week ends and had never witnessed any wild orgies. We had never seen any women staying there with him. I couldn't remember his even kissing anyone except Paulette in front of us.

The investigator in the district attorney's office didn't stop with the gun episode. From that he went on to embarrassingly intimate questions about our father, carefully putting them in a roundabout way so that, without his saying things in so many words, we would know what he meant. We couldn't believe our ears. He was asking us to testify about our father's morals! I was furious.

"What right have you to ask such questions?" I demanded. "About my own father! I don't have to answer you."

But of course in the end I did. "No, I haven't seen anything," I told him. "No women's clothes in his closets. No women staying in his house. Nothing!"

Syd was as vehement as I. We left the district attorney's office feeling a sense of shame and outrage. For a while we couldn't even look at each other.

Meanwhile Miss Barry's lawyers, who had filed suit for her in Superior Court, came to an agreement with my father's lawyers. In California, laws having to do with divorce and paternity cases are extremely partial to women. (Some well-informed people believe that this is because they've scarcely been modernized since 1849, when they were promulgated in an effort to entice the female sex to the state.) A woman's mere accusation that a man is the father of her child is sufficient grounds in California for forcing him to support both her and the child until the paternity suit is settled. Whatever the outcome of the trial, the money paid out during the interim need never be refunded.

Since my father had been formally accused by Miss Barry, he had no other recourse but to comply with the law, and it was arranged that he pay one hundred dollars a week temporary support and twenty-five hundred dollars immediately for Miss Barry's care. Added to this, forty-six hundred dollars was to be paid in installments for medical expenses. My father's lawyers, however, were able to get a stipulation that the child be submitted to medical tests five months after its birth to determine its paternity. If two of three physicians found negatively for my father, the suit was to be dismissed. Until such time as the matter was cleared up, the Chaplin name was not to be used on the child's birth certificate. This agreement, which was approved by Superior Court Judge William S. Baird, was signed by my father and his attorney, Loyd Wright, and by Miss Barry, her mother, Mrs. Gertrude Berry, and their attorneys, headed by John J. Irwin.

Since the beginning of June, my father, to escape reporters and possible process servers, had been hiding out on Layton Drive in West Los Angeles at the home of his good friend, Eugene Frenke, the well-known movie producer, and his wife, Anna Sten. To avoid further gossip Oona had been coming secretly to visit him there, sometimes spending the night at Anna Sten's invitation. Throughout that whole time the Frenkes were feeding Dad, and sometimes Oona, at a sacrifice to themselves, for they had to use up their precious ration stamps on their guests.

It was at the Frenke home that my father and Oona revised their marriage plans. Previously they had set the date for the first of June, when Oona should have passed her eighteenth birthday and would no longer need parental consent. Her mother, to whom she had confessed her love for my father, had approved the marriage from the first. But Oona had good reason to believe that her father, who had opposed her acting career so vehemently, would feel the same way about her marriage to Dad, who was at that time embroiled in such a widely publicized scandal.

The Barry case, with its promise of protracted litigation, had upset everything. There were two schools of opinion about the course to follow under the circumstances. Tim Durant felt my father should send Oona back East until the scandal blew over, so that she would not be involved in it. But Oona herself stood up against this suggestion.

"When a man is in trouble, the woman he loves and who loves him should be by his side," she said.

So they decided upon an elopement, setting the date for the sixteenth of June. The night before they left, Oona went to see the Frenkes.

"Gene and Anna, tomorrow I'm going to marry Charlie Chaplin," she said, speaking almost reverently. "Thank you so much for everything. As soon as I marry, you'll get all your ration coupons back."

But Frenke maintains the forgetful young bride never kept her word. "Oh, I forgave them long ago," he says with a laugh today. "But Anna, my wife, she's so straightforward, not compromising at all! To this day she can't forgive Charlie for those ration coupons."

My father and Oona drove up to Santa Barbara with Catherine Hunter, my father's secretary, and the late Harry Crocker, the newspaper columnist. They arrived at the Santa Barbara courthouse a little before nine in the morning. My father and Oona entered separately, my father seeming to be amused at first by all the secrecy, which was so much like his own brand of comedy. But when he entered the clerk's office the amusement faded and he became just another flustered bridegroom, fussing at his tie and picking imaginary flecks from his brown suit. He forgot to remove his hat, and when he went to sign his name his hand shook so he could hardly hold the pen.

Perhaps he was suddenly realizing he was letting himself in for a fourth marriage after the first three had ended so disastrously. Oona, on the contrary, was animated and happy. Though she was just eighteen and shy and quiet, where my father was concerned she knew her own mind from the start.

When the clerk asked Oona for her birth certificate, my father, who was fifty-four at the time, looked alarmed.

"Gosh, do I have to have one of those with me?" he asked.

They had to explain to him that it was only to prove Oona was of age; she looked so young. As soon as the license was made out, my father grabbed it without a word, leaving Mr. Crocker to attend to the two-dollar fee.

They drove on to the nearby town of Carpinteria, where the wedding took place in the home of Justice of the Peace Clinton Pancoast Moore, who was a seventy-eight-year-old retired Methodist minister. By coincidence, he turned out to be a former neighbor, having once lived just around the corner from my father in Beverly Hills. Throughout the brief ceremony my father and Oona clasped hands. Then Harry Crocker handed my father the simple gold wedding band he had bought the day before. He slipped it on Oona's finger and they were pronounced man and wife. My father gave Oona a quick kiss and accepted the marriage certificate from Mr. Moore. It wasn't until he got outside and looked at it that he saw it was made out to Chapman. It was the same name that had appeared years before on the telegram which first summoned my father to wealth and fame in Hollywood. He dashed back and asked Mr. Moore to change it.

When Miss Barry heard about the wedding she went into hysterics, but by the time my father and Oona returned from their two-week honeymoon in Santa Barbara everything had simmered down. Dad was able to bring his new bride in comparative peace to his house on the hill, and suddenly that house was a home again because there was a woman in it.

34

All that summer of 1943 I was only marking time, like so many other boys my age. Like Oona, I had passed my eighteenth birthday, and I was waiting for Uncle Sam to tap me on the shoulder. I had graduated from high school, but under the circumstances it would have been ridiculous even to think of entering college. So I just lived it up, taking girls to shows and parties and stuffing myself on rich malts. I wasn't yet smoking or drinking.

I got my greetings from Uncle Sam on October 7. Syd and my girl friend saw me off on the streetcar. Syd told me later he cried after I left. I've never seen Syd cry in my life and this is the only time I've ever heard of his doing so.

When I arrived at Fort MacArthur I was shown in by my

stepfather, Arthur Day, who had been drafted and was there ahead of me as an M.P. After a few weeks I was transferred from Fort MacArthur to Camp Haan, near Riverside. I was one of the two youngest soldiers in the outfit and I looked it. I wanted to prove I was a man, so, because I could speak French fluently, I volunteered for O.S.S. duty. Everyone advised me against it because the chances of coming back alive from that branch of the service were practically nil, if you could even survive the training.

But the hero bit had got me, so I took all the examinations and passed them. I thought I was headed for the life of a spy, but the Colonel turned me down because at a hundred and thirty-five pounds I was considered underweight for my height. I had to content myself with growing a mustache to appear more mature. I began to smoke as well and to drink 3.2 beer at the PX, because I thought drinking made a man of me. Besides, there was nothing else to do. I felt at loose ends, alone and homesick, separated from Syd and all my family, learning the hard work of war.

Then one day, passing the recreation room, I heard music and hurried in. A young man about twenty-three years old was at the piano tinkling it, and he had music in his finger-tips. I went up and began talking to him and then we introduced ourselves. He was Stan Keyava and he had come from the sleepy little town of Chico in Northern California. He was the oldest of seven children, he told me, and he'd been playing in a band in San Francisco before he had been drafted.

Stan and I became buddies. The first week-end pass I got I took him to Hollywood. Stan and my father spent about two hours that afternoon they met discussing music. But Dad didn't keep it at that. Before it was all over he had drawn everything possible out of Stan about his mother and father, his six brothers and sisters and all his relatives. My father, who had never had a real home life of his own, was curious about what it was like in a big family, a knowledge which later he was to acquire first hand.

By the time Stan and I took our leave Dad was treating him like old home folks, even urging him to bring his mother and father up to see him when they came to town. After that Stan came often with me to the house on the hill.

Though Dad likes to call himself the world's foremost peacemonger, he was proud I was in uniform. He always lectured me about taking my duties seriously. I never left for camp that he didn't put his arm around me and give me a pep talk.

"Charlie," he would say, "I want you to be a good soldier. If you don't do anything else be a good soldier."

But, my father's conception of the life of a soldier was as unrealistic in many ways as his portrayal of it in *Shoulder Arms*, his early satire on war. He was always warning me about sleeping on the cold ground in the open, which he said would give me pneumonia, as if I had any choice in the matter. He was horrified at Stan's and my descriptions of our infiltration courses. When we told how we had to crawl under barbed wire with machine guns raking the air just thirty inches off the ground he was deeply concerned. But he couldn't refrain from getting in a little wry humor about it either.

"Do be careful, boys," he always cautioned us whenever we took our leave. "Be sure to keep your tails down!"

That fall there was sadness in my life, too. My mother, alone now that kindly Arthur Day was in the army, went into her second nervous breakdown—a breakdown that was to be the main cause of her separation from Arthur in 1948. Again she became pitifully thin and dazed. Sometimes she was filled with such despair that she would think of suicide. But her old fear of my father was a thing of the past. One day in the midst of a black mood she phoned him and begged him to see her to discuss our future, Syd's and mine, because she was sure she would soon be dying.

It was five years since my father had last seen my mother— at my bedside in the hospital when I had had my appendix removed—but he drove out to her at once. He took her for a long ride, giving her advice, trying to comfort her and cheer her up. That week end he told me about it when I came with Stan to see him.

"I saw your mother the other day. She's a pretty sick girl," he explained. And suddenly I remembered he had said almost the same words to me when I was a child, perhaps now, as then, trying to help me understand how things were with her. "She was rather suicidal and very dramatic. I tried to make her realize that however dark things look they always work out."

My father paused, and then a wistful expression came over his face. He seemed to have retreated into old memories, memories in which I, his son, had no active part.

"I always thought your mother was the most beautiful girl I've ever known," he suddenly added softly.

Later my mother, too, talked to me about her last visit with my father. One remark of his stood out most clearly in her mind and was, perhaps, to make up to her for much of the grief of that first unhappy marriage. She said she had told him she was sorry things had started the way they had and had ended as they had between them. In reply my father had turned and looked at her a long while.

"If it will make you feel any better, Lita," he had said, "I'd like you to know there are only two women I've ever really loved in my life—you and the girl I'm married to now."

Yes, Dad really loved Oona. Everyone who saw them together noticed that. She was different from his three former wives. When she married my father she gave up all thought of acting, though success in that quarter was already within her grasp. Eugene Frenke, who had her under contract, wanted her to play an important role with his wife in *A Girl from Leningrad*. My father felt Oona should have her chance because of her extraordinary photogenic qualities, but he was pleased when Oona asked Frenke to release her from the contract. She had come to Hollywood to make a career for herself, but now that she was married to my father that was career enough for her. I never heard her voice any regret that that marriage was responsible for severing her last connection with her father. I asked Dad once whether Eugene O'Neill ever got in touch with him.

"Oh, we don't talk," he answered laconically, and that was all. I never heard either him or Oona discuss Eugene O'Neill personally, though sometimes my father would speak admiringly of his writing. Being an artist himself he never let grudges or alienations stand in the way of his appreciating a work of art. And I think this was all he ever really asked for himself from anyone.

From the first Oona had some magical touch about her where my father was concerned! Paulette had fought for years to get rid of those button-top shoes. They just quietly disappeared when Dad started dating Oona, and I've never seen them since.

There were a lot of other changes, too, subtle changes which are hard to describe. But they told me who had watched him so carefully for so many years that my father was happy for the first time in his life, that he felt security at last in a woman's love. I heard him put it into words for Tim Durant late one afternoon down at the tennis house.

"If only I had known Oona or a girl like her long ago," he said, and there was a tinge of wistfulness in his voice, "I would never have had any problems with women. All my life I have been waiting for her without even realizing it until I met her."

That fall was a comparatively peaceful period for the Chaplin family. The paternity suit Joan Barry had brought against my father was in abeyance. There wasn't even much stir when, in October, Miss Barry gave birth to a baby girl whom she named Carol Ann. But things were building up from another direction. Sometime that summer or fall, friends of Miss Barry filed two serious complaints against my father with the federal attorney general's office. The first was that he had contrived to deprive her of her civil rights when he bought her a ticket for the East following her arrest for vagrancy. The second was that he had violated the Mann Act, the "white slavery" act, by conveying her across state lines for immoral purposes, because he had paid her fare to New York and, ostensibly, back again, since she had used his money to return to Hollywood.

Acting on orders from Washington, the FBI performed its routine duty by investigating the matter and rounding up evidence. By January a dozen or so witnesses, including Miss Barry, were called in to testify before a federal grand jury. From then on until April, when the case was resolved, my father's private life made sensational headlines around the world, as it had at the time of my mother's divorce. Even soldiers at the front were kept informed by bulletins in army newspapers.

On February 11, my father and the six others implicated in the alleged conspiracy to deprive Miss Barry of her civil rights were formally indicted. Except for Police Judge Charles J. Griffin and Police Captain W. W. White, who were released on their own recognizance, bonds were fixed at one thousand dollars each. In addition, my father was separately indicted for violation of the Mann Act. If he were convicted of all the charges he could be sentenced to a minimum of twenty-three years in prison and a fine of twenty-six thousand dollars.

It was no wonder he appeared white and tense when on February 15 he arrived at the Federal Building accompanied by Jerry Giesler, the famous Los Angeles attorney whom he had retained to handle his case. All the way to the fifth floor, women clerks kept popping out of doors to get a look at my father. In the U.S. Marshal's office the usual battery of cameras was waiting. Light bulbs flashed and shutters clicked as Dad's fingers were pressed, one at a time, into the ink pad and then on a card. When it was over my father walked to the wash bowl and scrubbed his hands under the concentrated appraisal of a crowd of federal employees who had gathered to watch the show.

When he went to the booking desk to sign his arrest card, he kept trying to dip his pen into the capped ink bottle, finally realized his mistake and suddenly smiled. It was his only recognition of the latent comedy in the situation. He tucked away that fingerprinting scene, and later, so I hear, used it down to the last detail in his picture, *The King in New York*.

The trial itself started in late March and lasted ten days. United States Attorney Charles H. Carr acted as prosecutor and Federal Judge J. F. T. O'Connor was on the bench. Miss Barry's testimony was so lurid at times that my father sat through it flushed with embarrassment. She described in rich and imaginative detail the bedroom scene that she maintained took place in the New York hotel room when my father went East to make his speech. There was more imaginative and intimate detail to the scene she described at our house when she confronted my father with a gun.

When my father took the stand he denied emphatically that either scene had taken place. He gave the whole history of his relations with Miss Barry, frankly acknowledging that at one time he had been romantically involved with her. But he maintained this had all come to an end with his shelving of *Shadow and Substance* and her departure from Hollywood.

When he told his version of the gun episode and came to Syd's and my arrival on the scene, his voice broke as he described how he had talked to us while Miss Barry held the gun in the archway. Some reporters thought his acting at this point superb. I, as his son, know it was a genuine emotion; only Syd and I were ever aware of how deeply embarrassed he was when he slipped in the role of being a proper father.

Except for the two lurid bedroom scenes which Miss Barry described, and which my father swore from the witness stand never took place, her relation of events agreed quite consistently with my father's. And Mr. Giesler adroitly raised the question of who had been chasing whom in the romance.

Other people were caught in the glare of notoriety. A writer and a multimillionaire oil tycoon were called to the witness stand. The writer admitted going out with Miss Barry and being occasionally visited by her in his apartment. (At the later paternity trial his landlady was to testify that Miss Barry confided to her that she considered him a genius and that she was in love with him.) The millionaire also said he had seen Miss Barry frequently in Los Angeles, and in Tulsa, Oklahoma, where she had gone in November of 1942, almost immediately following her return to Hollywood from New York on my father's three hundred dollars. (She also visited Tulsa in early January of 1943.) Canceled checks proved that a number of her outstanding bills had been paid by a Tulsa law firm that numbered the millionaire among its clients. (At a subsequent trial Miss Barry was to testify that the millionaire took care of her bill at the Mayo Hotel in Tulsa while she was there.)

One witness testified about a weird odyssey Miss Barry made on the night and early morning of December 30 and 31, during which he acted as her chauffeur for part of the time. It began at eight o'clock when Miss Barry went to the Players restaurant with the writer and there saw my father and introduced the two men. She and the writer left the restaurant together but separated outside, Miss Barry going on to the witness's apartment, where the writer joined her shortly afterwards. But her escort left almost immediately and her volunteer chauffeur drove Miss Barry around a good part of the night trying to find him for her. When Miss Barry fell asleep in the car, he returned to his own apartment, left her outside and went in for a nap.

He came out after an hour or so to find Miss Barry lying on the sidewalk. He helped her up, saw that she was dizzy. Her speech was incoherent, her stockings torn, and she had a scratch on her forehead. She asked him to drive her to my father's place, which he did, leaving her there. According to Miss Barry my father drove her to the Beverly Hills police station. I can see why, after the gun incident which had so alarmed him, he should seek the protection of the law. But he did not sign a complaint. Miss Barry turned herself in.

Police Lieutenant Claude Marple, on duty at the time, said that Miss Barry was hysterical, had been drinking, but wasn't drunk. He noticed nothing unusual about her appearance. She was wrapped in a long silver-fox coat. The time was one thirty in the morning. At her own request, Marple drove her to the writer's apartment and left her. The writer himself testified that when he saw her she was disheveled and her dress was soiled, as though she had been lying in the dirt. There was blood on her head. Her stockings were torn and she was bleeding at both knees. The heel of one shoe was missing. He evoked a titter in court by saying that she was "in one of her states," indicating that he had seen her before in this condition.

That December 31 in his apartment, Miss Barry had painted her lips with iodine to simulate suicide and was taken by ambulance to the receiving hospital. It was shortly thereafter that she was found wandering on Olympic Boulevard, was booked at the Beverly Hills jail on the vagrancy charge, and received my father's ill-fated monetary assistance.

I go into these details, not to dredge up the unhappy past for its own sake, but to show the profound emotional turmoil of this apparently very ill girl who held my father's fate in her hands, and also to give some idea, at least, of the atmosphere of sensationalism that enveloped the Chaplin family at this period of their lives. It was as though a gigantic spotlight were trained on every move we made during those months.

There was always an atmosphere of tension at the house on the hill. When Stan and I went up on week ends now we often found Jerry Giesler sitting in one of the rattan chairs in the study. He was very calm, but Dad would be pacing back and forth, back and forth, as he does when agitated. Every now and then he would hurry over and tug at Giesler's coat and anxiously ask him about some point.

"Oh don't worry about it, Charlie," Giesler would answer, talking in the slow, comfortable tones of a father confessor. "Just let me get it all straight and I'll take care of everything."

Presently Giesler would rise to his feet and take a few strides in that relaxed manner of his, while my father would sit down and try to be calm. But he always looked as though he were just about to explode. Dad was concerned not only over himself but about Syd and me, who, as his sons, shared the spotlight with him. Every time Stan and I left, Dad would come over and put his hand anxiously on Stan's shoulder.

"Whatever you do, please keep Charlie out of the papers," he would beg. "Don't let him get out of line by a single step or they'll tear him to pieces."

Stan took his part seriously and almost ran himself ragged playing nursemaid to me. He kept guard over every glass of beer I drank at the PX and tried to censor all my conversations, for fear a brawl might start and I would be implicated. Sometimes he even had nightmares about it.

But it turned out to be Syd instead who almost made the papers. It was a Saturday night and I had come in alone from camp and was staying at Nana's place. Syd was living with a friend. He had been sick in bed, but when our former schoolmate, George Englund, who today is one of our better young film producers, dropped by to see him, Syd suddenly found he had a yen for a hamburger and a malt. He got out of bed, put on an old sweater and a pair of slacks, and didn't bother to comb his hair. George himself wasn't exactly dressed for a party. He had on a sweater and slacks, too, and he hadn't shaved. They looked like a couple of bums in search of handouts. But they didn't think it would matter because they didn't expect to run into anyone.

They went to a drive-in and were ordering their food when suddenly a squad car rolled up into the lot. A policeman got out of the car and pulled his gun and motioned Syd and George over. Without a word of explanation he clapped handcuffs on them and ordered them into the back seat of the squad car. When they asked what it was all about they were told tersely to shut up.

Suddenly the whole thing became very amusing to Syd, who couldn't resist hamming it up just as he had in school.

"I'm not going to talk until I get my mouthpiece," he proclaimed. "I don't want to fry in the chair."

The policemen looked put out and George nudged Syd to be quiet. They drove on for a while without talking. Then the policeman who was driving ventured some information.

"A woman's been attack-ted down the street here a ways," he said.

"She's been attack-*ted?*" my purist brother mimicked gleefully.

The policeman glared at him, and it was in that frame of mind that they came to the woman's house. She was lying stretched out on the couch, screaming hysterically, with friends gathered all around her trying to comfort her. Syd, who had forgotten how he looked in his old sweater with his thick black hair on end, was sure she'd see at once that he was the wrong person. The woman took only one look.

"That's the man," she yelled, pointing at him.

Syd turned white. It wasn't a laughing matter any more. He'd been identified. They took him down and locked him up.

I got a call about three thirty or four in the morning. It was Syd.

"Chuck," he said matter-of-factly, "they got me down here in jail on a rape charge."

I waited but he didn't say any more.

"Well, did you do it?" I asked at last, imbued as I was with the spirit of my father's trial.

"What do you mean, did I do it?" Syd demanded indignantly. "It's a mistaken-identity thing. Contact Dad."

So I had to beard my father, who had enough troubles of his own. I waited until six o'clock and then dashed up to see him. I remembered how in my childhood my father had enjoyed staying in bed until eleven or twelve o'clock. But he wasn't sleeping during the Mann Act trial. I found him already downstairs in his robe, pacing back and forth, talking to himself in a monotone, rehearsing what he was going to say in court that day.

"Dad," I said tentatively.

"Don't bother me now, son," he answered. "Can't you see I'm very busy? I haven't been able to sleep. This trial and everything . . ."

"Well, Dad, this is very important," I insisted.

He didn't answer. He seemed to have forgotten me. He went on pacing back and forth, talking to himself. The day was drawing on and Syd was still in jail. I got desperate.

Dad," I said more loudly, "they have Syd in jail on a mistaken-identity rape charge."

"Well," Dad said, not really hearing me yet, but just incorporating my information into his own line of thought, "I'll get him Giesler. I'll take care of it."

"But, Dad, he's innocent!" I almost shouted.

"I don't care, son," Dad answered. "We'll take . . ." Suddenly he did a double-take, stopped short and glared at me.

"Rape!" he shouted. "Mistaken identity! Innocent!"

He was more furious than I'd ever seen him in my life. It was as though his taut nerves had suddenly snapped.

"My God," he shouted, gesticulating in different directions at the same time, "if that even gets into the newspapers I'll sue the whole bloody police department. I'll sue every paper. Even if it's a fact I'll still sue. Mistaken-identity rape! They'll never see the mistaken-identity part. They'll look at the word *rape*. Do you realize what that means, son? Why, they'll take the whole Chaplin family and tar and feather them and ride them out of town on rails."

Finally my father got down to phoning. Meanwhile, around eight that morning, the woman came to the jail to make a more specific identification. She took one look.

"I'm sorry, this isn't the fellow after all," she said.

Shortly afterwards Syd walked nonchalantly in on us. But my father's phoning had its effect. That story didn't make the papers. It's never been told until this day.

On April 4, after five hours and one minute of deliberation, the seven women and five men of the jury declared my father innocent of the Mann Act charge. One of the jurors, Rowan T. Segner, a Pasadena banker, said later that the consensus had been that my father was motivated by kindness alone when he gave Miss Barry and her mother the train tickets to New York and the money later on.

Now that the ordeal was over, my father had difficulty holding back his tears. He kept fumbling with his Adam's apple and fussing with the knot of his tie, while the courtroom went into such wild applause that the judge had to threaten to clear it to restore order. Finally, supported by Giesler, who, according to reporters, seemed to be having some trouble with tears himself, my father made his way through the press of congratulatory people to the jury box.

"God bless you all," he said as he shook hands with each of the jurors. "I've always had an abiding faith in the American people and justice . . . and the press has been very fair, very fair—thank you."

When the news was telephoned to Oona, who was expecting her first child in August, she fainted with relief.

"I'm so glad I can hardly speak," she said afterwards, and she added almost as if it were an apology for an apparent desertion, "I didn't go to court with Charlie because he wanted me spared, but I would have sat right with him if he had permitted it."

Shortly after the Mann Act trial, Judge O'Connor moved to acquit all those who had been indicted on the charge of conspiring to deprive Miss Barry of her civil rights. But my father's trials were not yet over. By this time the blood tests of himself, Miss Barry and Carol Ann had been made by three noted pathologists, Dr. Roy W. Hammack, Dr. Newton

Evans, and Dr. Vernon L. Andrews. All three, working separately, had come to the same conclusion. They declared unequivocally that by these scientifically accurate tests my father could not possibly be the child's father, because she had a type of blood different from either his or Miss Barry's.

According to the stipulation previously agreed to by Miss Barry and my father, this should have ended all further litigation and Miss Barry's lawyer, John J. Irwin, felt honorbound to bow out of the picture. Attorney Joseph Scott took his place. Meanwhile, Superior Court Judge Stanley Mosk overruled the motion of my father's lawyers to dismiss the suit, pointing out that though blood grouping tests are accepted in the courts as corroborative evidence no decision in the United States had heretofore regarded them as conclusive, and they were not so regarded in California. He ruled, therefore, that "the ends of justice will best be served by a full and fair trial of the issues."

Judge Mosk was only declaring on a point of law, but Joseph Scott hailed his ruling as "a heroic and courageous decision." It was obvious that Mr. Scott was not going to regard the case as a simple paternity trial but as some kind of *cause célèbre.*

35

Life settled down to a happier state for my father after the Mann Act trial. In August Oona gave birth by Caesarean section to my charming little half-sister Geraldine. And Dad, who had been disappointed that Syd was born a boy, had his girl at last.

Nineteen days after Geraldine's birth, my father's first wife, Mildred Harris, died at the age of forty-three following an operation at Cedars of Lebanon hospital in Los Angeles. My father sent a spray of orchids, roses and gladioli to the funeral, which was held at Hollywood Cemetery. It was his last tribute to the first girl who won his heart in America.

Actually, that summer was only a period of uneasy truce for my father. Mrs. Gertrude Berry, Carol Ann's grandmother and guardian, was pressing for an early settlement of paternity suit. By June my father had paid more than ten thousand dollars for the little girl's support, which he thought a large sum of money to spend on a baby in a single year. Nevertheless, he did not cavil about continuing to support the child until the case came to trial. As I've pointed out before, his primary motive was not to escape monetary responsibility but to fight what he considered blackmail.

At Camp Haan during those months there was an air of growing uncertainty. Things were getting rougher in Europe and the East, and we all knew that it was only a matter of time before we would be in combat too. As time went by, boys began to get their orders right and left. One day Stan got his and we were separated and were not to see each other again until the close of the war. I had come to depend on him like a big brother. After he left I felt depressed and alone and began to drink more, thinking of what was awaiting me.

Sometime that fall I was transferred from Camp Haan to the 89th Infantry Division at Camp Butner in North Carolina and got my first look at German and Italian prisoners. I was surprised to find that they were just people, friendly and polite. It came to me with a shock that it was people such as these that I was going out to fight and kill and who were going to do their best to kill me.

From Camp Butner I went to Camp Miles Standish in Boston to wait embarkation, and I was there when the paternity trial started. My father, who felt that the results of the blood tests had made the paternity trial a routine affair, put it in the hands of his own lawyers, and Charles A. (Pat) Millikan defended him in court. This decision was made without taking two factors into account. One was that Miss Barry's new lawyer, Joseph Scott, even from his first appeal in Judge Stanley Mosk's court, obviously intended to rely on emotionalism, in contrast to the dignified and completely legalistic approach of Prosecutor Carr. The other was that the plaintiff would not be the formidable United States Government, in relation to which my father had been the "little man," but a beautiful and innocent eighteen-month-old child, who, with her attractive young mother, would be cast in the role of underdog.

In this situation my father needed Mr. Giesler's adroit showmanship to protect not only his interests but his reputation as well. Pat Millikan was capable and thorough, but he lacked Mr. Giesler's superb sense of the dramatic, and the trial was drama, or rather melodrama, from start to finish.

It began shortly before Christmas. I read about it daily in the papers. You couldn't escape it, really. There was little additional material to what had already been brought out at the Mann Act trial; the only really new evidence was the testimony of the three doctors, who stated unequivocally that scientific evidence in the form of the blood tests proved conclusively that my father could not possibly be the father of the child. So impressive was the testimony of these doctors that reporters on the scene felt my father had won the case. They were quick to note that apparently Mr. Scott thought so, too, for it was then that he pulled out all stops in an emotional attack on my father, apparently without considering the paradox of defaming the very name he was fighting to give the child. Even veteran court attachés registered shock at his strong language, saying that in all the years they had been around they had never before heard such intemperance in a courtroom.

Mr. Scott belittled my father unmercifully, referring to him among other things as a "gray-headed old buzzard," "little runt of a Svengali," "debaucher" and a "lecherous hound" who "lies like a cheap Cockney cad." There was no justification in fact for the epithets Mr. Scott hung on my father. Since the sensational headlines that had preceded his finally equable divorce from my mother in 1927, a period of some sixteen years, my father had not been touched by scandal. He had never been implicated in any charge of immorality until the Mann Act accusation, from which he was completely exonerated.

At one point in Mr. Scott's haranguing my father involuntarily turned to Judge Henry M. Willis.

"Your Honor, I've committed no crime," he remonstrated heatedly. "I'm only human. But this man is trying to make a monster out of me."

If only my father had called to mind that chapter in Dickens' *Pickwick Papers* which sets forth Sergeant Buzfuz' plea before the jury in the memorable breach-of-promise suit of Bardell against Pickwick, he might have been able to retain some sense of humor. As a seasoned actor he might then have found the poise to play his role with charm and convincing reasonableness. But even in moments of minor stress my father could never keep his head.

How could he maintain his equilibrium on the witness stand while Mr. Scott was not only deriding and needling him but even accusing him of purposely not remembering dates and places? The jury had no way of knowing that my father's faulty memory for numbers and names is an idiosyncrasy about which he has always been very sensitive. He just looked to them like an irascible villain caught at a crime and trying to lie himself out.

A sense of injustice so black and overpowering it washed away all reason, that was the Achilles heel Mr. Scott opened in my father—the cruel emotions, perhaps, of a long-ago Christmas Day in a London orphanage. My father sometimes told me about that day when he wanted me to realize graphically how much more fortunate my lot had been, and I used to think of it on Christmas when Syd and I were opening the mountains of toys Dad always lavished on us. In my mind's eye I would see another little boy sitting on a bench at a bare dining-hall table, crying empty-handed while all the other children received their small but treasured Christmas treats, a few candies and an orange apiece. The little boy alone had been singled out for deprivation because of some insignificant misdemeanor.

The feeling of being unjustly punished which my father experienced that day in the orphanage must have welled up during the ordeal of the paternity trial. And looking at the whole affair dispassionately, it does seem to be far more in the nature of a chastisement than an orderly inquiry into his actual responsibility in the case at hand.

"There has been no one to stop Chaplin in his lecherous conduct all these years—except you," Scott shouted to the jury. "Wives and mothers all over the country are watching to see you stop him dead in his tracks. You'll sleep well the night you give this baby a name—the night you show him the law means him as well as the bums on Skid Row."

The first trial resulted in a hung jury, though it was seven to five in my father's favor. It is interesting to see the opinions of the jurors. Despite the doctors' professional standing, the negative blood tests were discounted from the first. None of the jurors liked my father's actions in court. Those who voted for him did so because they felt Miss Barry had not proved her case.

At this point Judge Clarence L. Kincaid, who was to preside at the next trial, offered to arbitrate. Mr. Scott, doubtless feeling at a disadvantage because of the decision of the first jury, accepted the offer. My father refused. It was part of his stubborn integrity to try for a complete exoneration. During the second trial Mr. Scott continued his emotional attack, and my father, wearying of the whole thing, stopped showing up at court to testify, as was his prerogative in a civil suit. He wasn't there when the jury reached its verdict. It, too, completely ignored the scientific blood tests which the doctors claimed were infallible, and it was even less favorably impressed by my father than the first jury had been. It brought in a verdict, eleven to one, of guilty.

Following the original stipulation, Judge Kincaid allotted seventy-five dollars a week to Carol Ann, the sum to be increased to a hundred as her expenses grew greater. Furthermore, she was now legally entitled to claim the Chaplin name. Miss Barry had won her case, but the trial had not benefited her personally, for she had had to humiliate and embarrass herself by her many detailed allegations of intimacies.

My father suffered such a deadly blow to his reputation in this country that he has not yet completely recovered from it. The ugly image of a libertine which Mr. Scott superimposed upon his long years of uneventful domesticity both before and during his marriage to Paulette has also cast its shadow over the long period of his happy marriage to Oona. Yet I do not see how any man could have better proved himself a devoted husband and a good father than Dad has with Oona and their brood of seven children.

Others were hurt by the trial, too. Syd and I were shamed by the daily newspaper accounts, and Oona's little girl had to start life under the cloud of scandal. But I think the saddest victim of all was the little plaintiff of the case, eighteen-month-old Carol Ann, who was brought needlessly into the courtroom every day, exposed to the stares of the curious and made an object of notoriety around the world. It seems to me that a child's right to start life unhampered as much as possible by the mistakes of adults is as important as its physical welfare. I have a little daughter of my own now, and I should not like to see her exposed as Carol Ann was. Though I am neither judge nor lawyer, I feel strongly that something should be done to protect the children of disputed paternity cases from unsavory publicity, and that they should at least be provided with closed-court hearings.

As for the two juries, they did not escape severe censure from legal and medical authorities for their verdicts. In his book, *Disputed Paternity Proceedings*, published in 1953, Sidney B. Schotkin, Assistant Corporation Counsel of the City of New York, says, "The Chaplin verdict is contrary to science, nature and truth."

"In short," agrees Dr. Wladimir Eliasberg, a well-known

psychologist writing in the July 1946 edition of the *Southern California Law Review*, "the Chaplin jury let sentimental considerations turn logic out of doors and failed dismally in its task of weighing the evidence."

"The Chaplin case is a landmark in the miscarriage of justice," says Los Angeles attorney Eugene L. Trope, who has become an authority on the Chaplin case because of his own work with defendants of paternity cases. "It was humanly and scientifically impossible for Chaplin to have been the father of the Joan Barry child."

Mr. Trope, who in 1959 secured an acquittal in the much-publicized case of rodeo star Casey Tibbs vs. Leah J. Connor, says that my father's trial did, however, benefit others involved in paternity suits. Because of his fame and the wide publicity the case received, the attention of California lawmakers was vividly drawn to the state's antiquated attitude toward blood tests. In 1953 the California legislature passed a paternity ruling prohibiting further litigation in cases where the blood tests prove conclusively that a defendant cannot be the father of a child. Ironically, if Joan Barry had tried to bring her suit against my father in more recent years, he would have been completely exonerated by the findings of the three pathologists and there would have been no paternity trials.

And where are the principals in the case today? In 1946, Miss Barry married. At the time she said she was happily content with her new life of obscurity.

But in 1953, when she was committed to Patton State Hospital after having been found wandering in Torrance, California, it was revealed that she had tired of her quiet life. As in 1941 when she first met my father, she had come up from Mexico City, where she had been looking once more for theatrical work. Her marriage had proved a failure, and her husband, from whom she was separated, was not providing support for their two children. Today Dr. O. L. Gericke, the superintendent at Patton, in verifying my query about the case, discloses that the tragic Miss Barry is still a patient there "and will require treatment for an indefinite time."

The little plaintiff, who is sixteen years old now, is still receiving the hundred dollars a week support money from my father in far-off Vevey, my father who, for so long as I've known him, could never bear to see a child suffering want and privation. As he cried out in court that day, he isn't a monster after all, but only a human being with virtues and weaknesses like the rest of us.

36

On January 10, 1945, the 89th Infantry Division embarked for Europe. Our ship was overcrowded, and many of us had to sleep in the aisles. All the way over we had to zigzag to escape German submarines. In the English Channel we were trailed by four subs and kept firing depth charges at intervals. At last, one cold night, we came into Le Havre and walked up the pebbly beach—the pebbly beaches of France, I remembered them from my childhood.

It was one thirty in the morning by the time we climbed into the open vans waiting for us. The wind was blowing a blizzard when we passed through Le Havre, and I was heartsick as I stared at the rubble-strewn city and remembered how it had looked so long ago. Dreaming of warm billeting, we drove seventy miles through the freezing night to Camp Lucky Strike. But the soldiers who had vacated the tents to move up to the front had left the flaps open. It was as cold inside as out, and we had to pick our way carefully because the place was still mined. I found a little straw and put it on top of the snow in one of the tents and laid my sleeping bag on top of that and went to sleep without giving a single thought to my father's warnings about pneumonia.

We spent six weeks training in France, and because I knew French I acted as interpreter for the officers in the ordnance section.

Then we moved up to once beautiful Reims, a horrible rubble now, and so came to Luxembourg, our last stop before Germany. The citizens of Luxembourg welcomed us with cheers and bade us farewell with tears. And then we entered Aachen, our first German city. Once it had housed more than a million inhabitants. Now it was only a mass of debris. At Aachen we each got a notice from General Omar Bradley telling us that we were entering the combat area. They loaded us with ammo and grenades and we were moving again.

At Trier we heard at last the first sounds of war, the distant rumble of guns. We felt tense and frightened. This was it, we thought.

Ever since I left my family in California I had been writing my grandmother twice a week, and I continued to do so even now. I put something personal in each letter for my mother and something for Dad. Nana would show the letter to Mother and then mail it on to my father. Mother and Nana wrote me every week, but I heard from Dad only through Oona.

"We can't believe you're at the front lines, Charlie," Oona's letters would begin. "Neither your father nor I. Why, just a few months ago you were over here swimming and enjoying yourself." Then would follow all kinds of warnings, so that as I read along I could picture Dad standing at her shoulder, his hands behind his back, telling her just what to say. Dad was, of course, still warning me about catching my death of cold in foxholes.

I had been promoted to corporal by the time we moved up from Trier. I was camped in a foxhole behind a hill when they brought me the letter from my mother. Arthur Day had been shipped to New Guinea and was in a battle zone, Syd was in training, and my mother, feeling alone and deserted by her menfolk, was now deep in the throes of her second nervous breakdown. She wrote me that life was no longer worth living since we were all gone, that nothing mattered to her any more and she was going to kill herself.

Shocked, I read the letter over and over, my heart in my throat. Just then the sergeant, a tough, hard soldier, came by and took a long look at me.

"What's the matter, son?" he asked.

I told him, and suddenly I saw his face turn compassionate.

"Come along, we'll see the chaplain," he ordered.

The chaplain comforted me and then notified the Red Cross. I went back to the front while they got in touch with my family at home. Later I learned unhappily that they had given my mother a severe scolding. But all I heard then was that they had checked and everything was all right and I was not to worry. It was done in an inconceivably short time. How hard our government worked to keep up the morale of the soldiers at the front!

The next day we moved to the town of Gotha. It had just been captured and the civilians were still around, though there was rubble everywhere. In the center of the market place I saw the ruins of a circular opera house. It was an empty shell, yet somehow, miraculously, the names of the German great engraved on the ruined wall had not been disturbed. Goethe, Beethoven, Schiller, Wagner, Heine—they were all there, a melancholy reminder of the days of German culture. I read them over to myself and in my imagination I heard the strains of music that had once floated from the opera house in happier, peaceful days. I turned away and went to my billet, which was in a German radio factory, where we were housing the guns we had to repair. All the windows of the factory had been blown out and it looked like a haunted place. Once I had known a haunted house at Pebble Beach. How far away, remote in time and space, how delightfully childish it seemed. This was the front.

In Gotha I saw my first action. A Czechoslovakian running up to warn us that civilian snipers were plotting an attack was shot down by a nervous sentry for not knowing the password and not stopping when the warning shots were fired in the air. The Czech gasped out his story as he lay dying horribly, his chest torn wide open by the shell. We had no morphine to make it easier for him, just dressings and sulpha. He was the first man I had ever seen die.

The attack started before he died. It was close to twilight. Suddenly machine-gun tracer bullets started coming at us from the buildings across the street. I hit the dirt. I didn't even have my helmet on at the time. I had to crawl a hundred feet to my billet in the factory, scared and cursing every inch of the way, with the bullets hitting just above my head. I reached the billet and, lying on the floor, put on my helmet. The bullets were still coming in through the windows. I was the assistant bazooka man and the Lieutenant asked me to go out in the middle of the street, directly in the line of fire, and lob a few bazooka shells through the windows of the buildings across the way.

"We'll cover you, Charlie," he said.

I tried to follow his orders, but I was shaking so hard I couldn't coordinate.

"I'll do it," the Lieutenant told me. "You dive into the trench by the road and help the others there."

Coolly the Lieutenant sent off two bazooka shells and fired up both buildings while I dove into the trench where the rest of the platoon was stationed. There's where I almost got killed. It was quite dark now. You could tell the position of the guns only by the light flashes. I got so interested in drawing a bead on them that I forgot to keep my head down. Suddenly the fellow next to me shoved me.

"Duck!" he yelled.

I did—just in time. I didn't think anything of it then. There wasn't time to think. We went on firing until the light flashes stopped, then spent five hours in position waiting, and the waiting was even more horrifying than the action, because it was jet-black now. We felt like sitting ducks, not knowing if there was going to be another attack or where it would come from. We started joking and laughing hysterically over nothing to while the time away. And finally it was over and we got some sleep.

The next day we rounded up thirteen bodies of the enemy. Some of us had to stand guard over them while thick clouds of flies buzzed overhead and the relatives wailed hysterically. The rest of us went through the buildings to flush out any remaining snipers.

Chagrined by my performance with the bazooka, I was determined to be brave. I hurried to be the first to kick in the doors and look around and take the fire if there was any, but the Captain wouldn't allow it.

"No, let me," he said. He was as calm as a cucumber, a brave man.

That was the day President Roosevelt died. Back in the States they recessed the court session of my father's second paternity trial to mourn the president's passing, and in Gotha grown soldiers sat and wept like children. And I began for the first time to think seriously of death. Thoughts are dangerous at the front. I became dazed and silent. Now and then I shivered so hard my teeth rattled. When I walked I seemed to have lost my equilibrium; I kept banging into people, and I couldn't find the words to answer when they asked me what was wrong.

They said I was suffering a mild case of shock, so they took me to the first-aid station back of the lines and I stayed there for a short time. I begged them not to put it on my record and they listened to me. When I went back to the front I was a seasoned soldier.

Though the fear never left, war had become just a chore now. As a member of the ordnance crew it was my task to repair the guns on the front. A sudden image of Kay tinkering blissfully about Dad's cars with the parts strewn all round him in the quiet garage at home would sometimes come to me as I worked.

There was no quiet on the front. Every time we went out it was like a nightmare. We zigzagged up the hillside in our jeep. Just short of the brow we jumped out and carefully made our way to the guns, usually crawling there. We repaired them under the fire of the enemy, learning to duck when we heard the warning *Sh-sh-sh-sh* of a big shell. If you didn't move fast enough it was curtains.

One day I saw a friend of mine die that way. I didn't know he'd been hit until I saw blood oozing from a thousand little shrapnel holes in his chest. When we turned him over we saw that the blast had left his back a mangled mass of flesh. I looked at him and I almost started to cry. Who can describe the loneliness a soldier feels when he looks at the violent death of a friend and the shells are still coming over and he knows that at any moment one of them may have his number on it?

I began to drink more. I still didn't like the taste of it, but I found it warmed me and kept me from thinking and dulled the fear. Almost everyone drank and for the same reason. Everyone snatched what fun he could, knowing it might be his last. And we seldom talked romantically of the girl back home or our families or the nostalgic fun of our boyhood and youth, as is so often depicted in war movies. All we thought of was, "I'm scared. Oh, God, I wish we were all out of here."

By this time Syd was in the army, too. He had been sent over to Europe as a rifleman replacement in the 65th Infantry, a stranger taking a dead man's place in an already organized outfit. So it was even harder for him than for me.

After the war Syd was to tell us of his first hand-to-hand

encounter with death. Armed with a forty-five-caliber pistol, he was accompanying an officer who was going through buildings rounding up Nazis. They went into the second story of a house and came across a German officer. He surrendered and they told him to put his hands on top of his head. Then they began ransacking the room for private papers. While they were busy at this the Nazi turned, made a break for the door and started running down the steps.

"Shoot him!" the officer commanded Syd.

"You mean *kill* him?" Syd asked in horror. He couldn't believe he was actually being ordered to fire on a defenseless fellow man. He shut his eyes and pulled the trigger, and that was the way my independent, light-hearted younger brother was introduced to war.

One day the unbelievable happened. I received a long, personal letter directly from my father. He must have just seen a newsreel of soldiers working their way through mined houses, because the letter was full of warnings about booby traps. He was genuinely worried.

"Be careful where you walk, son," he wrote. "You might step on a mine and blow off your foot. It's not good to go through life maimed. Don't pick up strange objects, you might get a hand blown off."

He seemed especially concerned about pianos and singled them out for attention, warning me not to play on a strange one or to lift it or move it for fear the whole thing would blow up in my face. I suppose pianos troubled him so much because ever since I had shown an interest in music he had associated me with them. I had to laugh. Pianos were the least of my concern while bullets were flying overhead and shells were lobbing over and an occasional German plane was strafing us.

It was all a wearisome bloody frightening business, and a sickening one as well, when we came in to Ohrdruf and inspected the grim concentration camp surrounded with its barbed wire. The place was like a horrible nightmare, with its gas chambers that looked like shower stalls, its lime pits and the pyres made of railroad ties. We saw heaps of charred bodies on the pyres. Bodies were stacked in shacks. Partly decomposed bodies were in the lime pits. In the courtyard there was another pile of bodies, each with a bullet in the back of the head.

We brought the mayor of Ohrdruf and his wife to see what had been going on in their town. And they went away and hanged themselves.

Then our outfit was on the move again toward Berlin.

Two days after we had seen the concentration camp, there was great excitement among the men because word got out that five men and three officers were to be sent on a recuperation trip to the Riviera, the names to be chosen by lot. I couldn't believe it when the Sergeant told me my name was the first enlisted man's to be drawn out of hundreds. We drove straight from the front, dirty, unshaven, looking like bums.

At Nice we were given clean uniforms and we had a time for ourselves, two weeks packed as full of fun as we could, for all of us were thinking, "Maybe this is our last two weeks."

The two weeks came to an end too soon and we were back in the truck making our way to our outfit, and the scared feeling was with us again full force.

But when we came to Holland on May 8, 1945, we found dancing in all the streets of the Dutch cities. People swarmed round our truck and stopped us. Pretty girls grabbed us and hugged us, and everyone offered us beer. And so they made us understand the war was over. No more hiding in foxholes. No more sweating on ridges under the barrage of guns, no more killing and getting killed. We whooped it up and danced and sang and drank their beer and kissed their pretty girls, and finally we made our way to our outfit, but we were no longer going back to die.

I was sent almost immediately to Fort Leonard Wood, near St. Louis, Missouri, and there, by coincidence, I met up again with Stan and we renewed our old friendship. They kept us at Fort Leonard Wood for four months, and then Stan and I were sent west to Fort MacArthur and from there we were discharged on February 2, 1946.

I had two battle stars to prove I had been in combat, but suddenly the things of war were no longer important to me. I was a civilian again and glad of it. I persuaded Stan to go back with me to Hollywood and live with me and try to make a place for himself there. So Stan listened to me, and he says that I'm responsible for all his subsequent good fortune, that otherwise he would never have become an ASCAP composer writing special and original music for a number of top radio and television shows. Stan is married now and has four children. We're still close friends and tell each other our troubles and weep on each other's shoulders and celebrate with each other when the going is good. It is just as it was in the army days.

As soon as we got back to Hollywood I took Stan with me to the house on the hill. My little half-sister Geraldine was a year and a half old and scampering around the place. Oona was expecting her next baby shortly. But my father looked the same. He was sitting with his glasses on at his little table in the study and his pencil was racing over the yellow, lined paper before him as he worked on *Monsieur Verdoux*. Even the buzzer that looked like a doorbell was in its identical place. It was impossible to believe that a year and a half and a war lay between us and the last time I had walked in and found him sitting in that same position working on that same script. It might have been yesterday.

37

Ever since 1941, at least, my father had been working on and off at *Monsieur Verdoux*. He had taken time out for the screenplay of *Shadow and Substance* during that fateful interlude with Joan Barry, but as soon as that was over he had returned to the former script.

Dad had been introduced to the macabre story of the French Bluebeard by Orson Welles, who had been toying with the idea himself. One night after dinner at Dad's home they had discussed it. From that time on my father was haunted by it, and finally he asked Tim Durant to buy the idea from Welles. He never used Welles's idea, however, only the central character of Landru, who became Monsieur Verdoux in the picture.

From the first, friends had been dubious about the possibility of turning the gruesome plot into a comedy, but my father could not be dissuaded. *Monsieur Verdoux* was really as much a mission with him as *The Great Dictator*. It was to be his outcry against both the sufferings brought on by depressions and those caused by wars, with their mass killings, in particular the destructiveness of the atom bomb, which had so horrified him when it was dropped on Nagasaki and Hiroshima.

I think, however, that *Monsieur Verdoux* was more than a mission with my father. I feel that this picture served to objectify for him all the mingled fascination and horror he had felt throughout his life toward violence and the macabre—the gruesome newspaper story, especially if it concerned a child . . . the various sadistic punishments of different races which he would discuss with me at length . . . suicide and madness and the drama that precedes an execution, the condemned man's last meal and words and actions.

When I sent him some war souvenirs, a big Nazi flag, a German officer's dress sword and dagger beautifully carved and ornamented, he gave them back to me as soon as he could.

"I'm very proud of you, son, but I don't even want them here," he told me. "I can't bear to have them in the house." The horror in his face as he returned them was very evident.

Monsieur Verdoux served as an outlet for all these ambivalent emotions, and most especially for the destructive grief my father has always felt in the presence of the dark undercurrents of the human psyche. It was as though he hoped, with burlesque, to lighten the grimness inherent in life and to project it outside himself.

When I returned from the war that February the *Monsieur Verdoux* script was almost finished. Dad was as immersed in his subject as he had been in Hitler. He studied every detail of the life of the little murderer, and sometimes, thinking about him, he would be sunk in a depression that would last for hours.

"How could this man so methodically take these women out and cut them up and burn them in his incinerator, and then tend his flowers, with the black smoke coming out of the chimney?" he would suddenly exclaim in a tone of wonder.

In the next instant he would snap out of his brown study and start pantomiming the gruesome episode, turning it into such comedy that I couldn't help laughing. These uproarious scenes from *Monsieur Verdoux* which Dad depicted for me and any guests who visited him were the order of things throughout that spring of 1946. But when he went to film the picture he discarded most of the sequences he had tried out beforehand on us. I always regretted this, for I thought those spontaneous episodes far funnier than anything I saw on the screen. Perhaps it was because I had been spoiled in this way that I liked *Monsieur Verdoux* less than any of my father's pictures.

Dad had settled on his female lead months before I was discharged from the army, and he had at once begun writing his script around her without even notifying her of what he was doing. The girl was Martha Raye, the first of his leading ladies to have made movies in Hollywood before she came to my father. But as Martha says, her career has always been full of ups and downs and at the moment it was decidedly down. She was working at the Latin Quarter in New York when her phone rang one day.

"This is Charlie Chaplin," the voice at the other end said when Martha picked up the receiver.

"Oh, sure," Martha laughed, taking it for a gag, and hung up.

She gasped when Abe Lastfogel, her agent, got in touch with her and told her it actually had been my father.

"Why, to a comedienne that's almost like God calling you," Martha explains.

She was shaking when she phoned him back, but she managed to say yes when he asked if she could get to Hollywood in twelve days. All she could think of was that he was the King of Comedy, and she was to play opposite him.

The first day on the set was the first time they met, and as she talked to him Martha felt as though her knees were shaking hands with each other. They had lunch and then Dad, seeing how frightened she was, told her they would take two days to rehearse. But the two days couldn't erase Martha's awe. The great Charlie Chaplin! She had heard from others what a tyrant and perfectionist he was as a director.

For several days she went timidly around the set addressing Dad in a very dignified manner. It was Mr. Chaplin this, Mr. Chaplin that, until she became so tense and nervous she was almost ready to jump out of her skin. Then she decided to do something about it, something drastic no matter what the results. Syd, who by this time was out of the army too, and I were on the set the day Martha made her move. Dad was in the middle of one of his directorial stews and everyone was sweating it out with him.

"Chuck! Chuck!" Martha suddenly intoned. "How do you want me to do this bit?"

Dad looked around, startled. I guess it was the first time he had ever been called by that nickname. His eyes met Martha's and saw the challenging glint in them. Suddenly an amused look brightened his face. The tension eased. From then on it was "Chuck" all the time with Martha, and "Maggie" with Dad, because Martha's real name is Margaret Reed.

Martha had crossed her first hurdle. But she realized it wasn't enough. She had to keep asserting herself if she didn't want to be completely cowed by my father's personality. One day, in the middle of a scene, she broke everything up by stopping short.

"One hour!" she announced in a clarion voice.

"What . . . what do you mean?" Dad asked, too startled to be angry.

"Lunch," Martha explained tersely. "It's two o'clock and we haven't had lunch yet."

It was the first time on one of Dad's sets that anyone had dared call attention to the passage of time.

"You're so right," Dad agreed, and he dismissed the cast and crew for lunch.

After that, whenever Martha sang out "One hour!" Dad would knock off without a word. Those of us who knew his ways smiled to ourselves. For the only time in his directorial career, one of his feminine stars had dared to call his bluff.

Martha wasn't doing a picture with my father just for the ride. She was as eager to learn as Paulette and Jack Oakie had been. You saw her around the sets all the time, even when she wasn't needed, watching how things were done. And she sopped up every bit of instruction my father offered her. She found his advice especially helpful because her style of entertainment is based on pantomime. She learned from Dad to scale her pantomime to the size of her audience, as a speaker scales his voice—magnified pantomime for large theaters, less exaggerated for small ones. She learned that the trick sports clothes she was wearing to help put her jokes across weren't right.

"Low comedy requires beautiful clothes, good makeup and hairdress," Dad told her. "It's the gestures, not the clothes, that are supposed to get the laughs."

"He's right," Martha says. "But oh, he has cost me a lot of money—the money I've spent on clothes since!"

My father especially cautioned Martha not to come to the set too well rehearsed. It must have been the first time he had ever deprecated rehearsals for one of his feminine stars. But Martha was different from the others. She was an active pantomimist herself, and my father always felt that spontaneity was very important to his peculiar combination of low with pathetic comedy.

"If you get bored with yourself and aren't having fun

doing it," he explained to Martha, "the audience won't have fun watching you."

I think that because Martha was primarily a pantomimist, my father felt a sense of kinship toward her. He had great respect for her talents and seldom corrected her. He never tried to tone her down, though Martha, in her nervous concern, sometimes asked him if she was going too far.

"Don't worry," he told her. "I wrote you in that way. If you do anything wrong I'll let you know." Then he went on to give her another piece of advice.

"You can do anything if you don't have a vulgar mind, Maggie," he said. "Have a little pixyishness. Let them have fun, it won't be vulgar. Some can swear, others can't. It's like another gift, a talent. It's there or it isn't. You have to be what you are naturally."

When she confessed to him one day how nervous she was, my father suddenly began pouring out his own problems to her.

"I'm bloody nervous myself," he admitted, and went on to tell her that *Monsieur Verdoux* was an altogether new experience for him. He missed his talisman, the Little Tramp, who had walked out of *The Great Dictator* for good. He missed those familiar baggy pants, the derby and mustache. In their place was this strange, even repulsive character, a French Bluebeard. Out of his gruesome life he had somehow to construct a comedy and manage to keep it balanced dexterously on the borderline not only of tragedy but of the downright macabre.

"Why did he tell *me* about his nervousness?" Martha wondered. "He's the great Charlie Chaplin. He doesn't have to admit to weaknesses." It apparently didn't occur to her that there never was a lonelier man than Dad when he was in production.

There weren't nearly so many retakes on *Monsieur Verdoux* as on my father's previous pictures. He seemed to be racing to complete it, and he did so in the record time, for a

316

Chaplin picture, of twelve weeks; though it wasn't ready to be premièred until April of the following year.

Monsieur Verdoux wasn't a success in this country. It lacked appeal for American audiences, and in addition, it was boycotted by various groups. Some of them objected to the picture itself as making light of murder, but others made it plain that the boycott was directed not at the film but at my father. In May of 1947, for instance, a month after the picture opened, three hundred and twenty-five Ohio movie-theater owners tried to bring about a nation-wide boycott because they didn't believe screen time should be "dissipated upon a screen personality such as Chaplin." The picture that had been painted of my father as a licentious philanderer had succeeded in focusing attention on his personal life, and every fault of which he had ever been accused was now being blown up until it resembled a major crime. But I shall come to this subject later.

In Europe *Monsieur Verdoux* was hailed as a masterpiece and won several awards. It was particularly popular in France, the homeland of the murderer. Martha Raye was to have first-hand proof of this when, just after its release, she went over to do a road show for the occupation troops. Martha stopped off in Paris to purchase an outfit from Dior's establishment. She had only an hour or so, but Dior, who was putting on a fashion show at the moment, had a strict rule not to sell at such times. Martha was in despair when in walked Pierre Balmain, Dior's assistant at the time. He shrugged his shoulders when Martha introduced herself, because Martha Raye was nobody to him. Then he took a second look.

"Madame Verdoux!" he shouted exuberantly and threw his arms around her, kissing her on both cheeks in typical French fashion. After that anything she wanted was hers.

"Not even a gendarme would recognize me as Martha Raye," Martha told me. "But everyone knew Madame Verdoux."

As for those twelve weeks of work with my father, Martha sums it up in typical hyperbole. "I was honored," she told me seriously. "I would have done it for nothing—just to have the opportunity of working with him. Any comedian to this day asks me what it was like, I tell them, I tell everyone, that I look on it as the greatest experience in my life next to having my daughter."

38

I was out of the army. I was free. I was twenty-one. Suddenly life had become the most important thing in the world to me. I set out to enjoy it to the full—lots of relaxation, parties, girls. The ones I brought up to the house were no longer callow teenagers but more sophisticated young starlets. I wanted to cut a swath with them, so I sopped up my father's advice on how to woo and win a girl. After all, throughout his life women had been more or less throwing themselves into his arms.

"Most men put the wrong thing first in courting a girl," Dad used to tell Syd and me. "Always be a gentleman. Fascinate her by your mind first, not by your powers as a man. That comes much later."

Dad, for his part, was carefully looking over Syd's and my girl friends with the eye of a father who realizes his sons have reached marriageable age. He never exactly talked against any girl we brought up for dinner or a swim, but if he didn't approve of her he could be a devastating censor in the nicest way. He would just pantomime her, and when he did you would see every foible she had, highlighted in the most disconcerting way. He was always warning us about the opposite sex.

With all his advice floating into our ears, it is small wonder that Syd and I remained bachelors so long. Of course there are other factors as well. The four marriages each of our father and mother and the three of our grandmother tended to dampen our faith in the joys and stability of matrimony, I guess.

There was one young girl I brought up about this time who especially impressed my father. She was just about my age, twenty-one, an appealing little obscure starlet by the name of Norma Jean Dougherty who was under stock contract to Twentieth Century-Fox.

"Oh, she's a beauty," Dad used to tell me. "What a figure! I admire your taste, son, very much."

Dad liked to converse with Norma Jean. I don't know what they talked about, but I know he did most of the talking, because she was always so in awe of him.

"She *does* have a way of speaking, doesn't she?" he would tease me afterwards. And then he would mimic Norma Jean!

"Charrllieee," he would say in that wispy voice that has since become famous, "what are we going to do tonight?"

But despite his joking, Dad wasn't letting anything pass by, either. He could see how much I was coming to think of the beautiful little starlet.

"Just watch out, son," he said. "Don't fall in love yet. You have that education to take care of first."

But Dad didn't need to worry about Norma Jean and me. "Well, Charrllieee," she told me one day, "my name now is Marilyn Monroe."

Marilyn Monroe started going to the top fast, and it was the duty of her studio publicity department to keep her name in the papers by dating her here and there with other eligible young men. So she and I drifted apart, and I haven't seen her for years.

My father had never given up his dream of a college education for Syd and me, and all my life I had thought of following his wishes. But after the army I couldn't bring myself to take four more years of regimentation. It was the same with Syd and a lot of other boys whose education had been interrupted by soldiering. Dad was distressed.

"Stop playing with the girls and frittering away your time, Charles," he would lecture. "Get that education and then I'll take you into the studio and teach you the movie business from top to bottom. I'll even buy you that house you want so much."

Dad knew I had never given up my dream of becoming an actor and I had told him I planned to buy a house with the savings he had put away for me till my twenty-first birthday. His offer was tempting, especially as I knew it was genuine—he had never in his life broken a promise to me. And he always had such powers of persuasion. It was just like those Sunday afternoons of long ago when he sent me back to Black-Foxe full of enthusiasm and determination to make my mark in school.

Again I succumbed, at least to a certain point. To please him I took an extension course at the University of California at Los Angeles. But I couldn't help feeling I was only wasting time, and at the end of a year I gave up all thought of a formal education. I left U.C.L.A. and joined the Circle Theater group to which Syd belonged, branching out from there to the Hollywood Actors Laboratory.

Here in the acting field Syd and I again showed our different temperaments. Just as Syd had dared compete with my father on the tennis court, now he invited both his criticism and his coaching. I preferred to study under other teachers, though almost every day I came to watch my father drill Syd.

I admired Syd's courage in accepting Dad's coaching, but I didn't want it for myself. I idolized him too much, was too much in awe of the figure he cut in the theatrical world to feel I could give a genuinely independent performance under him.

This doesn't mean I didn't welcome his criticisms. Though I never rehearsed for him, he would come to see my finished performances and afterwards give me pointers. Usually his corrections would consist only of a shift of emphasis in some line. But sometimes he would suggest a realignment of a whole scene, as in Thomas Dekker's play, *The Shoemaker's Holiday*, in which I played the King.

He came to watch me perform at Actors Lab on opening night, the first time in my life he had seen me act. I was terrified, wondering how my performance would go over with him. For me there was no one else in the theater that night.

Suddenly in the middle of the play I heard his high-pitched spontaneous laughter above the others. Long ago as a child on the Ebell Theatre stage I had listened in vain for that distinctive laugh. Now I played my part with everything I had. My father came backstage afterwards to congratulate me.

"I never knew you were this good, son," he told me in an amazed voice, as if he were truly surprised I could act at all.

I asked him if he had any suggestions or criticisms. He had one that showed how close he kept to naturalism in his art.

"As the King, you're making too big a production of knighting people," he told me. "Kings just pull a sword out and go *poomp, poomp* on either shoulder, 'You are now a Knight,' all very matter of fact, because it's such a commonplace thing with them."

Everything Dad did on the screen was as offhand as his demonstration of a king's knighting habits. He had no use for the various schools of acting, Stanislavsky and Boleslavsky included, which taught the mechanics of the art.

"If you're good you don't have to worry about how to go about it," he would say. "It's intuitive."

After I had finished with Actors Lab I went back to New York to appear in *Now I Lay Me Down to Sleep,* and after that I did my second imitation of my father before an audience. It was a far cry from the childish performance at the Ebell Theatre.

Ken Murray asked me to appear in his show at the Roxy Theater, and I thought a long time before accepting his offer. But in the end I consented. I put on the little mustache and the derby and, twirling my cane, I acted out my father for about six thousand people.

The critics tore the show apart but they gave me rave notices. I stayed with Ken during his two-week run. Afterwards, Lou Walters of the Latin Quarter wanted to center another show on that act at a fabulous price, but I refused. The more I refused the more he raised his price. I was tempted, I must admit, but in the end I turned it down. I didn't want to be typed as an imitator of my father. I wanted to be an actor in my own right. So I came back to Hollywood. On the way I suddenly realized I would have to face my father and I began to wonder how he would feel about my imitating him.

I knew how vehement he was about people who tried to take advantage of his sons. Would he think Ken Murray had done just that? Would he think I was a fool ruining myself by imitating him instead of working out my own characterization? Would he figure I was just trying to ride in on his fame or make some fast money? Would he think I was presumptuous doing an imitation without consulting him first? What if he disowned me? I have a very fertile imagination, and now I pictured myself cut off from him for good. Yet I loved him and I wanted more than anything to keep his love.

Worst of all, after I got back to Hollywood, I was afraid even to face him and find out just how I stood. I waited two weeks, making excuses to myself for not phoning him. Then finally one day I went up. He was sitting on the couch in the living room awaiting me.

"How've you been, son?" he said when I came in. "I hear you did a very good job in your play with Fredric March."

"Thanks, Dad." I stammered.

"I hear you also played the Roxy Theater."

"Yes, Dad, I did."

"I hear you did an imitation of me . . ." He paused, a long pause. Then he concluded with a smile, ". . . that was very good."

What a relief! Seeing him sitting there in such good humor I asked myself what had made me so afraid of him. I felt a little foolish. He was my father, I was his son. That was how things had always been between us.

"I think that's very amusing," Dad was going on. "Will you do your imitation for me?"

Suddenly I was covered with confusion. "No, I wouldn't dare," I told him. "I just wouldn't dare."

He kept coaxing but I was too self-conscious. Neither then nor later could I bring myself to do that imitation, though he asked me often. I was able to do it without hesitation for another famous man, the late Walter Gieseking, the greatest coloratura pianist of our age, and had the satisfaction of hearing him laugh uproariously over it. But Dad is different. He's not only the master pantomimist of the world, he is also my father.

I can't say that the pantomiming bit I did for Ken Murray either helped or hurt my career. I've had the same problem from the beginning: I look like my father, many of my gestures resemble his. Casting directors are prone to type me as the Little Tramp or the drunk. I've even had to fight to keep from having my parts built up out of all proportion to the rest of the play just in order to display the son of the famous Charlie Chaplin imitating his father.

In the latter part of '51, when I was twenty-six, my father started filming *Limelight*, which he had been working on for the past five years. Syd had the young romantic lead. Even in a family there is type casting, and Dad needed someone very tall for the part to show off his own small stature. Syd, who is over six foot one, is the tallest in our family. Besides, my father had been working with Syd for several years and during that time had been writing the part around him. When I came back to Hollywood he pressured me to play a role in his picture too, no matter how small.

By this time he and Oona had four children, Geraldine, Michael, Josephine and little Victoria, who had been born just the previous spring. He was going to put the three older children in his picture along with Syd and me. He had a very sentimental reason for wanting to make *Limelight* what he called a family affair. He said he fully expected it to be his last as well as his greatest picture. As usual, he was back to retiring again, although speaking softly when he talked about it.

"Well," he would say, "I think your father is going to quit after this one. He's getting old."

At sixty-three, Dad was beginning to joke a little about his age. It was obvious he was becoming conscious of it, though even then he didn't attach too much importance to the number of years he had lived. He has always been young in spirit and he likes youth, or at least people young in spirit, around him.

The story of *Limelight*, which my father himself wrote, is in good part a symbolic autobiography in which he made ample use of the London music halls of his boyhood days. In it my father again played the role of a drunk, which had brought him to the attention of Hollywood when, back in 1913, he did it touring the United States with the Karno Company. But the characterization in *Limelight* is nostalgic rather than humorous.

The story concerns an old pantomimist who, through his addiction to alcohol, loses his place in the theatrical world. A young girl whom he saves from suicide rehabilitates him. She loves him, but he cannot believe his good fortune and encourages the romance between her and a shy young musician.

At the time my father wrote the picture he had no female star in mind. He decided on Claire Bloom at the last minute, because he felt he had put off production long enough.

Filming of the picture started in early December of 1951. The shooting schedule had been fixed at thirty-six days, but it took fifty to complete. And now, at last, it was Syd's and my turn to be targets of that drive for perfection which ever since our childhood we had seen focused upon others. After that experience I was more than ever convinced that my father's towering reputation and his seething intensity make it almost impossible for those working under him to assert their own personality. No one in the world could direct my father as he directs himself, but I feel that lesser actors in his pictures might profit from being directed by someone else.

With Syd and me he was, I believe, even more exacting than with the others. As his sons we could not appear to be favored, and so he went to the opposite extreme and even tended to make examples of us. He was especially tough on Syd as the young romantic lead, and sometimes I heard people around the set commiserating with him. But I never heard Syd himself complain. He kept his equanimity and learned from my father and was rewarded by being praised in the reviews for his fine performance.

Now that Syd and I were older and were in our father's profession as well, he began to confide in us more and to discuss with us what he was actually trying to get across in his pictures. It was his basic philosophy of life and it all came back to the Little Tramp. He talked much of the Little Tramp those days, for the pantomimist of *Limelight* is really the Little Fellow—the Little Fellow grown older and wiser, and more melancholy. Dad feels that the Little Tramp symbolizes the Little Fellow of the world who is always trying to better himself but never quite succeeds at it, and who leaves the stage of life as sad as he appeared on it. The theme gives away my father's own basic feeling of insecurity. Objectively he knows he is a great comedian. Objectively he has fame, wealth and the deep respect of his fellow craftsmen to back up this knowledge. Inwardly he is still the Little Fellow, with the unhappy feeling that he is something of a failure because he hasn't accomplished all he wished to do in life. That feeling of regret is apparent in his pictures, so that even when one of them ends happily it still conveys a sense of nostalgia and loss. It is the philosophy of a perfectionist who, try as he may, and work as hard as he can—as my father has certainly done all his life—still never achieves that final goal which seems always to hover tantalizingly just out of reach.

So far as technique is concerned, my father is prone to imitate the stage. He is a profound believer in showing the whole scene rather than a succession of close-ups, which he uses only when absolutely necessary. Close-ups, he used to explain, convey only an emotional effect. But the main thing is to show the picture of life as a whole—a picture to which the individual, no matter how important his role, merely contributes a share.

Syd and I were both proud to have done a picture with our father, to be able to say that we were directed by the King of Comedy. Yet I cannot say my sequence in *Limelight* was my favorite acting bit. I enjoyed more the comedy lead in *Oh, Men! Oh, Women!* which I played on tour in the British Isles in 1956. But my favorite role has always been that of Victor, the French proprietor in *All for Mary*, with Edward Everett Horton at the Pasadena Playhouse in 1957. In that role I had a chance to exhibit my talents in my own way. And when I read David Bongard's review in the *Los Angeles Herald Express*, I had the jubilant feeling that I was really being judged on my own abilities.

"A notable thing is the work of Charles Chaplin, Jr.," Mr. Bongard wrote. "He's a finished actor and displays a remarkable technical resemblance to the work of his comic father.

Nothing intentional. Just a quick gesture here and a twitch of the eyebrow there."

This was marvelous, for I had never wanted to be in competition with my father or to spend my life mimicking him, though I have to some extent inherited his pantomiming talents as he inherited them from his mother, my grandmother. I have wanted only to be worthy of my name—the name of Chaplin that stands so high in the theatrical world. I was sorry my father could not see me in this role.

39

I had brought a handicap back with me from my days in the army. Liquor hadn't been a problem to me during the war. I had drunk along with most of the other soldiers because I discovered that drinking relieves pressures. But in civilian life I suddenly found I was free, with no superior officers to answer to and no life-and-death duties to perform. I fell into the habit of indulging in alcohol as freely as I pleased.

I don't know why some people should find their refuge in drinking, while others are immune. I know we all have problems that have to be solved, so it's foolish to blame circumstances. It's something within us, something we don't ask for —call it fate or allergy as you please—that creates an alcoholic situation for some of us.

I had always thought of Syd as happy-go-lucky, but I discovered that he came out of the war with troubles, too, though drinking wasn't one of them. He who had always been the life of everything suddenly found he couldn't mingle with people. He would go to a party and sit in a corner and never say a word the whole evening.

When he got his first break on the stage, he took his problem to a psychiatrist. He wanted to pay for psychiatric treatment for me too, because he felt it had done him so much good.

"Hell, Chuck," he said, "I have all this money now. I can write it off my income tax."

I was deeply touched by Syd's generosity and goodness. But I shook my head. Syd and I both have always been so independent, each in his own way.

"No, Syd," I said. "I'd rather take care of it myself. It wouldn't help me any to sponge off you."

The public learned of my trouble—for the embarrassing part of an alcoholic problem is that it often makes a fool of you in front of the whole world—one New Year's Eve during the period I was studying at Actors Lab. I had a few too many and made the mistake of driving in that condition. I ended up in Lincoln Heights jail in Los Angeles. All the bunks were taken, so I put a piece of newspaper on the floor and stretched out on it. I wanted to die quietly in the jail cell among all the other unfortunates locked up with me. They were suffering in blessed anonymity, but I knew even as I lay there in the dark that I wouldn't be allowed that privilege.

After about twenty minutes, just as I had expected, all the lights went on. I could hear voices, feet, the clanking of doors. And suddenly about ten newspapermen, with a police guide, appeared right outside the cell. They were there to get a story about me, not because I was anybody in my own right but because I was the son of a famous man.

I realized my offense was a bad one. I was ready to pay the

penalty for it. But suddenly the unfairness of being singled out for added attention because my name was Chaplin filled me with blind fury. Normally I'm fond of newspapermen and a number of them are my good friends; I realize that a newspaperman has a job to do, too. But in that moment I hated them all. I began to call them every name I could think of, realizing all the time that I should control myself because I was at their mercy. But I just couldn't hold back the words. In the form of imprecations I poured out all the blind, suffering rage I felt, and in those moments I think I tasted to the dregs the terrible feeling of injustice my father had experienced when he was harried and ridiculed on the witness stand by Mr. Scott. There is no word to describe the blackness of that suffering, to be forced to stand without defense and be humiliated before your fellow man.

"Listen, I know they're going to make an example of me in court because of the heritage, whatever it is," I cried out to them. "But why do I have to bear this too?"

By this time I was threatening the photographers. But they only laughed at me and the policeman opened the doors and twisted my arm behind my back to get one last picture of me looking like a dangerous criminal.

I had been booked about two thirty in the morning, and by the time a friend arranged bail for me and I was released it was about six. I went out a free man, but all the same I felt like a criminal. I suffered terrible remorse, for my experiences had sobered me. I walked around aimlessly, waiting for the papers to come out. I bought them all without even looking at them.

"Something interesting happen?" the newsboy asked curiously.

"No, no," I said, averting my face because I knew without looking I would be on the front page.

I took all the papers and went to the office of my lawyer, Max Gilford. I looked a mess, unshaved and in my rumpled clothes. I told Max the situation. He tried to make me feel better.

"Well, I know, I've been drunk too," he said. "You have a hangover." And he ordered coffee for me.

While I drank the coffee we looked at the papers together. There I was on the front page with big headlines and a blown-up picture of me snarling behind bars like something in a zoo. Later I learned from Paulette that the story had made the papers even in France, where she was at the time.

What I saw made me feel worse than ever. Max looked at me sympathetically. He told me to go home and come back and discuss the situation with him the next day. I explained to him that my monetary situation was very low. I had bought a house with the money from the savings account which my father had had put away for me until my twenty-first birthday. And though I still received the proceeds from my trust fund, which amounted to some five hundred dollars a month, expenditures and debts of various kinds had sadly depleted this allowance. Max understood my situation. He told me not to worry, he would charge me only a fifty-dollar fee.

I left his office and went home to my mother and grandmother. They could see how I felt by how I looked, and they tried to cheer me up. But the worst hurdle was still ahead. I had to face my father. I could just imagine how the whole thing had struck him. I pictured him calmly glancing over the papers as he did every morning while he had a cup of coffee. I could see him this morning staring at the headlines and the dreadful pictures, suddenly jumping to his feet, pacing the floor, gesticulating and declaiming about his errant son—hurt, angry, all in one. How could I face him?

I waited until late in the day, figuring he might have recovered from the initial shock by that time, and then I phoned to ask if it was all right to come up. Of course it was. I shaved, showered and dressed and went to the house. I walked down the hall to the study. He was waiting for me. He wasn't ranting or raving. He was very quiet, almost expressionless in his calm.

"Sit down, son," he said. I sat down. He began to talk to me. He didn't mention the headlines, or the disgrace, or those terrible photographs. But I saw he was very worried.

"Drinking, you know, is quite bad, son," he said gravely. "It killed your grandfather when he was in his thirties. I hope you don't get like him. You know it hits you if you don't watch it.

"Of course," he went on, "we all make mistakes and they didn't treat you properly. But when you're drinking you shouldn't drive. You can get hurt that way. You can hurt others."

Listening to him talk, hearing the genuine concern in his voice when I had expected criticism, only made my remorse deeper.

"Well, I just feel terrible," I confessed to him.

What else could I say? I got up to go. Dad got up too. He came over and put his arm around me.

"Don't worry about it, Charles," he said. "If you need any help, let me know." I knew that he meant he would take care of the costs for me—the attorney, the fine—if I would let him.

I could have used his help. But it was I who had got myself into the mess and I figured it was my job to take care of it. I told him so.

"Okay, keep your nose clean," he said, trying to joke about it. But I could see a look of respect in his eyes, because I had refused his offer and was willing to take the responsibility for my own mistakes. Suddenly I felt a lot better.

My fine was a hundred and fifty dollars and I was put on probation for six months, during which time I wasn't to be seen at any public bars. I borrowed the money from the bank to pay my fine.

My father's concern for me lingered on long after the incident. I felt that he believed a weakness for drink is hereditary and that it had come to me from my grandfather and that I wasn't altogether to blame. So he kept a lookout to help me guard against it. I remember one night, during the probationary period, drinking too much at a big party at his place. I wasn't making a spectacle of myself, I was just sitting in a corner of the couch in a semi-doze, trying to make myself as inconspicuous as possible.

The next day Dad brought it up. "Son, you were a little high last night," he told me reproachfully. "I was watching you."

"I'm sorry, Dad," I answered. "I hope I didn't disgrace you." I began to apologize profusely.

"No, no, it was toward the end of the evening," he assured me to make me feel better. "You didn't make an ass of yourself. But after everyone left I had to help you up the stairs to your room. You were a little wobbly." And again he reminded me about my grandfather, who had died so young from drink. Always he remembered that. Always in his face was the grief and shock he must have felt long ago at the death of this man, at once so charming and so afflicted.

I'm a periodic drinker. Only once at the very beginning of my career did I fall down on a job because of it. It was after a quarrel with the girl who was my fiancée at the time. I drank too much and missed the plane to Boston, where I was to rehearse for *The Live Wire*, with Garson Kanin directing. I came in late in the afternoon. The rest of the cast had been at it all day and Kanin read me off in front of everyone. Of course I was terribly embarrassed, but I deserved it, so I couldn't very well resent his lecture, and we're friends to this day.

The next evening the stage manager, who was a good friend of mine, came up to me quickly and handed me my walking papers. But they were decent about it. I wasn't reported to Actors Equity. I didn't need that punishment. I was tortured with black remorse.

"What will Dad think?" I wondered. But I don't believe he ever heard about it. I was always grateful for that. He was so conscientious himself about his profession. It was mine, too, and it seemed to me I had failed both him and it. I was responsible for a black mark against the family name that he had built up through the years with his hard, undivided devotion to work. These were all the things I told myself afterwards. For days I didn't know what to do with myself. I didn't think, I just suffered. And I made up my mind that from then on I would leave alcohol alone when I was working. I have kept that pledge to myself so well that today I have a good reputation for sobriety while on a job.

To me acting is a vocation, a genuine calling, the work of creation. That feeling is what put me in awe of my father from the time I was a small boy and it is the reason I always phoned him before going to see him. When I went to New York, at the time my brother Syd was in *Bells Are Ringing*, I even called him up first, too, to be sure I wouldn't be interrupting him at his work.

"What are you talking about, Chuck?" Syd shot back, astonished at the formality. "Come on up, of course."

I went up and congratulated him on his success, but he only deprecated the whole thing.

"Aw, Chuck, damn it," he said, "I'm not an actor. I'm a businessman."

"A businessman!" I exclaimed. I was really shocked because I was thinking of Syd as a fine actor and here he was talking about art as though it were a business.

Syd is fortunate, of course. He has the objectivity I lack, though I don't for one minute believe he looks on himself as just a businessman. Deep down I know he is proud that everyone else says he's an artist.

It's my idealization of the acting profession that occasionally causes me trouble. I don't need it for a livelihood. I have three square meals a day from the proceeds of my trust fund. But I want more than this out of life. I want to achieve something worthwhile as an actor. And so when things are low and tough and it seems I'm getting no place in my career, when I have no answer if people ask, "What are you doing now, Charlie?" then is when I drink.

335

Being the son and namesake of a famous actor, especially if you want to be an actor yourself, has its drawbacks. You can't start fresh like other beginners, because you're already well known, even though you haven't done a thing to earn it. From the very beginning you run into ridiculous comparisons that can stymie you.

There was, for instance, the time I had an appointment with Theron Bamberger, the producer, to audition for a part in a play at the Bucks County Playhouse in Pennsylvania. I went into Mr. Bamberger's New York office for the interview and he kept me cooling my heels for more than half an hour. Finally, when I was called in, I found him with a paper spread open in front of his face. He didn't put it down or greet me or even look around it at me. For a while he didn't so much as speak; then he asked from behind the paper, "Are you as great as *he* is?"

What kind of answer could you give to a question like that? I just turned and walked out without a word. I heard him calling after me, but I didn't once look back.

For a number of years I have found myself having to face an additional handicap where my own particular name is concerned. It's the Communist label that was tagged on my father and that somehow seems to have carried over to me, frightening off producers who might otherwise be interested in me. Perhaps Sydney was wiser than I when he went to New York and concentrated on the stage. Fortunately, stage producers aren't so sensitive to mass public opinion as those of the film and TV industries. Out here, when my father left the country under a cloud and his pictures were boycotted, the name Charles Chaplin was considered poison at the box office. Yet I stayed on in Hollywood because it's my home and I like it, and I kept hoping to get that break that would vindicate me in my own right. But I can't say my choice hasn't made things tough for me.

I'm always asked the question. "Are you a Communist like your father?" the brash ones say.

This infuriates me, for I've never given anyone the slightest cause to doubt my loyalty to the United States. I willingly fought for my country in the last war and, if necessary, I would do so again against any enemy.

Other people put the question more fairly. "Is your father really a Communist?" they say, and they're the ones who are interested in hearing my side of the case.

I used to go into long, heated explanations about why he wasn't. But if you meet enough people and try to answer everyone, you spend the rest of your life explaining things. Now I have a different approach.

"Look, I think that's really a silly question," I'll tell them. "Why don't you look up the facts and figure it out for yourself? But if you want a short, straightforward answer, I'll tell you myself right now—he's not and he never was."

40

How did my father ever come to be considered a Communist, or even a fellow traveler? This is the second chief irony of his long career, just as getting labeled an immoral philanderer was the first.

David Raksin, who liked to think of himself in the thirties as a socialist, laughs when he recalls how his political views, mild though they were, were a bit too much for Dad, and how Dad used to twit him about them. When H. G. Wells came to this country in 1936, Dad even put the great novelist up to needling Raksin about his politics.

"Old man," Wells said in dignified British accents when they first met, "I hear you're rather pink."

"It depends on what you mean," Raksin replied, wary of being kidded.

"I mean it's a nice old-fashioned color," Wells replied tolerantly, while Dad smiled gleefully at David's discomfort.

But though Dad took flat exception to David's socialist views, he has always been sincere about his concern for the little man, as he demonstrated in his treatment of his own studio workers. He has always felt that the degradation of the very poor is the cruelest of all suffering. I remember how horrified he was by the wretched poverty he saw in India during his travels there, and how admiringly he spoke of Mahatma Gandhi, who joined with the outcasts when he could have lived a very comfortable life. Gandhi, he said, was not only one of the most brilliant men he'd ever met, but one of the most godlike as well.

Similarly my father at one time admired Ramsay Mac-Donald for showing interest in the rights of the common man. But during his trip to England in 1931, Dad paid a visit to MacDonald on his estate. While he was there he saw the Prime Minister unceremoniously order off a few people who were enjoying a picnic in a remote section of his grounds. My father, whose chief fault in the political field is perhaps that of being an idealist in this age of expediency, was scandalized. He would no longer have anything to do with Mac-Donald or even allow his picture to be taken with him.

My father's other deep conviction is that peace should somehow be brought to the whole world. He is almost a fanatic on this subject.

"Why can't we take all the leaders of the different countries who are opposing each other in war, strip them down to their trunks, put them in a ring and let them fight it out?" he used to say to me whimsically. "You would see all shapes and sizes—short and tall, lean and pot-bellied and knock-kneed—everything. And it would be such a ridiculous sight it would end strife right there."

Because he feels that nationalism engenders wars, my father has always been against drilling children in superpatriotism. He maintains that it only causes them to look down on those of other races and nations and that this results in nationalist states like Nazi Germany. That is why he likes to refer to himself as an internationalist. He had a deep admiration for Wendell Willkie, the 1940 Republican Presidential nominee, for his strong advocacy of a One World policy.

Outside these convictions my father's "politics" are extremely catholic. He will go through the various world systems, picking out the high points in each. On the one hand he used to praise Hitler's early concern for the common man and his interest in public works. On the other he approved of the way the Russians kept their artists from the front lines and generously subsidized them. It was only after the war that he realized the Communists, while carefully nurturing the physical welfare of their creative geniuses, were forcing them to direct their talents to propaganda purposes. And he became as disillusioned with them as he had been earlier with Prime Minister MacDonald. From the Far East he borrowed the peaceful mysticism of Buddhism to add to his potpourri, and his attachment to England has always been warm and sentimental. His roots are sunk too deep in the suffering of the Kennington slums to let him cast himself adrift from the anchorage of those squalid streets that gave him the symbol of the Little Tramp.

As for the United States, perhaps my father idealized this nation more than any other. He loved it—the people as a whole and individually, his house on the hill, the first real home he had ever possessed. He always felt he belonged here in America, with its promise of freedom in thought and belief and its emphasis on the importance of the individual.

My father enjoyed cementing together the odds and ends he had collected from various countries to create magnificent but utterly impractical utopias. This is his "politics," the fanciful, idealistic "politics" of an artist, which always delighted such seasoned statesmen as Sir Winston Churchill and President Roosevelt. He never preached his "politics" to Syd and me—he left us as free in that field as he did in the religious one—but he vastly enjoyed discussing his ideas with us and with anyone else who would listen. And since many of his theories seemed so outlandish to others, he could always count on stirring up a hornet's nest with them. Dad found an intellectual excitement in this kind of play.

For play it often was with him. I've heard him with mock seriousness arguing opposite sides of the same question within an hour with different people, just to test his ability to sway them to his side. To him this matching of wits was like an agile game of tennis, with words taking the place of the ball.

Sometimes, carried away by his enthusiasm, he would make high-flown statements which, after sober reflection, he was the first to discard. This put him in a dilemma, because he was so stubborn he could never bring himself to make retractions, especially to outsiders. But sometimes he would come close to it with Syd and me.

"Well, boys, I've changed my ideas about that setup I was discussing with you yesterday," he would say sometimes, chuckling deprecatingly as he always did when he had to beat a cautious retreat. "It's really not as good as I thought it was. As a matter of fact, it's terrible."

Another trait of my father's that was to cause him trouble during this period of his life is his intense curiosity about people, any kind of people. He liked occasionally to pay a visit to Skid Row in Los Angeles, and he would start his preparations several days in advance by allowing his beard to grow. In shabby clothes, to complete his disguise, he remained, so far as I know, unrecognized during these visits.

Sometimes when I was older I accompanied him. The chauffeur would drive us downtown and drop us off. From then on we were on our own. Dad would saunter around the grimy streets that perhaps reminded him of the London slums, and go into bars and sip a drink while he watched the people around him and listened avidly to their conversations.

He was always interested in unusual people. He liked to brag about having once made the acquaintance of gangsters.

"Of course," he explained, "I'm so well known, and many

341

of these people in the underworld admire the creative principle. They were so touched at meeting me that they even put their services at my disposal."

My father became very dramatic as he described the scene for me and repeated the gangsters' exact words: "Anyone, Charlie, if you want him out of the way, we'll take care of him for you. Just say the word."

Dad was fascinated by the gangsters, with their strange, perverted devotion to the creative, though he was more than glad to let them alone after their kind offer.

With this sort of curiosity about people, it isn't surprising that my father's tastes were completely heterogeneous where guests were concerned. A person who was interesting was always welcome at his home, regardless of political affiliations. His visitors included Republicans, Democrats, Socialists, reds and pinks without discrimination. As a matter of fact, though, there were very few Communists among the thousands who came to see my father during the last ten years of his residence here. There were many more pinks, because at that time the hue was considered rather fashionable. My father enjoyed their company not because of their politics, but because they had something creative to offer.

He deeply admired Henry A. Wallace, who came up to play tennis with him once. Harry Bridges and Paul Robeson were both guests at his place. And when the Dean of Canterbury, the Very Reverend Hewlett Johnson, known as the Red Dean because of his far-leftist views, visited this country, he too was entertained by my father, who considered him a very brilliant man.

My father's most controversial guest was Hanns Eisler, the composer. It made little difference to Dad that Hanns Eisler was the brother of Gerhard Eisler, who is now a propaganda leader in East Germany. He never inquired whether Hanns Eisler himself was a Communist. He saw in Eisler only a talented musician who had fallen upon hard times. My father ignored public opinion to help him, for he could never bear to see talent of any kind suffering deprivation.

This has always been a consistent characteristic of my father's personality. When Bill Tilden, the great tennis champion, was released from prison, where he had served a sentence on a morals conviction, he was almost destitute. Because of the nature of his offense it was impossible for him to get a job, and most of his former friends shunned him. Mr. Tilden had, in happier days, been a welcome visitor at my father's house. Dad had admired him as a true tennis genius, and because of this genius he felt obligated to help him. Dad never thought of protecting his own reputation. He lent his tennis court to Mr. Tilden, enabling him not only to keep up his practice but to earn a living by giving lessons. My father even bought a hundred and fifty dollars' worth of lessons for Oona.

Personally, Mr. Tilden, who was something of an autocrat, wasn't an easy man to help. He took over my father's court so completely that Dad himself had to ask permission to use it. He was also always having to straighten out arguments between his butler and the cantankerous Tilden, who became so difficult at last that most people would have thrown him out. My father only shrugged off his behavior with a laugh.

"God damn it," he said, "that's just the way I am with my work. When I'm in there I don't care who it is or what they're doing, I won't be bothered. I understand that in him."

It was the opinion of the columnists around town at the time that the spotlight focused on my father by the Joan Barry case was greatly responsible for making him look suspect in the field of politics also. For years Dad had been voicing his rather fanciful and sometimes very radical solutions to the world's problems without anyone's taking him seriously.

So far as I can ascertain, the first blunt accusation voiced against him was during the Mann Act trial. It was then that the Dies Committee investigating un-American activities first took my father to task for his second front speech in New

York back in 1942. By that time the second front advocated by my father had already been established and Russia was still our ally, so that accusation didn't carry much weight. But in 1945, between the two paternity trials, a second thrust was made against my father, this time from Senator William Langer, who said that he was going to introduce legislation to deport my father as an undesirable alien on moral grounds. The Department of Justice immediately replied that the existing law was adequate to deport my father if he were guilty of anything, but that there was not sufficient evidence to warrant such deportation.

In the spring of 1946 an incident occurred which again roused suspicions about my father's political affiliations. Konstantin Simonov, the Soviet poet and playwright who had been visiting Hollywood under the auspices of our own State Department, had enjoyed the hospitality of my father, of Lewis Milestone, the director, and of the late John Garfield. Before leaving, Mr. Simonov reciprocated their kindness by inviting them to a banquet aboard the Soviet tanker, the *S.S. Batumi*, then in Long Beach harbor. All three men accepted the invitation. Certainly it would have been a breach of both etiquette and international good will to have refused.

In the calmer atmosphere that prevails today, the importance that was attached to this incident appears somewhat foolish. At the moment our diplomatic status with Russia is the same as it was at the time of the Simonov incident in 1946, yet no one in this country is criticized now for visiting Russia itself, much less a Soviet tanker off our own shore. Indeed, the politically wise United States citizen, regardless of party, must derive some amusement over the identity of some of our top government officials who have since cavorted so cordially with Russian leaders here and on their own soil. Some of these officials are from the same camp that so mercilessly plagued my father for his "one-world" attitude in 1946.

My father has never made a single trip to Russia, and yet his casual visit with a Russian poet seemed to many people sure proof of Communist sympathy. Much was made of it in the papers at the time. And Jack B. Tenney, a California state senator, assigned two investigators to the job of finding out if anything un-American had been going on.

When the press called upon Milestone, Garfield and my father for comment, both Milestone and Garfield responded with reasonable statements. My father refused to make any comment. This brings us to another trait of his which has caused him a great deal of trouble. It is his lack of rapport with newspapermen. He has always been honestly afraid of the press because of the power it holds. I've never seen him so nervous as when preparing for an interview.

I remember the time some years ago when it was arranged for Louella Parsons to come by Black-Foxe, pick me up and take me out with her to the San Fernando Valley, where I was to meet Dad at a party. Dad anxiously coached me in what I should and shouldn't say during the long ride I was to make with her alone. I was still very young and he wanted to be sure I kept a discreet tongue in my head.

"Remember, son," he told me apprehensively, "she's a columnist and a very brilliant reporter. Try to give her short answers, no more than *yes* and *no* if you can help it."

I wasn't too impressed with Miss Parsons' reportorial abilities that day. She asked me a lot of questions but just in a nice, friendly way. She scarcely looked at me and seemed to pay little attention to my replies. She didn't take a single note. I couldn't understand why my father was so anxious about this perfectly innocuous conversation. But he met me at the party, took me aside and questioned me carefully about all the details. I thought he was making a lot of to-do about nothing until the next day I found my interview with Miss Parsons printed word for word, just as it had taken place. I realized then why my father had such a healthy respect for the newspaper profession.

Added to my father's natural reticence where reporters are concerned was his feeling that a good part of the press had turned against him after the paternity trials. It began to seem to him that reporters weren't trying to look at his side, but were deliberately lifting things he said out of context, changing the emphasis on others and sometimes even misquoting him. The breach between him and the press grew progressively wider and finally resolved itself in open hostility at a time when, more than any other, he was in need of good publicity. My father began to react in much the same way to reporters as he had on the witness stand under Mr. Scott's goading. Sometimes in the heat of anger he would state his case badly and then refuse to make any retractions. Actually, he was never fighting for the truth of what he was saying, but for the basic right to say what he pleased.

"A democracy is a place," my father pointed out, "where you can express your ideas freely—or it isn't a democracy."

Granted that, as the world's foremost pantomimist, my father is far more eloquent with his hands than his tongue, still, most of the replies he made to the criticisms which were leveled at him just after the war make sense when looked at in the more reasonable light of today.

His second front speeches, he explained, had been delivered at a time when close cooperation with Russia as our ally was imperative. He had merely been trying to help along relations between the two countries and he felt that his activities in this line had been helpful.

He had not become a citizen because he considered himself an internationalist, and because he did not wish to relinquish citizenship in the land of his birth. But he gave close friends who kept importuning him to relieve the pressure by becoming naturalized one more cogent reason for refusing.

"They are holding a gun at my back now. I can't do it," he said stubbornly.

To his critics my father pointed out that though he was not a citizen he was "a very good paying guest." I know for a fact that he poured millions of tax dollars into the United States treasury during his residence here. But at the time his statement was regarded as a smug dodge. People resented his explanations that though he derived only thirty percent of his income from the United States and seventy percent from abroad, he paid taxes to Uncle Sam on the entire hundred percent.

In the aftermath of the war his discussion of taxes in general was a sore point. He was quickly reminded that others had not only paid their taxes but had sacrificed their lives on the battlefronts as well. No one seemed to remember that though my father was too old for the front, he had gladly given his two sons to the war. He used to brag about our soldiering.

"I'm British but my sons are American," he would say proudly whenever he introduced us to anyone. "They were soldiers and fought at the front."

My father was challenged as well about the extent of his war efforts, which were compared unfavorably with Bob Hope's. Hope had traveled far and wide to entertain the troops. My father had done no entertaining at all.

"My type of artistry doesn't lend itself as readily as others to direct entertainment," he responded.

This again was a simple statement of fact, but it sounded like a feeble excuse because most people do not realize that there actually are two types of comedians. Only the stand-up comic like Hope can carry off the kind of impromptu entertainment that was demanded in the army camps. For my father, who was at his best among a circle of close friends, to come out cold before a strange audience and be funny was excruciating torture, with the dread of almost certain failure.

He tried it once at the request of the head of the personnel division of one of the big aircraft corporations near Los Angeles. One noon in the company's open-air theater where all the workers were gathered with their lunches, he laid, I think, the biggest egg of his career. No one laughed, no one clapped, apparently no one was even watching him. Everyone was too busy eating. My father came out of that experience unnerved and shaking.

"I'll never do it again, never," he said. "I can't. It's not my kind of entertaining."

My father pointed out, however, that he had donated his

time freely to the government and had made a number of speeches at its request. By this time, though, his speeches had become suspect and he was scarcely given credit for this bit of war effort.

To questions as to whether he was a Communist or a Communist sympathizer my father gave an unequivocal "No!" but he couldn't refrain from adding whimsically, "Life is so technical today. If you step off the curb with your left foot you're accused of being a Communist."

When he was questioned about Hanns Eisler he admitted to a warm friendship with the composer, but vehemently asserted he would never have anything to do with spies or treachery. Yet despite these forthright statements and explanations, the resentment toward my father and the belief that he was a Communist, or at least tainted with Communist associations, continued to grow.

One has to remember the conditions of the times to understand how this came about. With the close of the war Russia was no longer our ally but a large and powerful nation that deliberately broke the treaties we had made with her in good faith. We were so frightened by her sinister proportions that we forgot the wise counsel President Roosevelt once gave, "There is nothing to fear but fear itself." We became apprehensive that Russian agents were secretly undermining our institutions, and a great many things that had formerly seemed quite harmless now began to look suspect to us. The Un-American Activities Committee, in its search for Communists, started to interest itself actively in the entertainment world. It was not to be supposed that my father would escape their careful scrutiny.

In December of 1946 it was announced by Ernie Adamson, chief counsel for the committee, that my father would be subpoenaed to testify at public hearings in Washington, together with Will Rogers, Jr., and James Roosevelt. But six months later he had not been called and no specific charges had been brought against him.

Yet he was still being made the subject of controversy. He even provided the *pièce de résistance* of a heated debate in Washington, D.C., that June of '47. Representative John E. Rankin of Mississippi went so far as to refer to his pictures as "loathsome." Representative Chet Holifield of California came to the defense of Hollywood in general, but was cut short by Representative Joseph Martin for referring to the committee as the Un-American Committee.

By July of that year my father was exasperated beyond measure over a broadcast by Hy Gardner on N.B.C. Charging that it was full of innuendoes that he was a Communist and a liar, he immediately filed a three-million-dollar damage suit in federal court. But my father's spirited action did little to clear his name, especially as that same month Representative J. Parnell Thomas declared my father would be subpoenaed to appear before the House Un-American Activities Committee in Washington. For months afterwards the same nebulous rumor that he was on the verge of being called kept cropping up. Each time it did so it seemed to add a little more weight to the belief that he was a Communist or at least a fellow traveler.

In November, 1947, my father made one of those equivocal moves which cast a further cloud on his associations. When deportation proceedings against Hanns Eisler were at their height he cabled Pablo Picasso asking him to head a committee of French artists to protest to the American Embassy in Paris "the outrageous deportation proceedings against Hanns Eisler here, and simultaneously send me copy of protest for use here." I doubt if the incongruity of asking a confirmed Communist to intercede for a man being accused of communism in a noncommunist country ever even entered my father's head. He was an artist appealing to another artist to come to the aid of a third artist. But to many people his move smacked of insolence, and the newspapers roundly castigated him for his lack of etiquette rather than for any subversion. How could you call such an open move subversive?

In March of 1949, Oona gave birth to her third child.

Columnists expressed surprise at the length and very apparent harmony of this marriage, which should have done much to erase the ugly picture that had been painted of my father at the paternity trials. But apparently that picture had been too deeply etched to be expunged so quickly, and added to it now was the stigma of his alleged subversiveness.

In April of 1949 my father seemed to provide further proof of his inclinations to the left by lending his name as a sponsor of the Communist-organized World Peace Congress. Again, with his characteristic disregard for politics or "isms," he was attracted only to the words "world peace." He explained that he believed any move toward peace should be encouraged, no matter by whom it was sponsored.

That same April, Senator Patrick A. McCarran, chairman of the Senate Judiciary Committee, asked for legislation to expel subversive aliens from the United States. And Senator Harry P. Cain made it plain who was included by saying outright that the bill would provide for the expulsion of my father, who, he maintained, had been guilty of treason in sending the cablegram to Picasso.

Early in 1951, shortly before Oona had her fourth child, Representative Harold H. Velde announced again that my father was being investigated by the Un-American Activities Committee. If my father had been guilty of any subversion, no matter how minor, the committee's numerous investigations would surely have unearthed it and by this time he would have been called on the mat at once. But he never was called up because he had done nothing. He hadn't contributed to any front groups, had attended no cell meetings and had openly repudiated all political organizations of a subversive nature. There was never anything against him but the rumor.

My father would have welcomed the opportunity to clear his name. As I recall, he even contacted Washington at one time, asking to be allowed to testify. But he was ignored.

"They don't call me because they have nothing on me,"

he confided to me. "I am simply not a Communist and never have been."

My father wasn't the only one in Hollywood being investigated in those days. A score of film-land personalities were brought to the witness stand and subjected to questioning under the spotlight of television coverage, and many others besides my father were named as suspects but never given the chance to appear before the committee and clear their reputations. Only a very few leftists were actually unearthed, but some careers were damaged beyond repair by the public investigations and many others were forced into temporary eclipse.

Of course the entertainment world did not suffer alone under the wave of near-hysteria that, aggravated by the so-called police action in Korea, swept over our nation. During that period talented scientists, diplomats and educators, as well as many minor government workers, were harried or driven out of service. The tide was to abate only with the formal Senate censure of Senator Joseph McCarthy in the autumn of 1954.

During that period of grueling investigations a pall hung over Hollywood. Those in the entertainment world depend to a vital extent on public opinion for their livelihood, and most of the suspects named by the committee chose to suffer in silence and to keep themselves as inconspicuous as possible. It seemed the expedient thing to do. Not so with my father. As one of the most controversial individualists in the world, he spoke out loudly for the rights of the individual. Somehow it seems fitting that his fight should have been staged in this country, which has always prided itself on fostering individualism as against statism. Dad just couldn't be silenced from voicing at all times his stubborn conviction that in a democracy one should have the right to think as one pleases and to see whom one chooses so long as no harm is being done. You might say he fought primarily because he suffers from mental claustrophobia. He simply cannot bear to be shut up in a closet of proscription on thought. It stifles and oppresses him beyond endurance.

It must not be supposed that my father's fight for his convictions was made without sacrifice. When I came back from the East to play my part in *Limelight* I was saddened to see the effect his stand had had on his own life. It was no longer considered a privilege to be a guest at the home of Charlie Chaplin. Many people were actually afraid to be seen there lest they, too, should become suspect.

Tim Durant, the irreconcilable Yankee, solid as a New England rock in his loyalty, was around, and he did his best to bring back some of the old life, noting the irony the while. Once his phone had rung steadily with people calling him, offering him favors, wining him, dining him in the hope that he would extend them an invitation to the Chaplin home. Now it was Tim's turn to phone them and beg them to come up for a game of tennis. But they all backed out. The little tennis house and green lawn where once my father had held a gracious court were practically deserted on Sunday afternoons. I think my father must have been the loneliest man in Hollywood those days.

It was in that spirit, a spirit of haunting farewell, that he commenced work on *Limelight*, the nostalgic story of a pantomimist who had once been widely acclaimed but had fallen in later years into disfavor and eclipse.

41

On August 4, 1952, my father held his first preview of *Limelight*. It was a private showing for two hundred people. Such
well-known film personalities as David Selznick and the late
Humphrey Bogart and Ronald Colman came that night to
pay tribute to him. Then, as now, my father was respected in
Hollywood's inner circle as one of the town's authentic geniuses. But the audience also included a number of workers
who had served my father loyally since the *Gold Rush* days.

Dad was on edge with excitement, as he always was before
previewing one of his pictures. When the film ended he got up
to make a short speech. He went only as far as the phrase, "I
do want to say thank you . . ."

"No! No!" a woman in the audience suddenly cried out.
"Thank you!"

"Thank you! Thank you!" the cry was taken up by everyone until the room rang. It was the last accolade my father was to hear in Hollywood. And it was such an electric demonstration that columnist Sidney Skolsky described it as "the most exciting night I had ever spent in a projection room."

At the completion of *Limelight*, my father and Oona began to make plans for a vacation in Europe with their four children. Dad did so reluctantly; he was worried about leaving the country before his name was completely cleared. But Oona had never seen Europe and was as excited as a child at the prospect, and he did not want to disappoint her.

The night before they left, Tim Durant gave a farewell party in the back yard of his Beverly Hills home. It was an authentic clambake and all the fifty or sixty guests came in informal attire except Marlon Brando, who wore a dinner jacket. It is one of the few times Hollywood has seen Brando in formal dress, and he donned it out of admiration for my father.

That night Artur Rubinstein, who is a wonderful raconteur and pantomimist himself, held the floor most of the evening. A short man with a big front and little hands, he talked wittily about his travels in the Far East and did an imitation of the Kabuki players whom he had just seen in Japan. Imitating those players had always been my father's forte, but this evening he was strangely quiet and preoccupied. It was the first time I could remember that he hadn't been animated at a party. His air of sadness seemed to cast a shadow over the whole gathering, which even Mr. Rubinstein's gaiety could not lift.

Only once did my father's old brilliance as an entertainer among his friends shine forth that evening. He and Katherine Dunham, the great dancer-choreographer, suddenly began to dance together, and their performance was so striking that almost at once everyone stopped to watch. My father was taking on Miss Dunham's gestures and mannerisms, yes, even her personality. He seemed to be Miss Dunham, his every movement flowing with her feline grace and fluidity. It was the most extraordinary exhibition of pantomime any of us had ever seen, and some of us watched with a lump in the throat.

Was that amazing performance my father's swan song to the city he had chosen to make his home for so many years? It was the last that anyone in Hollywood was to see of the priceless entertainment with which he had graced so many parties in the past.

The next morning Tim Durant drove Dad and Oona and the four children to the train at Union Station in Los Angeles. On the way my father suddenly turned to Tim, and Tim saw there were tears in his eyes.

"You know, Tim," he said, "I have a presentiment I'm never coming back."

"That's nonsense, Charlie," Tim scoffed.

Dad just shook his head. "Yes, I really feel that," he insisted.

He boarded the train and it truly was his last day in California. But the melancholy premonition could not have troubled him before those final days here, because in the months past he and Oona had spent a lot of money, about fifty thousand dollars, fixing up the house. It was as though they had meant to live there forever. The changes were more widespread than any Paulette had ever dreamed of accomplishing. The wide, majestic hall had been roofed over at the second-story level to provide additional bedrooms for the growing family. My father was so proud of these rooms he liked to take his guests upstairs to show them off.

I wonder if that morning of his departure he didn't make a last-minute pilgrimage through all the rooms, new and old, of the house in which he had lived for close to thirty years. Did he pause longest in his familiar bedroom with the threadbare carpet—even Oona hadn't been able to persuade him to part with it! Did he make a last visit to his private woods, his swimming pool and tennis court at the foot of the stepped lawn? He had always marveled at having his own pool and court. Six acres isn't much of an estate for a multimillionaire, but he was proud of it.

So he bade all things his last farewell: his home, his hill, the town where he had found his fame and made a name for himself, and finally the very country where he had once dreamed of raising hogs in Arkansas. On September 17 he embarked for England on the *Queen Elizabeth*.

As soon as the *Queen Elizabeth* was well at sea, Attorney General James P. McGranery rescinded my father's re-entry permit and announced that a hearing was being set to see whether he was readmissible under the immigration laws. It was an extraordinary act, for the permit had been approved before my father left. Everything had been declared in order. Taxes had been paid up and, in 1948, he had been thoroughly investigated and cleared of all subversive and immorality charges by both the Immigration Service and the Justice Department.

Why did McGranery make this ill-advised move, which was to put the United States in a very bad light abroad? Among Dad's friends it was generally believed that the Attorney General had acted simply for political reasons.

The rescinding of the permit came as a shock to my father. From aboard the *Queen Elizabeth* he at once gave out a statement: "Through proper procedure I applied for a re-entry permit which I was given in good faith and which I accepted in good faith. Therefore I assume that the United States will recognize its validity."

The following day the Justice Department, perhaps to vindicate itself, indicated it had new facts on my father to back up its move. "There is plenty of information available," a spokesman for the department asserted point-blank.

Two days later Dad, arriving at Cherbourg, France, gave out another statement which began: "I have no particular political opinions. I love liberty, for which I could not be criticized in any democratic country."

In a speech on Oct. 2, a little more than a week later, Attorney General McGranery labeled my father an "unsavory character," but did not back up this derogatory statement with any of the facts his department claimed to possess. My father responded with another press statement: "I do not wish to comment on these vague accusations which, strangely enough, Mr. McGranery has seen fit to publicize while I am three thousand miles away from the United States.

"I again reiterate that through the proper channels I applied for and was given a re-entry permit by the government of the United States."

By this time the American Legion had adopted a resolution commending Mr. McGranery's action. But many other citizens, both those who admired my father and those who disliked him, felt the Attorney General had exceeded his rights in taking away the permit at a time when my father was unable to defend himself. Mary Pickford, who is far to the right in her political views, ably expressed the sentiments of these people when she said that it was "beneath the dignity of the great United States."

Meanwhile, over in Europe, Dad was being accorded a hero's welcome. Throngs greeted him in his native England and later all across the Continent. He was received by the Queen of England. President Auriol of France made him an officer of the Legion of Honor, the highest accolade in the power of that nation to bestow. And President Luigi Einaudi of Italy gave him a special audience and presented him with a gold medal on behalf of Premier de Gasperi.

It seemed that Europe was taking the occasion, not only to honor a famous man, but also to show up what was regarded over there as America's unjust treatment of him. And of course *Pravda*, the official Russian newspaper, took the opportunity to get in a gibe at us. Though there was much in my father's films that was not progressive, it said, the Chaplin case fully demonstrated the American government's demand that every actor and actress in motion pictures either put his talent in the service of war propaganda or face incessant persecution. We had earned ourselves a black eye everywhere abroad.

If the Attorney General had any proof to vindicate his move, surely now was the time to come forward with it. Instead of doing this he called in the F.B.I. and asked it to conduct another investigation into my father's private life, though that ground had been carefully covered before, when the Mann Act charge was filed. But the F.B.I. undertook the assignment again with all the thoroughness which has earned it a well-deserved reputation around the world.

After talking to the people who were questioned out here, I have come to the conclusion that the F.B.I. agents spent little time looking into my father's alleged political activities. And this could only mean he had come out of all the previous investigations bone-clean. The questioning centered primarily on his morals.

Most of the principals in the Joan Barry case were again interrogated, though the events had taken place eleven years before and my father had lived an exemplary life with Oona during the interim. My father's lawyer, Loyd C. Wright, was questioned and Tim Durant was called on three separate occasions. The witnesses were sternly reminded that perjury might mean a term on McNeil Island for them. The F.B.I. agents even questioned my mother about her divorce and any possible irregularities that might have taken place twenty-seven years before. They checked Paulette's divorce papers in Juárez, Mexico, and found them in order.

It is apparent that out of all these investigations sufficient grounds were never found for bringing any kind of indictment. The proof of this is that the Attorney General never held that public hearing, or any hearing at all for that matter.

In February of 1953, *Limelight* was ready for release and reviewers in general praised it as a good piece of work. Arthur Knight of the *Saturday Review* went so far as to list my father

as one of the three unequivocal geniuses of motion pictures—
the other two being D. W. Griffith and Sergei Eisenstein—
and to call his latest film his most important one.

"It is," said Mr. Knight, "in every sense a summing up, an
epitomizing of the comedian's fundamental philosophies and
attitudes about life, about love, about audiences, about comedy. Fundamentally, *Limelight* is not a comedy at all, but an
artist's testament limned in lovely poetry and poignant wit."

Al Hine, reviewing for *Holiday*, closed his praise of the
picture with the telling paragraph: "Chaplin is a genius and
admittedly a proud and difficult man . . . But all of us Americans might well remember that whatever we do to wound
our geniuses, the eventual evil to ourselves is larger than the
discomfort to them."

With the release date of *Limelight* so near, a new factor
entered into my father's complications with the government.
Four months had elapsed since the Attorney General's fruit-
less announcement that he was holding a public hearing on my
father's status. Yet the American Legion decided to go ahead
anyway and boycott *Limelight* until my father's innocence
was proved. Clubwomen joined the movement. And, surprisingly enough, Roy Brewer, chairman of the Hollywood Fed-
eration of Labor Film Council, strongly backed the American
Legion. It seemed strangely inconsistent to people in the industry for Mr. Brewer, after having allowed his union workers to help my father create the picture, to turn around and
ban it.

A few shocked voices were raised in protest across the
nation. One of these was the influential *New York Times*,
which devoted an editorial to the boycott. In speaking of the
punitive measures taken against a man who had not yet been
found guilty it said, "If this whole business of prejudgment
pressures and, what is worse, knuckling under to these pressures, doesn't smack of un-Americanism we should like to
know what does."

In Washington, D.C., the Very Reverend Francis B. Sayre,

Jr., Dean of the Episcopal Cathedral, devoted a Sunday sermon to the subject of censorship. "When any group of Americans . . . starts setting up its own little list of who is acceptable and who is not and then acting as though their judgment ought to be binding on all other Americans, then certain basic principles are being violated," he said.

But in the general tenor of the times these voices went unheeded. The boycott of *Limelight* was a success; but, ironically, its theme song, which of course Dad composed, moved rapidly into the hit bracket.

Meanwhile my father became discouraged by persistent press reports that if he returned to this country he could be held at Ellis Island for as long as two years while being investigated. In April of 1953 he turned in his re-entry permit to the United States Vice Consul, Kenneth R. Oakley, in Geneva, Switzerland, and settled down in Vevey. I wasn't surprised he chose Switzerland as his new home. Ever since I was a small boy he had told me how much he liked the little democracy. Like this country, it had always appealed to him for its way of life and its promise of freedom for the individual.

My father has lived in Vevey ever since, and his latest picture, *The King in New York*, which was filmed abroad, is his testimonial to the bitterness he felt at what seemed to him betrayal on the part of the United States. What isn't generally known, though, is that the first draft of that script was far more biting than the one my father finally used for shooting. After considerable reflection he toned it down decidedly.

In Europe my father continued to be his own controversial self, saying what he pleased and seeing whom he chose without causing any apparent consternation. He renewed his acquaintance with Picasso, not because of the painter's political associations, but because of his outstanding artistic talent.

In February of 1954 he and Oona created a stir when Oona gave up her United States citizenship to become a British subject. In that same year Dad entertained Chou En-lai, the

Chinese Communist Premier; was awarded an honorary membership in the Norwegian Actors Association; and was given the Peace Prize of fourteen thousand dollars by the Communist-sponsored World Peace Council. To add to his union of irreconcilables, he turned over part of the proceeds of the prize to Abbé Pierre, a Catholic priest and charity worker, and was immediately accused of irreverence by one of his vitriolic critics in this country.

England has honored him on several occasions. Understandably he has been a featured speaker at the sedate Dickens Fellowship society in London. Now and then he gets a call from the Russian Embassy in Switzerland inviting him for a visit. Every time it is the same amusing little drama. My father dresses up smartly in his formal clothes and goes to the Embassy. They greet him fulsomely and tell him how much the Russian people love and respect him for the fine artist he is. My father listens politely. After a while they come to the point.

"We'd love to have your pictures so the Russian people will know what a great artist you are," they say.

"Now, what about the financial arrangements?" my father asks.

"Well, we thought you'd be willing to show your subjects . . ."

"I will have you meet my business manager and discuss that with him," Dad says.

This always ends the interview. My father takes his leave each time with a feeling of disappointment, though he has no illusions about the Russians, never has had, really.

During his stay in Europe my father's biting comments about the United States have seen print from time to time. Over here, magazines and newspaper columns have periodically raked him over the coals. But in December of 1958 he and our government came to an equitable understanding over their much publicized tax dispute. That dispute was actually due to an honest misunderstanding and not to any recalcitrance on my father's part. When he turned in his re-entry permit he thought he had automatically given up residence in America. It never occurred to him that he had also to terminate it officially. He did this only after nine months, during which time the additional taxes accumulated. When he settled the bill with a five-hundred-thousand-dollar check to the United States Treasury the trial attorneys made it plain that the case had been one of honest dispute in which no criminality was involved. I can't help wondering if at the same time they weren't a bit regretful over closing the account of such a well-paying client.

42

I saw my father in Vevey in 1954, while Syd and I were in
Germany making a film together. As usual I phoned him first.
He seemed as surprised as ever, almost shocked, that after so
long an absence I should be so formal with him.

"Why, of course, come on up," he said.

I went up at once. It was just five days after Chou En-lai's
visit. For the second time in my life—the first having been
over his noncitizenship status—I took my father to task about
an action of his.

"My God, Dad," I said, "why do you have this fellow up
here to dinner? Do you know what you're doing? You're
going to have all the English-speaking people hating you."

"I can't help it if they take after me," Dad answered with

363

his usual stubborn logic. "I was curious about what made this man tick. Of course I don't agree with most of his policies. All the same he's a very interesting man, really, very intelligent."

Gangsters . . . the people on Skid Row . . . Einstein . . . musicians . . . H. G. Wells . . . Chou En-lai . . . my father's curiosity about people is boundless. He is just as curious about sights of interest. He likes to travel incognito with tourists and listen to the harangues of the guides. He has visited all the places of interest in the vicinity of his villa. And while I was there he insisted that I let his chauffeur drive me to the Castle of Chillon, which so inspired Lord Byron that after viewing it he wrote his memorable poem, "The Prisoner of Chillon," in a single night. Dad had been all through the place himself.

I found him living a very quiet life at Vevey. Everywhere there were only the green lawns and the leafage of the country, the sights and sounds of nature, the birds, the breeze in the shrubbery, the placid lake with its stately swans; and on quiet mornings the sounds of the firing range next door where the Vevey citizens practiced. Remembering how my father abhorred even the popping of firecrackers, I wasn't surprised at his exasperation over the noise of the guns or his resentment toward the agent for not having told him about it before he bought the estate.

Despite the firing range it was all too quiet for my tastes at Vevey. I was there five days and by the fourth day I felt my nerves beginning to shatter. Syd told me he lasted it out two weeks and then had to beat it back to the big city and the night clubs to restore his sanity. Dad loves the seclusion and can stay there for longer periods than we, but he and Oona now and then pack off to Paris or London to see the shows, the opera and the ballet and to enjoy the glamor of city life for a while.

I have reason to believe, however, that despite his pleasant life, Dad misses the old days of premières, of spotlights and enthusiastic fans. I remember the evening Oona and Dad and Syd and I all went to dinner at the Palace Hotel in Lausanne, Switzerland. During the course of the meal a crowd of college students appeared outside the door and it became obvious presently that they were waiting for my father. The maître d'hôtel offered to get us out another way, but Dad shook his head.

"It's all right," he said.

As we went through the front door, Syd and I tried to keep on either side of Oona and Dad to protect them. Though the crowd was friendly, it was charged with such youthful exuberance that it was more like a mob. A hulking fellow came up and slapped Dad jokingly on the back.

"Hi, Charlie, how are you?" he shouted.

The elbow of another knocked him in the eye. He was shoved this way and that by husky young people trying to get close to him and pulling at his coat for souvenir buttons.

We came close to being crushed before we could get into the car. Even after we were safely inside they kept tapping on the windows and shaking the chassis. They even put a few dents in the fenders before we could make our getaway. But Dad just sat there actually seeming to enjoy himself. It's a universal truth, I guess, that no matter how much an actor may like his privacy, the limelight and the accolades of his fellow men always act on him like heady wine.

During my stay in Vevey Dad asked me questions about how things were going in Hollywood, not too many but enough to make me feel he had missed it more than he cared to admit. But there was latent bitterness still in him. It is the bitterness of one who has idealized his love for someone or something and has been hurt by what he loves.

"Well, if they don't want me, I don't want to go back," was his attitude.

But altogether he has grown more mellow and philosophic with the years. I felt much of it was due to Oona's influence

—beautiful, shy, lovable Oona and her pixie children. Oona once said that she wanted ten children of her own, and it looks as though it wasn't a joke after all.

While I was at Vevey I noticed with amusement that my father, completely surrounded now by children of varying ages and sizes, was no longer timidly regarding babies as symbols and wondering what to do about them. He has learned his father role well since those long-ago days when he hovered uncertain and timid over Syd's and my cribs in the house on the hill.

What did we talk about during my stay with him? With the Castle of Chillon so near, it was natural that my father should dwell on the controversial poet. He spoke of Byron's clubfoot, the attraction he had for women, his bitterness toward life and his determination. It was this determination in Byron that most appealed to my own stubborn father.

He talked, too, about Edgar Allan Poe and his weaknesses, his bouts with liquor and his slovenly personal habits for which the people of his time condemned him, while his true greatness was realized only after his death. He spoke in the same way of Shelley, whose interest in Irish politics and unorthodox views of love had been the cause of his exile from England.

My father seemed to have become resigned to the fact that a living artist's work will always be judged more or less through the perspective of his personal life. From the first he never doubted that he himself was an artist and that his works were worthy of preservation. While such Hollywood geniuses as D. W. Griffith carelessly allowed their films to pass out of their control and deteriorate, my father carefully preserved his in special cans designed to ward off the destructiveness of time and the elements. Today his films are as fresh as when they were first made. Devoted Chaplin fans will also be interested to learn he has preserved most of his cutouts too. And many of these sequences, which were eliminated for story purposes, are funnier than those which were retained.

And to conclude, what of our family today? For the last few years I have been living with Nana, who is as sprightly as ever, in a small home in the San Fernando Valley. My mother, completely recovered from her last nervous breakdown and once again her old glamorous self, has been happily married since 1956 to Pat Longo, a trouble-shooter for the Union Bank of Los Angeles. Uncle Sydney is now living in Europe with his French wife. My brother Sydney is pursuing his success on Broadway. Paulette Goddard, my favorite ex, married Erich Remarque, the novelist, in 1958 and is living with him in Switzerland. But she never sees my father.

"We live on different mountains," she explains. She is still as vivacious and lovely as ever, and she still finds time for her acting career.

My father's correspondence habits remain deplorable. He confines himself to an occasional Christmas greeting. But when he learned of my marriage, on August 5, 1958, to actress Susan Magness, I received a congratulatory telegram from him and Oona and the six children. When, after Christmas, he learned that my wife and I were having first-year troubles and had separated despite the pending arrival, May 11, of our young daughter, Susan Maree, he decided that one of those earth-shaking occasions that call for a letter had arrived. At least he wrote me a brief but fatherly note, enclosing a check for a thousand dollars.

Nine months later, disturbed by my divorce from my wife, he sat down again. This time he wrote a much longer letter full of fatherly concern and the advice and philosophy of a man who has learned a great deal from life. The letter runs:

Dear Charlie,
Sorry I have not written before as no doubt you have heard I am writing my memoirs, which will take me at least another year to finish; but it takes up all my time drafting and redrafting.
I had a very sympathetic letter from your wife;

*she sounds quite charming. It is too bad you two can't
really get together. You have every reason to with
that beautiful baby of yours, who is, I am sure, a tremendous bond between you.*

*You will find, Charlie, as the years go by that
you need an anchorage, that is, someone you have
known over the years, and who is very close to you.
This child of yours is so beautiful that you must
make every effort to make her happy and in her
tender years nothing will give her more happiness
and security than the environment of both her parents.*

*I am seventy years old; and I think a great deal
about my children; and I think about you and what
you are doing with your life. You must not waste it.
You have talent, a good spirit and charm; because I
have seen you in the theater and know that your
capabilities are manifold—if you are serious about
them.*

*I don't wish this letter to be a lecture but I was
distressed to hear that you and your wife are divorced. She seems to me to be a very nice person. . . .*

*Do you hear from Sydney? I understand he is
doing well. You should be doing the same. You have
just as much talent. Write to me and let me know
your plans. . . .*

*Oona sends her love as well as the children. They
often speak of you and are very proud and enthusiastic about their little niece. They want to know
what you are doing and why you don't come over
and see them. They are growing: Geraldine is fifteen, Michael almost fourteen, Josi almost eleven,
Viki eight, Eugene six, Jane two and the baby three
days.*

> *Love,*
> *Father*

I know when my father speaks so poignantly of the necessity of an anchorage he is thinking of Oona, who came to him in his blackest trouble, bringing her loyalty and love. I remember how, long ago when we were just small boys, he confessed to Nana that he didn't believe anyone in the whole world had ever loved him enough. And I am glad that at last he has found Oona.

ABOUT THE AUTHORS

CHARLES CHAPLIN, JR., was born in Beverly Hills, California, in 1925. That the theatre was in his blood is borne out by his grandmother's claim that he could act before he could walk, and young Charles took great pleasure in imitating everybody—including his famous father.

With his younger brother Sydney, Charles, Jr., attended Black-Foxe Military Academy in Hollywood and later the Lawrenceville School in New Jersey. World War II interrupted his education; he was drafted before entering Princeton. After serving three years with General Patton's 89th Infantry Division and receiving two battle stars, he returned to California to begin formal dramatic training at U.C.L.A. He then joined the new Circle Theater group in Hollywood, making his debut in *The Time of Your Life*. Following appearances in other plays, he was selected by the Actors Laboratory as one of their eleven pupils, and he studied with them for a year and a half.

The next step was Broadway, and he was soon appearing behind the footlights with Fredric March and Florence Eldridge in *Now I Lay Me Down to Sleep*. Back in Hollywood, he played a bit part in *Limelight* with his father and brother, and later other screen roles. His dramatic career also includes the leads in the English productions of *Oh, Men! Oh, Women!* and *The Seven Year Itch*, and appearances at the Pasadena Playhouse.

N. and M. RAU have reported on the Hollywood scene for newspapers, magazines and major press services for more than twenty years. Mr. Rau is a native of Nashville, Tennessee, and Mrs. Rau was born in Swatow, China, where she lived for several years. The Raus, with their four sons and one daughter, make their home in Los Angeles.

PITTSBURGH FILMMAKERS
477 MELWOOD AVENUE
PITTSBURGH, PA 15213

PITTSBURGH FILMMAKERS
477 MELWOOD AVENUE
PITTSBURGH, PA 15213